HOME BREW RECIPE BIBLE

AN INCREDIBLE ARRAY OF 101 CRAFT BEER RECIPES,
FROM CLASSIC STYLES TO EXPERIMENTAL WILDS

CHRIS COLBY

EDITOR OF *BEER & WINE JOURNAL*

PHOTOGRAPHY BY
TED AXELROD

PAGE STREET
PUBLISHING CO.

PAGE STREET
PUBLISHING CO.

Copyright © 2016 Chris Colby

JUN 15 2017

First published in 2016 by
Page Street Publishing Co.
27 Congress Street, Suite 103
Salem, MA 01970
www.pagestreetpublishing.com

Distributed by Macmillan, sales in Canada by The Canadian Manda Group.

19   18   17   16   1   2   3   4   5

ISBN-13: 978-1-62414-314-4
ISBN-10:1-62414-314-8

Library of Congress Control Number: 2016932018
Cover and book design by Page Street Publishing Co.

Photography by Ted Axelrod

Printed and bound in China

Page Street is proud to be a member of 1% for the Planet. Members donate one percent of their sales to one or more of the over 1,500 environmental and sustainability charities across the globe who participate in this program.

TO MY WIFE JENNIFER, WHO PUTS UP WITH ME. ME!

CONTENTS

2

DARK ALES: ROASTY AND DELICIOUS 49

3

AMBER ALES: SUMPTUOUS SPECIALTY MALTS 83

4

PALE ALES: FROM WELL-BALANCED TO HOP HEAVEN 105

5

DARK AND AMBER LAGERS: RICH, MALTY AND SATISFYING 153

PREFACE

We learn best by doing. That's the idea behind this book. By reading through these recipes and brewing the ones that interest you, you can learn while you brew, quickly absorbing knowledge of useful techniques and ingredients. There is no order to the lessons interspersed throughout the book—just read about and brew the beers that interest you and pick up the relevant knowledge as you go. I'm assuming that you've brewed before, though brewers at any level should be able to follow the recipes.

You might wonder where these recipes came from. Most of them came from my own brewing notebook. I have been a homebrewer since 1991 and have records for close to 300 batches of beer in that time. Plus, I've "winged it" innumerable times. For most of my beers, I have detailed notes on how they were brewed and how they tasted. Many have been tweaked multiple times and rebrewed, a few as many as 30 times.

As a homebrew writer and editor for more than 15 years, I've covered a lot of topics and seen a lot of beer recipes—both from homebrewers and commercial brewers. I've read several professional brewing texts and have even dug into brewing science literature. (I have a PhD in biology from Boston University.) Even better, I've been able to sit and talk to many highly trained and accomplished professional brewers—and maltsters and hop growers—over the years. So, the recipes that don't come directly from my own notebook come from the accumulated experience of brewers everywhere. I'm also presenting recipes from four fellow homebrewers—James Spencer, Denny Conn, Mark Schoppe and Dan Ironside.

I hope you brew and enjoy as many of these recipes as you can and expand your brewing horizons in doing so. You can find more information about homebrewing at my website—*Beer and Wine Journal* (beerandwinejournal.com). Skoal!

MAKING THE MOST OF THESE RECIPES

If 100 random homebrewers all brewed the same recipe, there would be 100 different results. The best of the lot would be equal to—or better than—the best commercial beer of that type. The rest would vary from good to … not so good. The differences would come from variations in the freshness of the ingredients, the water used, the brewers' equipment and differences in the skill levels of the brewers. These days, a lot of what separates good beer from bad is known, but it can get lost in the tidal wave of brewing information on the Internet. With that in mind, here are my tips regarding the major issues that you need to understand in order to make the best beer from these recipes.

First of all, if you are new to brewing, follow these recipes as closely as you can reasonably manage. Don't add, subtract or substitute ingredients. If your homebrew shop doesn't carry a particular ingredient, order it online. Measure everything— weights, volumes, temperatures, etc.—as carefully as you reasonably can. You don't need to be ludicrously precise, but resist the urge to just "wing" anything. Also, read the instructions and follow them when you brew. Make a checklist to help you remember the steps, if needed. Don't take the recipe list and brew following the instructions from the last beer kit you made or from another homebrew book. The ingredients and procedures work together to make the beer.

THE MOST IMPORTANT THING

The most important aspect of brewing is also the least glamorous—cleaning and sanitation. You can't brew quality beer unless your equipment is spotlessly clean and properly sanitized.

When you prepare for a brewing session, clean every surface of your brewing equipment, paying special attention to any surface that will contact chilled wort or beer. Inspect your equipment after cleaning it and reclean if everything is not spotless. Whatever you use to sanitize your equipment, follow the directions carefully. More concentrated sanitizing solutions may not be more effective and are harder to rinse. Some sanitizers do not need to be rinsed. If that's the case, don't. Know that if you (or any unsanitized object) touch a sanitized surface, it is no longer sanitary. Clean, if needed, and sanitize it again.

Cleaning your equipment often requires a bit of "elbow grease." Spotlessly clean equipment is required to brew clean beer.

Also, don't think that you can sanitize your hands. Even though products called hand sanitizers are sold, they don't render your hands sanitary to the degree that you can touch chilled wort or surfaces that will contact chilled wort. Keep your hands clean while you brew, avoid touching surfaces that will contact wort and skip the hand sanitizer.

Avoiding contaminants in your beer involves more than just cleaning and sanitizing your equipment. Bacteria and wild yeast cells are very small. If you have ever been in a dark room with sunlight streaming in from one small hole, you have probably seen tiny motes of dust floating in the air—even in a room that appears clean when the lights are on. Those tiny bits floating on air are gigantic compared to bacteria and yeast cells. And, like the dust, they are suspended in the air all around you. As such, you should always minimize any time that chilled wort or fermented beer is exposed to the environment. If possible, cover the vessel and do whatever you need to do as quickly as possible. For example, if you are chilling your wort with an immersion chiller, cover your brew pot or kettle as best you can with a (sanitized) lid. Or, if you are bottling beer, cover your bottling bucket with aluminum foil, and work as quickly as possible to get the beer bottled. Act as if a steady stream of potential contaminants is raining on your brew day—because they are.

Also know that some environments have more potential brewery contaminants than others. For example, the dust produced by a grain mill is loaded with lactic acid bacteria. As such, mill your grain away from any area that will have exposed wort or beer.

Finally, any contaminant in your wort has to compete with the brewers yeast for resources. Pitching an adequate amount of the yeast, such that they quickly colonize the wort and start fermentation, will suppress the growth of many types of bacteria and wild yeast.

FRESH INGREDIENTS

It is important to brew with only fresh ingredients. You cannot brew quality beer from stale malt or cheesy hops. Malted grains are like any food product made from grains, in that they will go stale in time. It is easy to tell if malt has gone stale—just chew a few kernels. If you can identify when bread, cereal or crackers have gone stale, you'll be able to tell in malt.

Malt extract also goes stale. When it does, it darkens and begins to taste stale. A quick check of the freshness is to dilute some in water and examine the color. Dilute a small amount of malt extract in a glass of water so the specific gravity (SG) is about SG 1.048. If the malt extract is supposed to be light—or extra light or Pilsner—it should be pale to golden in color. If it looks amber, it's stale. You can confirm this by tasting it.

Whole malts and grains stay fresh longer than crushed grains. If you have a grain mill, wait until brew day to mill the grains.

Keep hops bagged and frozen. A deep freeze, not a frost-free freezer, is the best place to store hops.

Stale hops turn brown and smell cheesy. Use only fresh hops in your beers.

A gap tool used for testing spark plugs can measure your mill gap.

Grain mills may be motorized or cranked by hand.

When crushed, barley hulls should be broken into two to three pieces.

Hops become brown as they age and start smelling cheesy. If you take hops—whether pellet or whole—and rub them in your hands, the aroma should be of fresh hops. If the aroma is lacking or has a cheesy quality, do not use those hops. Hops that are green are usually fresh. Hops are harvested once a year in each hemisphere. Advanced homebrewers might want to wait until the year's crop becomes available and buy their hops in bulk. Ideally, store the hops in a non-frost-free freezer. If not, a frost-free freezer will work. Barley can be harvested twice a year in each hemisphere, but it is stored in grain elevators; malt is produced continually throughout the year.

Yeast needs to be healthy and abundant to properly ferment wort. Liquid yeast comes with an expiration date and should be kept cool—refrigerated at your home—until used. Making a yeast starter is one way to ensure that you have a healthy pitch of yeast ready on brew day.

Most beer is over 90 percent water, so always check that your water is suitable for brewing. Municipal tap water will have chlorine compounds (chloramines) to keep the water fresh in the pipes. However, you don't want these in your brewing water. Either filter the water through a large carbon filter (like an under-the-sink model) or use one Campden tablet per 20 gallons (76 L) to chemically neutralize the chloramines. Just crush a tablet and stir it into the water; the chemical reaction occurs in less than a second.

Advanced brewers will eventually seek to add minerals (or acids) to their water to get the best brewing results. (See the section opener in Chapter 2 on page 50 for brewing water recommendations.) Once your brewing liquor (the water you will brew with) has been prepared, taste it. If it does not taste good, it won't make good beer.

FERMENTATION

For most homebrewers, conducting an ordered fermentation is what makes or breaks their beer. An ordered fermentation is one that starts quickly, proceeds steadily and finishes at a reasonable final gravity (FG). What "quickly," "steadily" and "reasonable" are depends on the yeast strain and the beer. For most ales, fermentation should start within 24 hours, and

Fermentation should start within 24 hours.

Maintain a proper and steady fermentation temperature.

Always pitch an adequate amount of yeast.

may do so much earlier. For an average strength ale, primary fermentation should take about a week, with the specific gravity of the fermenting beer changing every day. (You don't need to take a gravity reading every day, however.) And finally, in most cases, the final gravity should be roughly a quarter of the original gravity or lower.

Stronger beers take longer to ferment and finish at higher final gravities. Lagers take longer to start and to ferment, as they are fermented at lower temperatures. The three biggest keys to running an ordered fermentation are pitching an adequate amount of yeast, establishing the correct fermentation temperature and thoroughly aerating the wort prior to fermentation.

PITCHING RATE

Each recipe in this book gives a recommended yeast starter size. This should raise the optimal number of yeast for each fermentation. The yeast starter volumes for the strongest ales and lagers get quite large. In the case of very strong lagers, you may want to raise the yeast by brewing a batch of low-gravity lager beer. You can almost always get away with making a starter smaller than prescribed.

In fact, beer made from a starter that is half the volume recommended will have a slower start than one with the correctly sized starter, but will otherwise likely be fine. (All the yeast need to do is replicate once in the fermenting beer to reach the density equivalent of pitching the larger starter.) Progressively smaller starters will yield beers with progressively more fermentation byproducts, especially in yeast strains known for them. Specifically, underpitching English ale strains known for their ester production will increase ester production, resulting in an overly fruity smelling beer.

If you aerate the starter once or twice a day, and swirl the contents to rouse the yeast, you can make a smaller starter than recommended. The starter sizes recommended here assume you aerated the starter wort well and let the fermentation proceed without intervention. With daily aeration and rousing the yeast, you can use half the recommended starter size.

TEMPERATURE

The temperature at which beer ferments influences the character of the beer. Warmer fermentations lead to more fermentation byproducts while cooler fermentations (with a yeast strain's specified range) lead to "cleaner" beer. In ale fermentations—which are usually conducted between 65–72°F (18–22°C)—the pitching rate and fermentation temperature ensure a smooth fermentation with a pleasing level of esters (and other elements in some strains). In lagers—which are usually fermented at 50–55°F (10–13°C)—the pitching rate and fermentation ensure a "clean" beer.

The brewer needs to ensure that the fermentation temperature is within the yeast strain's preferred range. And, he or she should also strive to keep the fermentation temperature

A small tank of oxygen, as used by welders, can supply oxygen to your chilled wort.

reasonably steady. In the case of strong beers, this may require some extra effort to control the temperature around high kräusen (the most vigorous stage of fermentation). To actively manage fermentation temperatures, many homebrewers use a refrigerator or chest freezer equipped with an external thermostat. Others simply restrict their brewing to the times of year when ales can be brewed at ambient temperature.

When monitoring fermentation temperature, remember that fermentation itself gives off heat and the fermenting beer will be warmer than the ambient temperature. As such, you need a way to measure the temperature of the beer, not the air in the room or chamber it is fermenting in. The simplest solution, which works well on buckets and glass carboys, is a strip thermometer that attaches to the bucket or carboy.

AERATION

Yeast require oxygen to reproduce. They incorporate oxygen into molecules (sterols) used to build their cell walls. In brewing, chilled wort is aerated prior to fermentation and this helps the yeast population grow to a density that will rapidly ferment the wort.

Air or oxygen can be bubbled through wort by hooking either an aquarium pump or small oxygen tank (used for welding) to an aeration stone. A HEPA filter placed between the source of gas and the stone will filter out any contaminants. Bubbling air for 6 to 12 minutes through wort should be enough to aerate it. Bubbling oxygen through the wort for 1 to 2 minutes will also work. Most homebrewers cannot directly measure the oxygen content of their wort. (If you could, around 10 ppm would work well for most yeast strains.)

However, if you are using a 2-micron aeration stone, and adjust the stream of air (or oxygen) so that it produces tiny bubbles that rise all the way to the surface, you will almost assuredly be fine if you aerate for the times indicated. When fermenting a strong beer (over 8 percent ABV), you may want to aerate the wort more than once. After the initial aeration, wait a few hours, and then give the wort another shot of air or oxygen. Do not aerate once vigorous fermentation starts.

Most of the gas you bubble into wort will diffuse out of solution fairly rapidly. As such, be sure to pitch your yeast promptly after aerating your wort.

DIACETYL

As yeast ferment, they give off the primary products of alcoholic fermentation—ethyl alcohol and carbon dioxide (and heat). However, they also excrete other metabolic byproducts, some of which are not wanted at high concentrations in beer. The most important of these unwanted byproducts is diacetyl.

Diacetyl gives beer a buttery or butterscotch flavor and aroma and contribute a tongue-coating slickness that most beer drinkers do not find appealing. Yeast gives off the precursor to diacetyl (alpha acetolactate) during fermentation, and the precursor gets converted to diacetyl in the fermenting beer. (This happens most rapidly when oxygen is present.)

Healthy yeast, however, will absorb the diacetyl late in the fermentation, lowering its level in the finished beer. Most ale yeast strains will reduce the levels of diacetyl to below their sensory threshold by the end of fermentation. However, most lager strains will leave some residual diacetyl if something is not done to get rid of it.

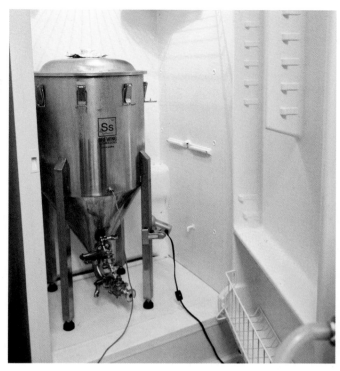

A fermentation refrigerator allows you to ferment beer at any temperature.

Most commonly, lager brewers will employ a diacetyl rest to lower the amount below the threshold. This is done by letting the fermentation temperature rise—often to around 60°F (16°C)—at the tail end of fermentation. The increase in temperature causes the yeast to become more active and they take in the diacetyl.

Lager brewers may also kräusen a beer. Kräusening is the introduction of a small amount of vigorously fermenting beer into lager beer that has almost finished fermenting. The yeast in the kräusen beer scrub diacetyl from the wort and also help the primary yeast finish the fermentation.

Diacetyl can also occur if the beer is separated from the yeast near the end of fermentation. Even in ales, it's good to let the beer sit on the yeast at least a day after primary fermentation has ended. Diacetyl is also produced by some contaminating microorganisms.

Beer should be shielded from oxygen at all times.

OXYGEN

Yeast requires oxygen at some point in its propagation cycle to remain healthy. However, once beer is fermented, oxygen has only negative effects. Exposure of beer to oxygen causes it to go stale faster than it would if shielded from oxygen. Stale beer can have a cardboard-like flavor or—in bigger beers—take on a Sherry-like quality. (The latter is actually desired in some aged ales.) In homebrewing, there are a number of steps when the beer is exposed to oxygen.

Any time beer is transferred from one vessel to another, the beer is exposed to air. When racking beer to a secondary fermenter, it is best to rack to a vessel with as little headspace as possible. When racking to a Corny keg, the brewer should purge the headspace after the beer has been transferred.

To do this, place the lid on the keg and turn on the CO_2. Adjust the regulator to apply a small amount of pressure. (Anything in the vicinity of serving pressure is fine.) Lift the safety release valve for a second or two then release and wait for the keg to come back up to pressure. This vents the air in the headspace and replaces it with CO_2. Repeat this venting two or three times. A brewer can also fill a keg with water, push the water out with CO_2 and then rack the beer into the keg—under a cloud of CO_2.

Obviously, the beer is exposed to air when bottling. However, the renewed fermentation spurred by the priming sugar will mean that active yeast cells take up some of this oxygen. Still, have everything ready to go before racking the beer from your fermenter to the bottling bucket. Then bottle as quickly as you can reasonably manage and get the bottles capped. You don't need to rush, but don't waste any time at this stage.

You should also not store beer in containers that are permeable to oxygen. The PET bottles that soda comes in are slightly permeable to oxygen. They are fine for short-term storage—up to maybe a few months—but you should not put beer in them if you don't intend to drink it fairly soon. Glass bottles or stainless steel kegs are completely impermeable to oxygen (although tiny amounts of oxygen can get in through the lining in the bottle caps or gaskets sealing the keg).

TANNINS AND ASTRINGENCY

Tannins are a class of molecule that are present in relative abundance in a lot of plant material. In beverages, they lend an astringent mouthfeel that can be mistaken for bitterness. In a red wine, tannins are said to give the wine "structure." Essentially, they (in conjunction with the acids) keep the wine from simply being a sweet, alcoholic mess. In most beers, however, noticeable astringency is not wanted.

The husks of barley have tannins. So does the green matter in hops. So, for that matter, does the plant material in most spices and parts of many fruits. Brewers cannot avoid extracting some tannins from all the plant material in their ingredients.

Tannic acid is the molecule that gives tannins their name.

However, they can strive to extract an amount below the level at which it becomes a problem. Two common ways that excessive tannins can end up in beer are oversparging and sparging with water that is too hot.

For every grain bed, there is a maximum amount of wort that can be collected before the runnings become overly tannic. Near the end of sparging, when little sugar is left in the grains and the pH has risen to near 5.8, tannins become more soluble. Continuing to collect wort beyond this point means gaining a tiny amount of sugar at the expense of an astringent beer (and a requirement to boil the wort longer to condense it).

To avoid this, stop sparging when the pH of the final runnings reaches 5.8 or the specific gravity falls to 1.008. You can also taste the runnings to see if they are astringent. If you are a batch sparger, don't collect more than two batches of sparged wort (in addition to the first wort).

While pH plays a role in extracting tannins, so does temperature. Near the end of sparging, if the temperature of the grains is over 170°F (77°C), unacceptably high levels of tannins are extracted. So limiting the amount of sparge water and its temperature will help you keep the tannins below an acceptably high level.

In a few beers, a hint of astringency can be a good thing. Some big beers are meant to have a wine-like edge to them and so a little astringency can be welcome. Likewise, in some flavored beers, a little tannin is part of the expected flavor. For example, if you flavored a beer with red grapes, you'd expect some grape tannin in the flavor.

CONCLUSION

Those are the major issues that most brewers—home and pro alike—have to contend with. If you keep these issues under control, odds are your beer will be of high quality. The recipes in this book were written with all of these things (and more) in mind. If you follow the procedures closely, you will avoid these issues.

SECTION 2

THE RECIPES

These recipes have a lot of detail in order to describe how to make the best possible beer from the list of ingredients. Here are some details that might help you make better sense of them.

Most of the numbers in this book are expressed to two significant digits unless more precision is required. In many cases, further precision would be useless—for example, expressing hop amounts to three significant digits would mean these weights would be given to the nearest tenth of a gram. Most homebrewers don't have a scale or balance that accurate, and there is no reason they would need to. Follow the ingredient amounts as closely as your equipment allows, but don't sweat small measurement errors.

For the all-grain recipes, I give the amount of strike water (water used for mashing) and a temperature. This temperature should work if your grains and equipment are around "room temperature." If not, adjust it so you hit the mash temperature specified. If your actual mash temperature is within 2.0°F (1.1°C) of the target, you are doing fine. (Within 1.0°F [0.55°C], is even better.)

In the extract recipes, I specify either dried malt extract or liquid malt extract, although you can use whichever type is available or convenient to you. Keep in mind that dried malt extract yields 45 "gravity points" per pound, while liquid malt extract usually yields around 37.

The recipes were brewed using pellet hops for kettle additions and whole hops for dry hopping. However, using different forms of the hops should not change the recipe drastically.

The recommended yeast starter sizes should give you the optimal cell count for each beer. You can almost always "get away" with a smaller starter, but it will take longer for the beer to start fermenting and characterful yeast strains will produce more esters (or whatever byproducts they are known for). The recommended starter sizes are quite large for the strong lagers and strongest ales, but these beers are the most difficult to ferment correctly. Taking the time to make a reasonably sized starter will ensure all your work on brew day is not for naught.

I know homebrew setups differ and thus I do not specify a lautering method. You can fly sparge, batch sparge or use brew in a bag (BIAB) methods. Likewise, I do not specify how to separate the trub from your chilled wort. I simply give my chilled wort time to settle, but you can use hop screens or strain the (chilled) wort as you transfer it to your fermenter. I also do not specify how to chill your wort. I use an immersion chiller. If you use a counterflow or plate chiller, the late hops may contribute more IBUs than these recipes expect. The difference should not be large, however.

For every all-grain recipe, I give the pre-boil wort volume expected if you fully sparge the grain bed. For the biggest beers, these volumes can be quite large and would take hours to reduce via boiling. I expect many brewers will collect and boil a more manageable amount of wort. Your extract efficiency will suffer a bit, but you can make up any lost gravity by adding malt extract in the boil or malt in the mash tun. (Adding 4.0 ounces [110 g] of dried malt extract to 5.0 gallons (19 L) of wort raises the specific gravity by 2 "gravity points.")

Fire up your burner, it's time to brew!

Speaking of extract efficiency, I assume 70 percent for all these recipes. Adjust the amount of base malt if your efficiency differs from this. And, I use a hop utilization curve that is almost the same as Tinseth's.

I give an amount of priming sugar that will yield an appropriate level of carbonation for each of these brews. For many of the English ales, this is lower than craft beer drinkers are used to. If you like your beers fizzy, up the amount of priming sugar so you hit around 2.5 volumes of CO_2.

The point of these recipes is to make good beer, not to blindly follow instructions. Take good notes when you brew, then taste your beer critically.

If recipes from this book seem to be consistently too hoppy or not hoppy enough (compared to expectations), yield an original gravity (OG) consistently over or under the expected OG by a certain amount, adjust the ingredient amounts to reflect how the recipes turn out on your system. Hop utilization and extract efficiency varies among homebrewers. These recipes are all formulated consistently, so if you consistently get better or worse hop utilization or extract efficiency than assumed here, you'll know to make adjustments when you brew any of these beers.

1

BEERS MADE WITH MALT EXTRACT: BRILLIANT BEGINNINGS

This section features 10 recipes for beers made with malt extract. There are all-grain versions for each of these recipes, but the recipes were designed as extract recipes that will produce superior beer if you use fresh ingredients and follow the procedures carefully. The beers here run the gamut of colors and strengths. Each recipe either demonstrates a useful extract brewing technique or highlights a common ingredient.

In the other sections of this book, I give instructions on how to prepare brewing liquor (water with minerals dissolved in it) for different colored beers. For this extract section, I will keep it simple. Some of the water in every batch—including some added to the brew pot, plus the water added in the fermenter—is meant to dissolve (or further dilute) the malt extract. This water should be as soft as possible. (Soft meaning not having a lot of minerals dissolved in it.) Ideally, you can use distilled water or reverse osmosis (RO) water for this portion of the batch. If you have naturally soft tap water, you can carbon filter it and use that. For the water that you use to steep or mash the grains, some simple water treatment may help.

Any time grains are being steeped or mashed, a little calcium in the water is a good thing. So, for all these beers, start with 2.0 gallons (7.6 L) of distilled water or RO water and add one teaspoon of calcium. For balanced beers, do this by adding half a teaspoon of calcium chloride and half a teaspoon of gypsum; for hoppy beers add one teaspoon of gypsum. If you are brewing a pale beer, between 0 and 10 Standard Reference Method (SRM), you're done. If you are brewing an amber beer, between 10 and 20 SRM, add half a teaspoon of baking soda (sodium bicarbonate). If you are brewing a dark beer, over 20 SRM, add between three-quarters and one full teaspoon of baking soda, depending on how dark the beer is—three-quarters of a teaspoon for brown ales and similar colored beers and one teaspoon for the darkest porters and stouts.

Measuring to the nearest quarter teaspoon is not the most accurate way of measuring mineral content in water, but it will work well enough. You do not have to have your water chemistry extremely fine-tuned for it to benefit your beer. Use the 2.0 gallons (7.6 L) of treated water as the source of your water for steeping or mashing grains. Use distilled (or very soft) water for the rest. If you are making a hoppy beer, add another teaspoon of gypsum—per 5.0-gallon (19-L) batch—as you boil your wort.

BOAT RIDE FOR THREE IPA
SESSION IPA

Session IPA is a lower-strength version of an American IPA, which is usually fairly strong (5.5–7.5 percent ABV). A good session IPA delivers all the hop flavor and aroma of an IPA, but with slightly less bitterness on account of its lower original gravity. Some people would simply call this beer a hoppy American pale ale, and that's fine. The grain bill is, however, modeled on an IPA and produces a slightly drier beer with less caramel flavor than a typical pale ale. Call it what you like, it's a dry, 4.5 percent ABV pale ale full of hop flavor and aroma.

5.0 GALLONS (19 L) AT 4.4% ABV
OG = 1.045, FG = 1.011
46 IBU, 4 SRM

+ Wyeast 1056 (American Ale), White Labs WLP001 (California Ale) or Fermentis U.S.-05 yeast
+ a 1.1-qt. (1.0-L) yeast starter is recommended for the liquid yeasts
+ 5.0 lb. (2.3 kg) light dried malt extract (or 6 lb. 2 oz. light liquid malt extract)
+ 0.75 oz. (21 g) Warrior hops at 16% alpha acids, boiled for 45 minutes (41 IBU)
+ 0.5 oz. (14 g) Simcoe hops at 13% alpha acids, boiled for 5 minutes (5 IBU)
+ 1.0 oz. (28 g) Cascade hops at 6% alpha acids, added at knockout (0 IBU)
+ 0.5 oz. (14 g) Simcoe hops (dry hops)
+ 1.5 oz. (43 g) Cascade hops (dry hops)
+ 2 tsp. (4 g) gypsum, boiled for 45 minutes
+ 0.50 tsp. Irish moss, boiled for 15 minutes
+ 5.0 oz. (140 g) corn sugar, to prime bottles for 2.5 volumes of CO_2

If you are using the Wyeast or White Labs yeast, make your yeast starter two to three days ahead of time. Both yeasts will perform better if you make a yeast starter two to three days ahead. Add 2.0 gallons (7.6 L) of water (preferably distilled) to your brew pot and dissolve the malt extract. Once the extract is dissolved, add water to make (at least) 3.0 gallons (11 L) and bring to a boil. Add the Warrior hops and gypsum once the wort (unfermented beer) is boiling and boil for 45 minutes.

Add the Irish moss with 15 minutes left in the boil. When 5 minutes remain in the boil, add the first charge of Simcoe hops. Then, immediately after the boil ends, add the first charge of Cascade hops. If the volume of the wort looks like it will dip below 2.5 gallons (9.5 L) at any time during the boil, add water to keep the volume to at least 2.5 gallons (9.5 L). Use a smaller pot of boiling water to top up the kettle, if needed.

(continued)

Light malt extract is made from 2-row pale malt and is used as a base for a lot of beers, but it isn't the only type of malt extract available. Substituting Pilsner malt extract for the light malt extract would produce a very similar beer, but with a hint of the characteristic sweetness of Pilsner malt. A blend of half light malt extract and half wheat malt extract would yield a beer with a little bit of the "zing" from wheat. If you made a blend of one-third Munich malt extract with the remaining two-thirds being light or Pilsner malt extract, you would add a bit more color and malt character to the beer.

A kitchen scale can be used to weigh specialty grains.

Chill the wort to 68°F (20°C). Transfer to your primary fermenter and add water to make 5.0 gallons (19 L) of wort. Aerate the wort thoroughly and pitch the yeast. Let the beer ferment at 68°F (20°C). When fermentation stops, let the beer settle for two to three days, then rack to a secondary (separate) fermenter with the dry hops. (Ideally, use a carboy [container] with little or no headspace left when the beer is transferred.)

Let the dry hops contact the beer for five to six days, then rack the beer to a keg or bottling bucket for bottling. Carbonate to 2.5 volumes of CO_2. Keg or add priming sugar and bottle.

ALL-GRAIN OPTION

Replace the malt extract with 8 pounds 10 ounces (3.9 kg) of U.S. 2-row pale malt. Mash at 150°F (66°C) in 12 quarts (11 L) of water. Collect about 5.6 gallons (21 L) of wort. Boil hard for 45 minutes, adding hops at times indicated in recipe list. You may have to top the volume up with water near the end of the boil. An all-grain version of this recipe will be slighter lighter in color and likely slightly better attenuated, for a slightly lower FG (and correspondingly higher ABV).

TIPS ON USING MALT EXTRACT

The wort for this beer is made entirely from malt extract—there are no base grains to mash or specialty grains to steep. This beer is focused on the hops, so a complex grain bill is not desirable.

Malt extract is condensed wort. Wort is the sugary liquid that gets fermented to produce beer. Brewery grade malt extract, the kind homebrew stores sell, is ready to be reconstituted with water and boiled. The extract itself only needs to be heated to the point that the wort is sanitized. However, if the extract is not hopped, you will need to boil hops in the reconstituted wort to extract their bitterness.

Malt extract comes in liquid and dried powder forms. Both can be used interchangeably. Dried extract can be stored longer than liquid, but is a little darker in color compared to a liquid malt extract made from the same wort. Liquid malt extract should be purchased fresh, stored in a cool place and used within a couple months. Dried malt extract should likewise be stored in a cool place but will last longer (up to eight months). Dried malt powder should be stored away from humidity or else it will absorb water and harden.

Dried malt extract contains less water than liquid malt extract. Therefore, when substituting one for the other, you'll need more liquid extract for a given amount of dried extract (because a larger part of the weight of liquid extract is water). When substituting liquid malt extract for dried malt extract, multiply the amount of dried malt extract by 1.2. For example, if a recipe calls for 2.0 pounds (0.90 kg) of dried malt extract, but you wanted to use liquid malt extract, you would need 2.4 pounds (1.09 kg) of liquid malt extract. Conversely, when converting an amount of liquid malt extract to dried malt extract, multiply by 0.8. The density of malt extracts varies, but these conversion factors should work well enough in almost all homebrewing situations.

ARNOLD'S AMBER ALE
AMERICAN AMBER ALE

Amber ales are similar to pale ales, but are usually slightly less hoppy and show more caramel malt flavoring. And of course, as the name implies, they are red or amber in color. The two styles overlap considerably, though, and very hoppy red ales do exist. This amber ale is an average-strength beer that's full-bodied and balanced. It is moderately bitter, with hop flavor and aroma from American hops.

5.0 GALLONS (19 L) AT 5.3% ABV
OG = 1.056, FG = 1.015
35 IBU, 10 SRM

+ Wyeast 1272 (American Ale II) or White Labs WLP051 (California V Ale) yeast
+ A 1.5-qt. (1.5-L) yeast starter is recommended
+ 12 oz. (340 g) caramel malt (40°L)
+ 8.0 oz. (230 g) caramel malt (60°L)
+ 2.0 oz. (57 g) caramel malt (90°L)
+ 5 lb. 8 oz. (2.5 kg) light dried malt extract (or 6 lb. 12 oz. [3.1 kg] light liquid malt extract)
+ 0.66 oz. (19 g) Magnum hops at 12% alpha acids, boiled for 60 minutes (30 IBU)
+ 0.75 oz. (21 g) Mt. Hood hops at 6% alpha acids, boiled for 10 minutes (6 IBU)
+ 0.50 oz. (14 g) Liberty hops at 4% alpha acids, boiled for 0 minutes (0 IBU)
+ 0.50 oz. (14 g) Santiam hops at 6% alpha acids, boiled for 0 minutes (0 IBU)
+ 0.50 oz. (14 g) Liberty hops (dry hops)
+ 0.50 oz. (14 g) Santiam hops (dry hops)
+ 0.50 tsp. Irish moss, boiled for 15 minutes
+ 5.0 oz. (140 g) corn sugar, to prime for 2.5 volumes of CO_2

Make your yeast starter two to three days ahead of time. In your brew pot, heat 1.0 gallon (3.8 L) of water to 163°F (73°F). Place the crushed caramel malts in a steeping bag and steep them in the hot water for 45 minutes. Hold the temperature of the steeping grains (malts) around 152°F (67°C). (You don't have to be very accurate with the temperature when steeping grains, anywhere within 10°F [5°C] of this target is more than good enough.)

After the grains have steeped, stir in roughly half of the malt extract, add water to make (at least) 3.0 gallons (11 L) of wort, and bring to a boil. Do not let the wort volume drop below 2.5 gallons (9.5 L) during boil. (Top up with boiling water, if needed.) Once boil starts and the first bits of hot break show, add the Magnum hops and boil for 60 minutes. Add the remaining hops at times indicated.

(continued)

Add Irish moss with 15 minutes left in boil. Stir in the remaining malt extract in the last 10 minutes. (Dissolve it in a small amount of wort first to make it easier to stir in.) Chill wort to 68°F (20°C) and transfer to fermenter. Add water to make 5.0 gallons (19 L) and aerate thoroughly. Pitch yeast and let ferment at 68°F (20°C). When fermentation is complete, add dry hops to a secondary fermenter and rack the beer onto them. Dry hop for seven to 10 days, then keg or bottle. Carbonate to 2.5 volumes of CO_2. Keg or add priming sugar and bottle.

ALL-GRAIN OPTION

Replace the malt extract with 9 pounds 10 ounces (4.4 kg) of U.S. 2-row pale malt. Mash the grains at 153°F (67°C) in 14 quarts (13 L) of water. Collect about 7.0 gallons (27 L) of wort and boil hard for 90 minutes to reduce the volume to 5.0 gallons (19 L). Add hops at times indicated in the recipe list.

CRYSTAL AND CARAMEL MALTS

Crystal malt is a type of malt that originated in Britain to add body and caramel flavor to beer. Crystal malts are produced by stewing pale malt, then kilning it. Crystal type malts go by a variety of names. Many U.S. maltsters call their crystal type malts caramel malts. In Germany, some maltster's crystal malts carry the prefix "Cara," for example, CaraMunich. Crystal, caramel, and "Cara" malts with same color rating will be similar, but not exactly alike.

Differences in the varieties of barley used and differences in how different maltsters prepare their crystal-type malt lead to differences in the flavor and aroma of these malts. This recipe calls for caramel malts, which is what most U.S. maltsters call their crystal malts. But, you can substitute English crystal malts or German "Cara" malts with the same color rating for a similar result.

You can also adjust the color ratings and relative amounts of the three caramel malts. A higher percentage of low color malts—for example, a mix of crystal (20°L), crystal (30°L) and crystal (40°L)—would produce a lighter-colored, less caramel-flavored beer. Conversely, a blend using darker malts would result in a darker one with more caramel flavors. Dark crystal malts, over 60°L can additionally have a raisin-like character and the darkest crystal malts—such as Dingeman's Special B malt at 150°L—may also impart a roasted character.

This beer gets its color and caramel flavor from caramel malt. The grains are steeped to extract their color and the sugars inside them. Later, malt extract is dissolved to supply most of the fermentable sugars. This "extract plus grains" formulation is how many old school homebrew recipes worked. And, this approach can work well when the specialty grains are a focal point of the beer. (All other extract recipes in this book incorporate a small amount of base grains, necessitating a small mash instead of simply steeping.)

RECIPE OPTIONS AND NOTES

Lovibaud is a color scale used in describing malts.

This amber ale is on the light side of the style, colorwise. You can darken it, without changing the flavor much by adding 2–3 ounces (roughly 60–90 g) of any darkly roasted grain, including chocolate malt, roasted barley or black malt. Of these three, black malt adds the least amount of roasted aroma. Many brewers use small amounts of black malt as a way to adjust beer color, without changing the flavor.

LOCKS OF FREJYA
BLONDE ALE

Blonde ale, sometimes called golden ale or even light ale, is found in the lineup of many brewpubs. The basic idea is to offer a beer that might interest those who have only ever tried light lagers. The best blonde ales are pleasantly malty-grainy, with just enough hop bitterness to provide balance. This recipe uses a blend of Pilsner malt and Vienna malt, with just a touch of light crystal malt, to give the beer a rounded malt profile.

5.0 GALLONS (19 L) AT 4.9% ABV
OG = 1.049, FG = 1.011
24 IBU, 4.9 SRM

+ Wyeast 1056 (American Ale) or White Labs WLP001 (California Ale) yeast
+ A 1.6-qt. (1.5-L) yeast starter is recommended
+ 1 lb. 13 oz. (820 g) German Pilsner malt
+ 12 oz. (340 g) Vienna malt
+ 7.0 oz. (200 g) crystal malt (20°L)
+ 4 lb. 8 oz. (2.0 kg) light liquid malt extract
+ 0.33 oz. (9.4 g) Summit hops at 17% alpha acids, boiled for 60 minutes (21 IBU)
+ 0.25 oz. (7.1 g) Willamette hops at 5% alpha acids, boiled for 15 minutes (2 IBU)
+ 0.25 oz. (7.1 g) Willamette hops at 5% alpha acids, boiled for 5 minutes (1 IBU)
+ 0.50 oz. (14 g) Willamette hops at 5% alpha acids, boiled for 0 minutes (0 IBU)
+ 0.50 tsp. Irish moss, boiled for 15 minutes
+ Optional: 1 vial Clarity Ferm or 8 g (~3 tsp.) Polyclar AT (PVPP)
+ 5.25 oz. (150 g) corn sugar, to prime for 2.6 volumes CO_2

Make your yeast starter two to three days ahead of time. In your brew pot, begin heating 2.0 gallons (7.6 L) of water to a boil. Aim to reach boiling when the small mash is done. In a separate, large (8-quart [8-L] or larger) pot, heat 1.0 gallon (3.8 L) of water to 161°F (72°C). Place the crushed grains in a steeping bag and submerge them in the second pot. The temperature should settle in around 150°F (66°C). Let this mash rest at 150°F (66°C) for 60 minutes, then slowly heat the mash to 168°F (76°C), stirring constantly.

In a third pot, heat 2.0 quarts (1.9 L) of water to 170°F (77°C) to use as sparge water. Place a large colander over your brew pot, set the grain bag in it and pour the wort through it (to filter out solid pieces of grain); then, rinse the grains with the sparge water. You should yield about 3.0 gallons (11 L) of wort. Stir in roughly a quarter of the malt extract and bring the wort to a boil. Do not let wort volume drop below 2.5 gallons (9.5 L) during boil. (Top up with boiling water, if needed.)

Once the boil starts and the first bits of hot break show, add your hops and boil for 60 minutes. Add remaining hops at times indicated. Stir in the remaining malt extract in the last 10 minutes. (Dissolve it in a small amount of wort first to make it easier to stir in.) Chill wort to 68°F (20°C) and transfer to fermenter. Add water to make 5.0 gallons (19 L) and aerate thoroughly. Pitch yeast and ferment beer at 68°F (20°C). Optionally, add vial of Clarity Ferm at beginning of fermentation or stir in Polyclar AT after fermentation finishes. These items increase the clarity of the finished beer. Keg, or add priming sugar and bottle.

ALL-GRAIN OPTION

Omit the malt extract and increase the amount of Pilsner malt to 8 pounds 2 ounces (3.7 kg). Mash at 150°F (66°C) for 60 minutes in 12 quarts (11 L) of water. Collect 6.0 gallons (23 L) of wort and boil for 60 minutes, adding hops at times indicated in the ingredient list.

PARTIAL MASH

When brewing using a partial mash, the brewer combines wort made in a small mash with reconstituted malt extract. Performing a small partial mash differs little from simply steeping specialty grains, at least in terms of the procedure. You just need to pay more attention to the temperature, and also the volume of water the grains "steep" in. You'll also likely want to rinse them (with roughly half to the full amount of water used in the mash). However, in both cases you're basically soaking grains in hot water.

In the case of steeping grains, you are simply dissolving the colors and flavors from the grain husks and the fermentables inside the grains. In a mash, you are doing this, plus dissolving starch from the interior of the grain. By holding the partial mash at the specified temperature (and mash thickness), these starches are degraded into fermentable sugars by enzymes from the grain.

A small partial mash brings the aroma of the base grains to the beer. When malt extract is made, some of this aroma is lost. As such, beers made entirely from malt extract have a very light malt aroma and may seem somewhat like alcoholic iced tea. Steeping specialty malts adds the aroma of those malts, but the aroma of base malt is also important to making the best beers.

Most of the extract beers (or extract options) in this book employ a small partial mash—3.0 pounds (1.4 kg) of grains per 5.0-gallon (19-L) batch. It's very manageable for anyone who has done an "extract and steeped grain" beer, and produces superior results. Also, since malt extract is more expensive than a comparable amount of malt, the brewer also saves a bit of money.

RECIPE OPTIONS AND NOTES

You can substitute 12–24 ounces (340–680 g) of table sugar for an equivalent amount of the liquid malt extract. This will produce a beer that is drier, and slightly lighter in color. Because plain sugar is 100 percent fermentable, while malt extract is typically around 75 percent fermentable, this substitution also increases the alcoholic content of the beer slightly (from 4.9 percent ABV to 5.0 percent ABV).

SPITFIRE BITTER
STRONG BITTER

As the name implies, strong bitter is a comparatively strong ale in the bitter family. Strong bitters frequently have some caramel character with toasty and biscuit-like notes from English pale ale malt (and sometimes other specialty malts, such as biscuit malt). The aroma and flavor of English hops are prominent, and—again, as the name implies—are relatively bitter. They do not rival American IPAs, or even most American pale ales, in terms of bitterness, however.

This recipe produces a beer reminiscent of Fullers ESB, a malty, moderate-bodied beer with the flavor and aroma of English hops (especially Kent Goldings).

5.0 GALLONS (19 L) AT 5.9% ABV
OG = 1.059, FG = 1.013
34 IBU, 10 SRM

+ Wyeast 1968 (London ESB) or White Labs WLP002 (English Ale) yeast; A 2.1-qt. (2.0-L) yeast starter is recommended
+ 1 lb. 14 oz. (850 g) English pale ale malt (3°L)
+ 1 lb. 2 oz. (510 g) crystal malt (60°L)
+ 4.0 lb. (1.8 kg) light dried malt extract
+ 1.0 lb. (450 g) corn sugar
+ 0.75 oz. (21 g) Target hops at 10% alpha acids, boiled for 60 minutes (28 IBU)
+ 0.33 oz. (9.4 g) Northdown hops at 8.5% alpha acids, boiled for 10 minutes (3.8 IBU)
+ 0.33 oz. (9.4 g) Challenger hops at 7.5% alpha acids, boiled for 5 minutes (1.9 IBU)
+ 0.50 oz. (14 g) Kent Goldings hops at 5% alpha acids, boiled for 0 minutes (0 IBU)
+ 0.50 oz. (14 g) Kent Goldings hops (dry hops)
+ 0.50 tsp. Irish moss, boiled for 15 minutes
+ 0.25 tsp. yeast nutrients, boiled for 10 minutes
+ 4.5 oz. (130 g) corn sugar, for priming to 2.4 volumes CO_2

Make your yeast starter two to three days ahead of time. In your brew pot, heat 2.0 gallons (7.6 L) of water to a boil. Aim to reach boiling when the small mash is done. In a separate, large pot (8-quart [8-L] or larger) heat 1.0 gallon (3.8 L) of water to 163°F (73°C). Place the crushed grains in a nylon steeping bag and submerge them in the second pot, and let the temperature settle in to around 152°F (67°C). Let the mash rest at 152°F (67°C) for 60 minutes. You may need to add heat occasionally to maintain this temperature. Slowly heat the grain and water mixture to 168°F (76°C), stirring constantly.

In a third pot, heat 0.50 gallons (1.9 L) of water to 170°F (77°C) to use as sparge water. Place a large colander over your brew pot and set the grain bag in it. Pour the wort from "steeping" the grains through the grain bag.

(This is to filter out any solid pieces of grain.) Then, carefully rinse the grains with the 170°F (77°C) sparge water. You should yield about 3.0 gallons (11 L) of wort.

Stir in roughly half of the malt extract and 1 pound (450 g) of corn sugar and bring the wort to a boil. Once the first bits of hot break show, add the Target hops and boil for 60 minutes. Add remaining hops at times indicated. Add Irish moss for final 15 minutes of the boil. As the boil progresses, do not let the wort volume drop below 2.5 gallons (9.5 L). Top up with boiling water, if needed.

Stir in the sugar, remaining malt extract and yeast nutrients in the last 10 minutes. (Dissolve it in a small amount of wort first to make it easier to stir in.) Chill wort to 68°F (20°C) and transfer to fermenter. Add water to make 5.0 gallons (19 L) and aerate thoroughly. Pitch yeast and ferment beer at 68°F (20°C). Dry hop for seven to 10 days. Keg, or add priming sugar and bottle.

ALL-GRAIN OPTION

Omit the malt extract and increase the amount of pale ale malt to 8 pounds 12 ounces (4.0 kg). Mash at 152°F (67°C). Collect about 6.4 gallons (24 L) of wort and boil for 90 minutes, adding hops at times indicated.

BOTTLE CONDITIONING

Bottle conditioning is a simple way for homebrewers to carbonate their beer. Some commercial beers, including many English ales, are bottle-conditioned. The basic idea is that fermented beer is primed with sugar and sealed in bottles. Yeast in the beer consume the sugar and turn it into carbon dioxide (and ethanol). Since the bottle is sealed, the carbon dioxide cannot escape. The gas saturates the beer and builds up pressure in the headspace of the bottle, giving the beer its fizz.

Bottle-conditioned beers must be stored upright and will form a layer of yeast on the bottom. You will need to pour the beer off the yeast and into a glass to enjoy it.

The level of carbonation achieved depends on the residual level of carbonation after fermentation and the amount of sugar added. Although fermented beer may seem flat, it does retain some carbon dioxide (CO_2). How much of it the beer retains is a function of temperature. Cooler fermentation retains more carbon dioxide. See the two charts on my website (beerandwinejounal.com/residual-co2) to fine-tune your level of carbonation. Your target level of carbonation minus the residual level of carbonation (in volumes of CO_2) gives you the amount of carbonation that must be produced by the sugar.

To minimize the amount of yeast at the bottom of your bottles, let the beer fall completely clear before bottling it. When priming the beer, boil the priming sugar in as little water as you can manage. Place the priming solution in your bottling bucket and rack the beer into it. Stir so the sugar is evenly distributed, but stir quietly so you minimize the amount of oxygen that enters the beer. Bottle the beer and cap the bottles as quickly as you can, again to minimize the beer's exposure to oxygen. Store the bottles somewhere warm—around 80°F (27°C), if possible—for about two weeks, then take one bottle and chill it for a few days. If it is carbonated, cool the rest of the batch.

RECIPE OPTIONS AND NOTES

Some British ales have a distinctly biscuit-like flavor. Sometimes this is achieved by adding biscuit malt. If you like that character, try swapping between 4.0–8.0 ounces (110–230 g) of biscuit malt (or Victory malt) for an equivalent amount of the crystal malt. Four ounces (110 g) in a 5.0-gallon (19-L) batch will lend a very subtle biscuit note. Eight ounces (230 g) in the same-sized batch will have a strong biscuit character.

MAN IN BLACK PORTER
AMERICAN PORTER

American porter is a stronger, hoppier version of an English porter. It was among the first styles of beers American brewers began producing during the craft beer revolution. It's a malty, full-bodied beer that features roasty flavors from darkly roasted grains, with black malt being used frequently as the primary dark grain. The roast character is matched with aggressive hopping from American hops. All told, American porter is a moderately strong, intensely flavorful ale.

5.0 GALLONS (19 L) AT 6.2% ABV
OG = 1.064, FG = 1.016
45 IBU, 36 SRM

+ Wyeast 1056 (American Ale), White Labs WLP001 (California Ale) or Fermentis U.S.-05 (dried) yeast
+ A 2.1-qt. (2.0-L) yeast starter is recommended
+ 3 lb. 10 oz. (1.6 kg) U.S. 2-row pale malt
+ 12 oz. (340 g) caramel malt (60°L)
+ 3.0 oz. (85 g) caramel malt (90°L)
+ 8.0 oz. (230 g) chocolate malt
+ 8.0 oz. (230 g) black malt
+ 4.0 lb. (1.8 kg) light dried malt extract
+ 0.66 oz. (19 g) Nugget hops at 13% alpha acids, boiled for 60 minutes (31 IBU)
+ 0.75 oz. (21 g) Columbus hops at 15% alpha acids, boiled for 10 minutes (15 IBU)
+ 0.75 oz. (21 g) Willamette hops at 5% alpha acids, boiled for 0 minutes (0 IBU)
+ 5.0 oz. (140 g) corn sugar, to prime bottles for 2.5 volumes of CO_2

If you are using one of the liquid yeasts, make your yeast starter two to three days ahead of time. Crush the pale malt separately from the other malts. Mix the crystal malt and the dark malts together. Line an 8-quart (8-L) beverage cooler with a large steeping bag. Heat 5.5 quarts (5.2 L) of water to 163°F (73°C). Add a couple cups of hot water to the cooler, then add the same volume of pale malt, stir and repeat until you've used up all the pale malt. Then add roughly 6.0 ounces (170 g) of the mixed roasted and specialty malts in the same fashion on top of the pale malts.

Add the rest of the water, if needed, so you have 4.0 pounds (1.8 kg) of grain in the cooler and 5.5 quarts (5.2 L) of water. Let this sit, at 152°F (67°C), for 60 minutes to mash. (The temperature will likely drop 4–5°F [2–2.5°C] in this time. This is fine.) While the malts are mashing in the cooler, steep the remaining specialty malts at 150°F (66°C) in 7.0 quarts (6.6 L) of water in your brew pot.

(continued)

Partial mashing can be a step towards all-grain brewing.

In a separate pot, heat 5.0 quarts (4.7 L) of water to 170°F (77°C). When the mash is done, remove the steeping grains from your brew pot, and stir in roughly 3.0 pounds (1.4 kg) of the malt extract. Heat this to 150°F (66°C) and hold the wort in your brew pot around 150°F (66°C) as you collect the wort from the cooler. Recirculate the wort in the cooler, and run off the wort as you normally would—collect a cup or two of wort and pour it in the brew pot, then pour the same volume of sparge water on top of the grain bed. Wait about 30 seconds between each round of collecting wort and adding sparge water. When you run out of sparge water, simply drain the rest of the liquid from the cooler. When you are done, you should have about 3.5 gallons (13 L) of wort in your brew pot.

Bring the wort to a boil, add the first dose of hops, and boil for 60 minutes. Add the other hops at times indicated. Stir the remaining malt extract into the wort in the last few minutes of the boil. (The best way to do this is to put a portion of the dried malt extract in a separate pot, then ladle hot wort onto it. Once dissolved, pour it into the boil. Stir the wort, and then repeat until all the extract is stirred in.) Chill the wort to 68°F (20°C). Transfer to your fermenter and add water to make 5.0 gallons (19 L). Aerate this wort, and pitch the yeast. Ferment at 68°F (20°C). Keg or bottle condition, aiming for 2.5 volumes of CO_2. Keg or add priming sugar and bottle.

ALL-GRAIN OPTION

Omit the malt extract and increase the amount of pale malt to 10 pounds 6 ounces (4.7 kg). Mash the grains in 15 quarts (14 L) of water. Your mash temperature should be 152°F (67°C). Collect around 8.0 gallons (30 L) of wort and boil to reduce to just over 5.0 gallons (19 L), adding hops at times indicated.

COMBINING STEEPING AND PARTIAL MASHING

This porter uses a technique that combines the steeping of specialty grains with a partial mash. In this beer, the pale malt is mashed and the specialty grains that can be steeped, are steeped. This procedure works well for most partial mash formulations of porter and stout.

Dark grains are acidic. In a full mash, adding some carbonates to the water can offset the acidity because the percentage of dark grains is unlikely to be over 15 percent. A partial mash, however, will contain all the dark grains in the recipe, but a smaller amount of base grains. As such, the percentage of dark grains in the small, partial mash may be much higher. This can cause the pH of the mash to drop too low, inhibiting the ability of the starch-degrading enzymes to work properly.

A simple solution is to steep any specialty grains that do not need to be mashed separately, and lower the amount of dark grains in the small mash. In a countertop partial mash, you perform the mash in a small cooler, so your brew pot is free to steep any additional specialty grains. This makes for a slightly more complex brew day, but it is far from unmanageable.

FRANK'S GUESTS
IRISH RED ALE

Irish red ale is a fairly low-gravity, balanced ale. Although similar to English session ales, Irish red ales usually show less caramel character and have a slight roasted grain "bite" that may be most noticeable in the aftertaste.

5.0 GALLONS (19 L) AT 4.2% ABV
OG = 1.044, FG = 1.011
23 IBU, 13 SRM

+ Wyeast 1084 (Irish Ale) or White Labs WLP004 (Irish Ale) yeast
+ A 1.1-qt. (1.0-L) yeast starter is recommended
+ 3 lb. 6 oz. (1.5 kg) U.K. 2-row pale ale malt
+ 5.0 oz. (140 g) crystal malt (40°L)
+ 5.0 oz. (140 g) roasted barley (300°L)
+ 2 lb. 10 oz. (1.2 kg) light dried malt extract
+ 0.75 oz. (21 g) First Gold hops at 8% alpha acids, boiled for 60 minutes (22 IBU)
+ 0.25 oz. (7.1 g) Fuggles hops at 5% alpha acids, boiled for 5 minutes (1 IBU)
+ 0.50 tsp. Irish moss, boiled for 15 minutes
+ 4.5 oz. (130 g) corn sugar, for priming to 2.4 volumes CO_2

Make your yeast starter two to three days ahead of time. In your brew pot, heat 5.5 quarts (5.2 L) of brewing liquor (see page 12 in the Section 1 opener) to 163°F (73°C). Place the crushed grains in a large steeping bag and submerge in brew pot water. Mash at 152°F (67°C) for 45 minutes, stirring and heating briefly every 10 minutes to maintain the mash temperature. In a separate pot, heat 5.0 quarts (4.7 L) of water to 170°F (77°C). When the mash is done, heat it to 170°F (77°C) for a mash out. Lift bag and let it drip into the brew pot until you can move it over to the cooler without splattering too much wort.

Scoop or pour the wort from the brew pot into the cooler. Recirculate the wort until it is clear, then run off. Sparge steadily over 60 minutes (collect about a cup of wort from the cooler every 90 seconds) to collect about 10 quarts (9.5 L) of wort. Add about 2.0 quarts (1.9 L) of water to the brew pot, and start heating it as you collect the wort. You should yield about 3.5 gallons (13 L) of wort.

When you're done collecting the wort, stir in roughly one-third of the malt extract and bring the wort to a boil. Add the first dose of hops and boil wort for 60 minutes. Add other hops at times indicated. Add Irish moss for final 15 minutes of boil. Stir in remaining malt extract in the last 10 minutes of the boil. Chill wort to 68°F (20°C), then rack to fermenter. Add water to make 5.0 gallons (19 L), aerate wort thoroughly, and pitch yeast. Ferment at 68°F (20°C). After fermentation stops, let the beer settle for seven to 10 days or rack to a secondary fermenter to clear. Rack to a keg or bottling bucket. Carbonate to 2.4 volumes of CO_2. Keg or add priming sugar and bottle.

(continued)

ALL-GRAIN OPTION

Omit malt extract. Increase the amount of pale ale malt to 7 pounds 12 ounces (3.5 kg). Mash at 152°F (67°C) in 11 quarts (10 L) of water. Mash for 60 minutes, and then collect around 5.0 gallons (19 L) of pre-boil wort. (If you collect too much more from this relatively small grain bed, you may run into problems with extracting excessive amounts of tannins.) Add water so you have enough to boil vigorously for 60 minutes and be left with just over 5.0 gallons (19 L). (And you can add water during the boil, if your initial estimate is low.) Boil for 60 minutes, adding hops at times indicated.

COUNTERTOP PARTIAL MASHING

Countertop partial mashing is one way to easily manage a fairly large partial mash. A 8-quart (8-L) beverage cooler is lined with a large steeping bag, and 4.0 pounds (1.8 kg) of grain are mashed in it. Alternately, the grains can be mashed in your brew pot and then transferred to the cooler for lautering (as in this recipe). You do not need to modify the cooler in any way for this to work well. This amount of grain will yield roughly 2.5 gallons (9.5 L) of wort at a specific gravity around SG 1.044. You can boil your hops in this wort—and a small amount of dissolved malt extract—and add the bulk of your malt extract near the end of the boil.

To collect the wort, you just drain a cup or two from the cooler and pour it in your brew pot. Then, add the same amount of sparge water to the top of the grains and repeat until the sparge water is gone. (For a 5.0-gallon [19-L] batch, you'll need 5.0 quarts [4.7 L] of sparge water—slightly less than the amount of water originally added to the cooler.)

Once the sparge water is gone, simply drain the rest of the wort—a cup or two at a time—until no more wort flows out of the grain bed. From this point on, your brew day is the same as any typical brew day using malt extract.

Cleanup is fairly simple because the grains are contained with the cooler. Just let them cool, perhaps overnight, and then lift out the bag and dispose of the grains. (Turn the bag inside out and rinse well to remove stray pieces of grain husk stuck in the mesh.)

You can do a small mash in your brew pot or in an insulated cooler.

BB-35 BROWN ALE
AMERICAN BROWN ALE

American brown ales showed up on the menus of many brewpubs in the early days of the craft beer revolution, and they are still popular, crowd-pleasing brews. Although the styles can overlap a bit, American brown ale is most often a stronger, hoppier version of an English brown ale.

Because of their early popularity among homebrewers in Texas, some homebrewers call the hoppiest interpretations of this style Texas brown ale. Brown ales are full-bodied brews that typically have a moderate amount of roast character, backed up by some sweetness from caramel malts. Although hoppier than most English versions, the hop character should not overshadow the malt profile in this beer.

5.0 GALLONS (19 L) AT 5.4% ABV
OG = 1.056, FG = 1.014
30 IBU, 23 SRM

+ Wyeast 1056 (American Ale), White Labs WLP001 (California Ale), or Fermentis U.S.-05 yeast; A 1.6-qt. (1.5-L) yeast starter is recommended
+ 1 lb. 3 oz. (540 g) U.S. 2-row pale malt
+ 10 oz. (280 g) caramel malt (40°L)
+ 8.0 oz. (230 g) caramel malt (60°L)
+ 3.0 oz. (85 g) caramel malt (90°L)
+ 8.0 oz. (230 g) chocolate malt
+ 4 lb. 10 oz. (2.1 kg) light dried malt extract
+ 0.70 oz. (20 g) Northern Brewer hops at 9% alpha acids, boiled for 60 minutes (24 IBU)
+ 1.0 oz. (28 g) Willamette hops at 5% alpha acids, boiled for 10 minutes (6.7 IBU)
+ 1.0 oz. (28 g) Willamette hops at 5% alpha acids, boiled for 0 minutes (0 IBU)
+ 5.0 oz. (140 g) corn sugar, to prime bottles for 2.5 volumes of CO_2

If you are using one of the liquid yeasts, make your yeast starter two to three days ahead of time. Heat 2.0 gallons (7.6 L) of water to a boil in your brew pot. Aim to reach boiling when the small mash is done. In a separate, large (8 quart [8-L] or larger) pot, heat 1.0 gallon (3.8 L) of water to 163°F (73°C). Place the crushed grains in a steeping bag and submerge them in the second pot. The temperature should settle in around 152°F (67°C). Let the mash rest at 152°F (67°C) for 60 minutes, then slowly heat it to 168°F (76°C), stirring constantly.

In a third pot, heat 2.0 quarts (1.8 L) of water to 170°F (77°C) to use as sparge water. Place a large colander over your brew pot, set the grain bag in it and pour the wort through it. (This is to filter out any solid pieces of grain.) Then, carefully rinse the grains with the sparge water. You should yield about 3.0 gallons (11 L) of wort. Stir in roughly half of the malt extract and bring the wort to a boil. Do not let wort volume drop below 2.5 gallons (9.5 L) during boil. (Top up with boiling water, if needed.)

(continued)

RECIPE OPTIONS AND NOTES

One option when brewing this beer is to increase the amount of hops to make it a Texas brown ale (or something approaching a brown IPA, if you prefer). Increasing the amount of bittering hops to around 1.25 ounces (35 g) will increase the bitterness to just short of 50 IBU. (This assumes 9 percent alpha acids.) You could also increase the amounts of the two late hop additions by 20 to 50 percent to add more hop flavor and aroma to the more bitter brown ale.

Once the boil starts and the first bits of hot break show, add the Northern Brewer hops and boil for 60 minutes. Add the Willamette hops at the times indicated. Stir in the remaining malt extract in the last 10 minutes. (Dissolve it in a small amount of wort first to make it easier to stir in.) Chill wort to 68°F (20°C) and transfer to fermenter. Add water to make 5.0 gallons (19 L) and aerate thoroughly. Pitch yeast and ferment beer at 68°F (20°C). Keg, or add priming sugar and bottle.

ALL-GRAIN OPTION

Omit the malt extract. Increase the amount of pale malt to 9 pounds 4 ounces (4.2 kg). Mash at 152°F (67°C) in 14 quarts (13 L) of water. Mash for 60 minutes, and then collect about 7.0 gallons (27 L) of wort. Boil to reduce to 5.0 gallons (19 L)—which may take 90–120 minutes—and add hops at the times indicated.

STEEPING VS. MASHING

Most of the malt extract recipes in this book are really partial mashes. All this means is that, in addition to the specialty grains being steeped, some base grains are also incorporated into the recipe. Because base grains are used, the "steeping" needs to be done within a certain temperature range (148–162°F [64–72°C]) and at a certain water-to-grain ratio (generally in the vicinity of 1–2.5 quarts (1–2.5 L) of water to every pound (450 g) of grain (2.1 pounds–5.2 L/kg). Other than that the mechanics are the same.

Specialty malts, including most crystal type malts and darkly roasted grains, can be steeped at virtually any temperature and water-to-grain ratio. All that occurs when they are steeped is that the colors and flavors come from the husks, and the sugars in their interiors are dissolved. Base malts—the kind that generally comprise over 80 percent of any all-grain grist—need to be mashed. This is because their interiors are starchy and this starch needs to dissolve and be degraded by enzymes in the malt. Base grains include malts labeled brewer's malt, pale malt, pale ale malt, Pilsner malt, Vienna malt and Munich malt.

If you do not know whether a malt needs to be mashed, or if it can be steeped, you should check the manufacturer's webpage. Or, you can simply avoid the issues and always "steep" your grains within the window of temperatures and water-to-grain ratios in which grains are mashed.

HALDANE'S HEAVY PALE ALE
ENGLISH IPA

IPAs are everywhere these days, and the IPAs that currently crowd our beer shelves in the U.S. are descended from English IPAs. Like the American IPA, English IPA is a stronger, drier, hoppier version of its corresponding pale ales. English IPAs cover quite a bit of ground, stylistically. English IPAs tend to have more malt character than American IPAs, however, and may have nutty, biscuity notes along with some caramel flavor.

5.0 GALLONS (19 L) AT 6.4% ABV
OG = 1.065, FG = 1.015
55 IBU, 6.2 SRM

+ White Labs WLP007 (Dry English Ale), Wyeast 1098 (British Ale) yeast, Fermentis Safale S-04 yeast
+ A 2.1-qt. (2.0-L) yeast starter is recommended
+ 2 lb. 2 oz. (960 kg) U.K. pale ale malt (3°L)
+ 8.0 oz. (230 g) crystal malt (30°L)
+ 5.0 oz. (140 g) biscuit malt
+ 8.0 oz. (230 g) cane sugar
+ 5.0 lb. (2.3 kg) light dried malt extract
+ 1.33 oz. (38 g) Target hops at 10% alpha acids, boiled for 60 minutes (50 IBU)
+ 0.50 oz. (14 g) Fuggles hops at 5% alpha acids, boiled for 10 minutes (3.4 IBU)
+ 0.50 oz. (14 g) East Kent Goldings hops at 5% alpha acids, boiled for 5 minutes (1.9 IBU)
+ 0.50 oz. (14 g) East Kent Goldings hops at 5% alpha acids, boiled for 0 minutes (0 IBU)
+ 0.50 oz. (14 g) East Kent Goldings hops at 5% alpha acids, dry hops (0 IBU)
+ 0.50 tsp. Irish moss, boiled for 15 minutes
+ 4.75 oz. (130 g) corn sugar, to prime for 2.4 volumes of CO_2

If you are using one of the liquid yeasts, make your yeast starter two to three days ahead of time. Heat 2.0 gallons (7.6 L) of water to a boil in your brew pot. Aim to reach boiling when the small mash is done. In a separate, large (8-quart [8-L] or larger) pot, heat 1.0 gallon (3.8 L) of water to 163°F (73°C). Place the crushed grains in a steeping bag and submerge them in the second pot. The temperature should settle in around 152°F (67°C). Let the mash rest at 152°F (67°C) for 60 minutes, then slowly heat it to 168°F (76°C), stirring constantly. In a third pot, heat 2.0 quarts (1.8 L) of water to 170°F (77°C) to use as sparge water. Place a large colander over your brew pot, set the grain bag in it and pour the wort through it. (This is to filter out any solid pieces of grain.) Then, carefully rinse the grains with the sparge water. You should yield about 3.0 gallons (11 L) of wort.

(continued)

This recipe uses biscuit malt to increase the biscuit-like flavor in this ale. Not everyone enjoys this character, and you can decrease the amount or omit the biscuit malt and replace it with the same amount of crystal malt (30°L). This yields a beer of basically the same strength (and color), but with less biscuit and more caramel flavor.

Stir in roughly half of the malt extract and bring the wort to a boil. Do not let wort volume drop below 2.5 gallons (9.5 L) during boil. (Top up with boiling water if needed.) Once the boil starts and the first bits of hot break show, add the Target hops and boil for 60 minutes. Add the remaining hops at the times indicated. Add Irish moss for final 15 minutes of boil.

Stir in the sugar and remaining malt extract in the last 10 minutes. (Dissolve it in a small amount of wort first to make it easier to stir in.) Chill wort to 68°F (20°C) and let sit for between 20 minutes to 2 hours to let the hop debris settle. Keep the brew pot covered during this time. Then transfer the wort to the fermenter. Add water to make 5.0 gallons (19 L) and aerate thoroughly. Pitch yeast and ferment beer at 68°F (20°C). Dry hop for seven to 10 days. Keg, or add priming sugar and bottle.

ALL-GRAIN OPTION

Omit the malt extract and increase the amount of pale ale malt to 10 pounds 10 ounces (4.8 kg). Mash at 152°F (67°C) in 16 quarts (15 L) for 60 minutes. Collect around 7.0 gallons (27 L) and boil to reduce volume to 5.0 gallons (19 L), adding hops at times indicated.

HOPS: TO BAG OR NOT TO BAG

This recipe uses a fair amount of (pellet) hops. In hoppy beers, brewers are always faced with the problem of how to separate the spent hop debris from the wort. If some hop material carries over to the fermenter, it's not the end of the world. However, lots of hop "gunk" in your fermenter is not desirable. This recipe solves the problem by letting the chilled wort sit (covered) for at least 20 minutes. In this time, the largest bits of hop material will have settled to the bottom of the brew pot. Longer settling times will give smaller particles time to settle and yield progressively clearer wort.

Another solution is to place your hops in a small mesh bag and place the bag in your brew pot. When the boil is over, fish the bag out to remove the hop debris. This is simple, but is has some downsides. For one, the amount of bitterness and aroma extracted from the hops is lowered slightly. Also, unless the hops are given a lot of room in the bag, it's possible that some will clump together. The result will hop clumps with dry interiors. The dry areas will not have contributed anything to the beer. For this reason, it is best to fill a hop bag only one-third full. The remaining volume allows the hop pellets to expand and wort to flow around the pellets.

There are other solutions for dealing with hops, including kettles with false bottoms or hop screens. (The solution you choose also depends on whether you use pellet or whole hops.) I think letting the chilled wort settle is a good choice because you get the most from your hops, and don't need any further equipment or gadgets to aid in the separation—just let gravity and time do their thing. I usually occupy myself during the settling period with cleaning up or other tasks.

CALCIFIED DUBBEL
BELGIAN-STYLE DUBBEL

Dubbels (or doubles) originated in the Trappist monastic brewing tradition as beers intermediate in strength between Trappist singles and tripels (triples). The name is an indicator of the beer's strength, but dubbels are not literally twice as strong as singles. Dubbels are dark beers with a rounded dark malt profile and a dry finish. Their aroma is fruity and may additionally show signs of pepper, cloves or other phenolic aromas. These aromas are yeast products, not the result of actual spicing. The level of bitterness, coupled with the dry finish of the beer, combine to yield a surprisingly quaffable beverage, given its alcoholic strength of 6 to 7.6 percent ABV.

The grain bills of actual Belgian dubbels vary greatly, but many American homebrew versions have "calcified" around the idea of using Special "B" malt for the dark caramel flavor and darker grains, usually chocolate, for color. This recipe is strongly in that homebrewing tradition, although the style itself could be approached with very different malts and sugars.

5.0 GALLONS (19 L) AT 7.1% ABV
OG = 1.070, FG = 1.015
30 IBU, 15 SRM

+ Wyeast 3787 (Trappist Ale) or White Labs WLP530 (Abbey Ale) yeast
+ A 2.3-qt. (2.2-L) yeast starter is recommended
+ 2 lb. 5 oz. (1.1 kg) Munich malt
+ 8.0 oz. (230 g) Special "B" malt (150°L)
+ 3.0 oz. (85 g) chocolate malt
+ 1.0 lb. (450 g) cane sugar
+ 5 lb. 2 oz. (2.3 kg) Pilsner dried malt extract
+ 2.5 oz. (71 g) Saaz hops at 3.5% alpha acids, boiled for 60 minutes (30 IBU)
+ 0.50 tsp. Irish moss, boiled for 15 minutes
+ 5.0 oz. (140 g) corn sugar, to prime bottles for 2.5 volumes of CO_2

Make your yeast starter two to three days ahead of time. Heat 2.0 gallons (7.6 L) of water to a boil in your brew pot. Aim to reach boiling when the small mash is done. In a separate, large (8-quart [8-L] or larger) pot, heat 1.0 gallon (3.8 L) of water to 163°F (73°C). Place the crushed grains in a steeping bag and submerge them in the second pot. The temperature should settle in around 152°F (67°C). Let the mash rest at 152°F (67°C) for 60 minutes, then slowly heat it to 168°F (76°C), stirring constantly.

(continued)

RECIPE OPTIONS AND NOTES

In Belgium, dubbels are very diverse. Some are made with just Pilsner malts and sufficient dark sugars to adjust the color. You can take this (or any decent) dubbel recipe and adjust the amount and color of the crystal malts (Special "B" is a dark crystal malt), so long as the beer doesn't end up with a strong caramel sweetness.

You can get your dark color either from dark roasted grains (as done here), from dark sugar additions in the kettle or a blend of the two. You can use virtually any blend of Munich malt, Vienna malt and Pilsner for your base malts. You can also add small amounts of other specialty malts—including Belgian biscuit malt or aromatic malt—to give a more complex malt character. (Keep in mind that the yeast is going to make the aroma complex, even with a simple malt bill.) Not every possible combination of ingredients will yield a wonderful beer, but you have a lot of "wiggle room" to tinker with this recipe and still have a beer that's recognizably a dubbel. As long as the original gravity (1.062–1.075) and color (10–17 SRM) are in the right range, you're on your way.

In a third pot, heat 2.0 quarts (1.8 L) of water to 170°F (77°C) to use as sparge water. Place a large colander over your brew pot, set the grain bag in it and pour the wort through it. (This is to filter out any solid pieces of grain.) Then carefully rinse the grains with the sparge water. You should yield about 3.0 gallons (11 L) of wort. Stir in roughly half of the malt extract and bring the wort to a boil. Do not let wort volume drop below 2.5 gallons (9.5 L) during boil. (Top up with boiling water if needed.)

Once the boil starts and the first bits of hot break show, add the hops and boil for 60 minutes. Add Irish moss with 15 minutes left in the boil. Stir in the remaining malt extract in the last 10 minutes. (Dissolve it in a small amount of wort first to make it easier to stir in.) Chill wort to 68°F (20°C) and transfer to the fermenter. Add water to make 5.0 gallons (19 L) and aerate thoroughly. Pitch yeast and ferment beer at 72°F (22°C). Keg, or add priming sugar and bottle.

ALL-GRAIN OPTION

Omit the malt extract and add 8 pounds 10 ounces (3.9 kg) of Pilsner malt to the recipe. Mash at 152°F (67°C) in 15 quarts (145 L) for 60 minutes. Collect around 7.5 gallons (29 L) and boil to reduce volume to 5.0 gallons (19 L), adding hops at times indicated. To avoid a prolonged boil, you may choose to collect less wort and add a small amount of malt extract or sugar near the end of the boil to make up the difference. Take a gravity reading as you near the end of the boil, and let this be a guide to how much to add. (One pound [450 g] of dried malt extract adds 9 "gravity points" to 5.0 gallons [19 L] or wort.)

KETTLE SUGARS

In much all-grain brewing, all of the wort sugars are formed in the mash and boiled in the kettle (or brew pot). However, adding sugars to the boil also has a long history in brewing. Obviously, when homebrewing using malt extract, malt extract is added to the kettle. But there are other times sugar is used.

Sometimes sugar is added to wort simply to boost the strength of the beer without increasing its body. Simple sugars, like sucrose and glucose, are completely fermentable. They are consumed by the yeast and converted entirely to ethanol and carbon dioxide (and heat). So, adding cane sugar (sucrose) or corn sugar (glucose) increases the original gravity (OG) of a beer, but not the final gravity (FG). And, it does so without directly adding any flavor to the beer. (Alcohol, of course, has a flavor. And, the added stress of more sugar may cause the yeast to produce more byproducts, such as esters.)

Other forms of sugar add flavor and perhaps color to the beer. Beer can be brewed with caramelized sugars, molasses, treacle, invert sugar or honey. This beer is brewed with simple cane sugar, but some homebrewers like to make their beers using Belgian candi sugar, which comes in light and dark colors and adds a certain flavor to their beers.

KING LUPULOR
AMERICAN DOUBLE IPA

This is a double IPA—big, and very, very hoppy. Double IPA is a pale beer, but it will be hazy due to the large dose of dry hops. Double IPAs have great foam stands and the aroma is overwhelmingly of hops. This wonderful floral aroma is backed up by a lot of bitterness. In fact, given the solubility of iso alpha acids in wort—not to mention the point at which your tongue gets saturated with bitterness—you won't find a beer that tastes more bitter than this.

5.0 GALLONS (19 L) AT 7.5% ABV
OG = 1.072, FG = 1.014
100+ IBU, 5 SRM

+ Wyeast 1056 (American Ale), White Labs WLP001 (California Ale) or Fermentis U.S.-05 yeast; A yeast starter is not required
+ 3.75 lb. (1.7 kg) Pilsner malt
+ 8.0 oz. (230 g) caramel malt (30°L)
+ 4.0 lb. (1.8 kg) light dried malt extract
+ 1.0 oz. (28 g) Warrior hops at 16% alpha acids, boiled for 60 minutes (60 IBU)
+ 0.75 oz. (28 g) Summit hops at 17% alpha acids, boiled for 60 minutes (48 IBU)
+ 0.75 oz. (21 g) Ahtanum hops at 6% alpha acids, boiled for 0 minutes (0 IBU)
+ 0.75 oz. (21 g) Cascade hops at 6% alpha acids, boiled for 0 minutes (0 IBU)
+ 0.75 oz. (21 g) Amarillo hops at 9% alpha acids, boiled for 0 minutes (0 IBU)
+ 1.0 oz. (28 g) Ahtanum hops (dry hops)
+ 1.0 oz. (28 g) Amarillo hops (dry hops)
+ 1.5 lb. (680 g) cane sugar
+ ¼ tsp. Irish moss, boiled for 15 minutes (in step 1)
+ ¼ tsp. Irish moss, boiled for 15 minutes (in step 2)
+ 5.0 oz. (140 g) corn sugar, to prime bottles for 2.5 volumes of CO_2

OVERVIEW: If you are using one of the liquid yeasts, make your yeast starter two to three days ahead of time. Make 2.0 gallons (7.6 L) of wort on day one. Pitch yeast. Make 3.0 gallons (11 L) of wort on day two and add to fermenting beer.

STEP 1: In your brew pot, heat 2.5 quarts (2.4 L) of brewing liquor to 159°F (71°C). Place roughly two-fifths of the crushed grains—a little less than 2 pounds (0.9 kg)—in a large steeping bag and submerge in brew pot liquor Mash at 148°F (64°C) for 60 minutes, stirring and heating briefly every 10 minutes to maintain the mash temperature. In a separate pot, heat 2.0 quarts (1.9 L) of water to 170°F (77°C). When the mash is done, heat it to 170°F (77°C) for a mash out. Lift the bag and let it drip into the brew pot until you can move it over into a colander. Set the colander on top of your brew pot.

(continued)

RECIPE OPTIONS AND NOTES

Believe it or not, one option when brewing this recipe is to add even more hops. Although the beer cannot be any more bitter, it's possible to pack more hop flavor or aroma into it. You could add some hops near the end of the boil (in the 5–15 minute range), add more dry hops or double-dry hop.

Double-dry hopping is when you dry hop the beer, remove the dry hops and then add a second dose of dry hops. The amount of hops you add is up to you, but keep in mind that hops absorb wort and you'll lose a little volume of beer for every bit of hops you add. For best results, experiment by increasing the amounts slightly each time you brew this until you hit a level you like.

Rinse the grain bag with the 170°F (77°C) water. Add roughly 1 pound (450 g) of malt extract to the wort. Add water to make a total volume of 2.5 gallons (9.5 L) and bring to a boil. Boil for 60 minutes adding two-fifths of the hops at each time indicated. (You do not have to be super-accurate in measuring out two-fifths of the hops. That is 40 percent of the total. If it's easier, just add half the hops—50 percent—and you'll be fine.)

In the last 15 minutes of the boil, stir in 1 more pound (450 g) of malt extract, two-fifths of the cane sugar and the first dose of Irish moss. Make sure you have 2.0 gallons (7.6 L), or slightly more, at the end of the boil. Add water—preferably boiling water—if this is not the case. Chill wort to 68°F (20°C), then rack your 2.0 gallons (7.6 L) of wort to your fermenter. (If you let the chilled wort sit, covered, for about an hour, you'll give it time for the trub to compact and yield more wort. You can also save the trub in a sanitized container overnight in your refrigerator and add the fresh wort to your chilled wort the next day.) Aerate wort thoroughly, and pitch yeast. No starter is needed if your yeast is fresh. Ferment at 68°F (20°C).

STEP 2: Repeat what you did in step 1, but make 3.0 gallons (11.4 L) of wort instead of 2.0 gallons (7.6 L). Mash the remaining grains at 148°F (64°C) in 2.8 quarts (2.7 L) of water. Mash out to 170°F (77°C). Rinse grains with 1.5 quarts (1.4 L) of 170°F (77°C) water. Add 1 more pound (450 g) of malt extract to the wort and add water to make 3.5 gallons (13 L). Boil for 60 minutes, adding the remaining hops at their appropriate times.

Add the remaining malt extract, sugar and Irish moss in the final 15 minutes of the boil. Make sure you have 3.0 gallons (11 L), or slightly more, at the end of the boil. Add water—preferably boiling water—if this is not the case. Chill the wort and let the hop debris settle, but do not aerate it. Check to make sure the wort temperature is 68°F (20°C)—or very close to that—and rack into fermenting beer. Do not aerate the fresh wort or the combined wort unless fermentation of previous day's wort is very sluggish. Continue fermenting at 68°F (20°C).

POST FERMENTATION: After fermentation stops, let the beer settle for two to three days, then rack to secondary fermenter. Dry hop for seven to 10 days, then rack to keg or bottling bucket. Carbonate to 2.5 volumes of CO_2.

ALL-GRAIN OPTION

Omit the malt extract. Increase the amount of Pilsner malt to 10.5 pounds (4.8 kg). Mash at 148°F (64°C) in 14 quarts (13 L) of water. Collect around 7.0 gallons (27 L) of wort and boil to reduce to 5.0 gallons (19 L) of wort. Add hops at times indicated.

TEXAS TWO-STEP

Boiling a dense wort, made at least partially from dissolved malt extract, and diluting it with water in your fermenter is a convenient way to homebrew. However, the denser the wort, the more color it picks up during the boil and the lower your hop utilization. When brewing the lightest, hoppiest homebrews with malt extract, you need to make some adjustments. This is one way to do it.

In the Texas Two-Step, you make part of your wort one day, and the rest the next. That way, you can boil each part at (or near) working strength. You also use the first of the two brews as your yeast starter. For best results, the two "steps" should be roughly equal in volume. (In this recipe, it's a 40:60 split, which is fine.)

And, you should brew the second step 16 to 24 hours after the first. This gives the yeast some time to grow in the first batch of wort. Do not aerate the second wort if the beer is strongly fermenting, and be sure you have cooled your second wort down to fermentation before adding it. If it is too hot, it will stun or kill the existing yeast. Once the two batches of wort are combined, finish the beer as you normally would.

2

DARK ALES: ROASTY AND DELICIOUS

This section gives the recipes for 13 dark ales. They range from an OG 1.038 (4.0 percent ABV) dry stout to an OG 1.099 (9.9 percent ABV) imperial stout—with other stouts, porters and other dark beers in between. The color of these beers ranges from 20 SRM to more than 40 SRM.

If you are treating your water, you should aim to have at least 100 ppm calcium (Ca^{+2}) ions, and between 220 ppm and 440 ppm bicarbonate (HCO_3^-), with the lower end for beers being around 20 SRM and the upper end for beers around 40 SRM. (When the boil starts, you may want add 50 ppm more calcium.) You do not have to adjust your water chemistry to match your beer's SRM exactly. Being in the ballpark is all you need.

If you are making your water by adding minerals to 5.0 gallons (19 L) of distilled or RO water, start by adding 7–14 g of sodium bicarbonate ($NaHCO_3$, baking soda), with the low end of the range corresponding to beers around 20 SRM and the high end corresponding to beers around 40 SRM. (Note: Some brewers claim that your brewing water should not contain more than 50 ppm sodium [Na^{2+}] Others say levels up to 100 ppm Na^{2+} are fine. Still others say levels up to 250 ppm Na^{2+} are fine. Over these limits and the beer will have a metallic taste, it is claimed.)

Following the instructions above, your water would contain 100 to 200 ppm sodium. If you brew a beer and it has a metallic taste, try reducing your sodium levels next time. Then choose a calcium addition depending on how much you want to accentuate the hops. For a balanced beer, add 4 g of calcium chloride ($CaCl_2$*$2H_2O$) and 4 g of calcium sulfate ($CaSO_4$*$2H_2O$, gypsum). For a beer in which the hops are to be accentuated, add 8 g of calcium sulfate ($CaSO_4$*$2H_2O$, gypsum). You will need to prepare more than 5.0 gallons (19 L) of brewing liquor for the all-grain versions of these beers.

For the extract versions, you only need to prepare brewing liquor (water with the correct mineral additions) of the grains you steep or mash. Use distilled water, RO water or naturally soft water for diluting the malt extract.

If you have a water report that describes what is in your water, you can use brewing software to plan your mineral additions. Remember to treat your water to remove any chlorine compounds, if present (as they are in all municipal water sources).

POGUE MAHONE STOUT
DRY STOUT

Despite the misguided idea that some beer drinkers hold—that dark beers are strong beers—dry stout is a low-gravity ale. Although low in strength, it is very flavorful—with the roast character in commercial examples ranging from pleasantly chocolate-like to aggressively coffee-like.

This is a balanced dry stout, in the tradition of Murphy's. It has a relatively mild roast character, well balanced by just enough hops. These days, most commercial Irish dry stouts are served via nitrogen—either pushed with a mix of nitrogen and carbon dioxide on tap or from a can with a widget in it. However, in my opinion, this stout tastes best carbonated as a regular beer would be.

5.0 GALLONS (19 L) AT 4.0% ABV
OG = 1.038, FG = 1.007
32 IBU, 34 SRM

+ Wyeast 1098 (British Ale), White Labs WLP007 (Dry English Ale) or Fermentis Safale S-04 yeast
+ A 1.1-qt. (1.0-L) yeast starter is recommended
+ 5.0 lb. (2.3 kg) 2-row pale ale malt (3°L)
+ 2.0 oz. (57 kg) caramel malt (80°L)
+ 4.0 oz. (110 kg) chocolate malt
+ 11 oz. (310 g) roasted barley (500°L)
+ 12 oz. (340 g) cane sugar
+ 0.75 oz. (21 g) Target hops at 11% alpha acids, boiled for 60 minutes (31 IBU)
+ 0.25 oz. (7.1 g) Kent Goldings hops at 5% alpha acids, boiled for 5 minutes (0.9 IBU)
+ 0.75 tsp. Irish moss, boiled for 15 minutes
+ 4.0 oz. (110 g) corn sugar, to prime to 2.2 volumes of CO_2

If you are using one of the liquid yeasts, make your yeast starter two to three days ahead of time. Heat 7.6 quarts (7.2 L) of brewing liquor to 160°F (71°C) and mash in crushed grains. Mash at 149°F (65°C) for 60 minutes, stirring every 15 minutes, if you can do so without losing too much heat from your mash tun. Heat or add boiling water to mash out to 168°F (76°C). Recirculate wort until clear, and then run off. Sparge steadily over 90 minutes to collect about 3.9 gallons (15 L) of wort.

Add water to yield a pre-boil volume that will yield 5.0 gallons (19 L) of wort after a 60-minute boil. On most homebrew setups, this would be 6.0–6.5 gallons (23–25 L). Boil wort for 60 minutes. Add hops and Irish moss at times indicated. Stir in cane sugar in the final 10 minutes of the boil. Chill wort, and then rack to fermenter. Aerate wort thoroughly and pitch sediment from yeast starter. Ferment at 68°F (20°C). Keg or add priming sugar to carbonate to 2.2 volumes of CO_2.

(continued)

MALT EXTRACT OPTION

Add 1 pound 14 ounces (850 g) of light dried malt extract to the recipe. Lower the amount of pale ale malt to 1.9 pounds (880 g). In your brew pot, steep the 3.0 pounds (1.4 kg) total of crushed grains in 4.1 quarts (3.9 L) of water at 149°F (65°C) for 60 minutes. (This is really a mash, so follow the temperature and volume guidelines closely.)

After steeping, place the grain bag in a large colander over your brew pot. Rinse the grains with 2.0 quarts (1.9 L) of 170°F (77°C) water. Add roughly half of the malt extract to the wort collected and adjust the wort volume with water to make 3.0 gallons (11 L) of wort. Boil for 60 minutes, adding hops and Irish moss at times indicated. Add the sugar and the remaining malt extract in the final 10 minutes of the boil.

DON'T OVERSPARGE LOW-GRAVITY BEERS

Collecting too much wort from a grain bed extracts excess tannins. This leads to astringency in the finished beer. In most moderate-strength to strong beers, this rarely occurs. However, in the case of low-gravity beers, some brewers will sparge until they reach their desired pre-boil volume. In some cases, they overshoot the volume of wort that can be safely collected from a given weight of grain.

If you use continuous sparging, monitor the late runnings and stop collecting when the pH climbs above 5.8. This usually corresponds with the specific gravity dropping below 1.008–1.010. When you reach this point, stop collecting wort and add water to make your required pre-boil volume. In this book, I suggest an amount of wort to collect for each recipe—0.65 gallons per pound of grain (5.4 L/kg). Use this as guidance, but not the final word, on how much wort to collect.

BALLINGARRY MINES STOUT
DRY STOUT (II)

Dry stout is a dark session ale. Although very flavorful, it is not sweet or full-bodied—hence the "dry" in the name. Roasted barley gives this beer an aromatic, coffee-like character, and this is matched by more hop bitterness than in the previous dry stout recipe (page 51). The mouthfeel of this stout, which is reminiscent of Guinness, can be accentuated by dispensing the beer with a 75:25 mix of nitrogen and carbon dioxide.

Beer dispensed with "stout gas" is under about 30 PSI in the keg. It requires a special gas tank to hold the gas mix. You also need a regulator that will fit the tank and regulate the serving pressure. Finally, you will need a tap that restricts the flow of beer. This keeps the beer from shooting out of the tap from the high pressure. It also encourages nitrogen to break out of the solution, producing the cascade effect you see when a Guinness is poured in a pub. The equipment required (and full instructions) are frequently sold as a package at many homebrew shops.

5.0 GALLONS (19 L) AT 4.2% ABV
OG = 1.041, FG = 1.009
39 IBU, 37 SRM

+ Wyeast 1084 (Irish Ale) or White Labs WLP004 (Irish Ale) yeast
+ A 1.1-qt. (1.0-L) yeast starter is recommended
+ 6 lb. 4 oz. (2.8 kg) English pale ale malt (3°L)
+ 1.0 lb. (450 g) flaked barley
+ 1.0 lb. (450 g) roasted barley (500°L)
+ 1.0 oz. (28 g) Target hops at 10% alpha acids, boiled for 60 minutes (37 IBU)
+ 0.50 oz. (14 g) East Kent Goldings hops at 5% alpha acids, boiled for 5 minutes (1.9 IBU)
+ 0.75 tsp. Irish moss, boiled for 15 minutes
+ 4.0 oz. (110 g) corn sugar, to prime to 2.2 volumes of CO_2

Make your yeast starter two to three days ahead of time. Heat 11 quarts (10 L) of brewing liquor to 161°F (72°C) and mash in grains. Mash at 150°F (66°C) for 60 minutes, stirring every 15 minutes, if you can do so without losing too much heat from your mash tun. Heat or add boiling water to mash out to 168°F (76°C). Recirculate wort until clear, and then run off.

Sparge steadily over 90 minutes to collect about 5.4 gallons (20 L) of wort. Add approximately half a gallon (2 L) of water and boil wort for 60 minutes, adding hops and Irish moss at times indicated. Chill wort, then rack to fermenter. Aerate wort thoroughly and pitch sediment from yeast starter. Ferment at 68°F (20°C). After fermentation stops, keg or bottle and carbonate to 2.2 volumes of CO_2. Or dispense with a 75:25 mix of nitrogen and carbon dioxide. Keg or add priming sugar and bottle.

(continued)

MALT EXTRACT OPTION

Add 2.5 pounds (1.1 kg) of light dried malt extract to the recipe. Decrease the amount of 2-row pale ale malt to 2.0 pounds (910 g). Place the crushed roasted barley in a nylon steeping bag and steep it at 150°F (66°C) in a brew pot. This will require about 1.5 quarts (1.4 L) of water. Place the flaked barley and crushed pale ale malt in a nylon steeping bag and mash them in 4.1 quarts (3.9 L) of water in your brew pot. The mash temperature should be 150°F (66°C). Hold this temperature for 60 minutes. Stir frequently and add heat to maintain temperature as needed.

After mashing, lift the grain bag from the brew pot into a large colander. Place the grain bag with roasted barley on top of it. Place colander over brew pot then pour "grain tea" from the steeped roasted barley into your brew pot. Next, rinse grains with 3.0 quarts (2.9 L) of water at 170°F (77°C). Stir in roughly half the malt extract and add water to bring wort volume to 3.0 gallons (11 L). Bring wort to boil and boil for 60 minutes. Add hops and Irish moss at times indicated. Stir in remaining malt extract in last 10 minutes of the boil.

BLACK MALT VS. ROASTED BARLEY

Black malt is malted barley that is roasted at similar temperatures and durations as coffee. Roasted barley is unmalted barley roasted in a similar manner. Both are roasted to around 500°L and contribute a roasted character to beer. However, because one is malted and the other isn't, their characteristics differ. Most important, roasted barley is highly aromatic. Its smell is reminiscent of coffee. In contrast, the aroma of black malt is very subdued. Roasted barley provides the coffee-like aroma and flavor in dry stout.

Black malt is often used in porters for a dark, roasted character without as much aroma. Small amounts of black malt are also used to adjust color in many beers. In a 5.0-gallon (19-L) batch, 2.0–3.0 ounces (57–85 g) of black malt will darken wort by 8.5–11 SRM, but not add any appreciable roasted aroma or flavor.

BOOMBALLATTY BROWN ALE
BRITISH BROWN ALE

Brown ale is a dark, balanced ale with less roast character than a stout or porter. It can be as light as session ales, or closer to a moderate-strength beer. Brown ales frequently get much of their roasted character from chocolate malt and are usually balanced towards being full-bodied and slightly sweet rather than dry.

Hopping is most often restrained. The best brown ales have a complex malt profile—with elements of roasted grains, caramel and biscuit—yet still give the overall impression of a balanced, quaffable ale. A small amount of fruity esters from English yeast can round out the beer, but should not be intense.

5.0 GALLONS (19 L) AT 4.0% ABV
OG = 1.044, FG = 1.013
28 IBU, 23 SRM

+ Wyeast 1968 (London ESB) or White Labs WLP002 (English Ale) yeast
+ A 1.1-qt. (1.0-L) yeast starter is recommended
+ 6.0 lb. (2.7 kg) U.K. 2-row pale ale malt (3°L)
+ 1.0 lb. (450 g) mild ale malt (4°L)
+ 12 oz. (340 g) crystal malt (45°L)
+ 7.0 oz. (200 g) crystal malt (60°L)
+ 7.0 oz. (200 g) U.K. chocolate malt (400°L)
+ 1.0 oz. (28 g) First Gold hops at 7.5% alpha acids, boiled for 60 minutes (28 IBU)
+ 0.75 oz. (21 g) Fuggles hops at 5% alpha acids, boiled for 0 minutes (0 IBU)
+ 0.75 tsp. Irish moss, boiled for 15 minutes
+ 3.5 oz. (100 g) corn sugar, to prime for 2.0 volumes CO_2

Make your yeast starter two to three days ahead of time. Heat 11 quarts (10 L) of brewing liquor to 165°F (74°C) and mash grains at 154°F (68°C). Hold at this temperature for 60 minutes, stirring every 15 minutes if possible. Mash out to 168°F (76°C) by adding direct heat or boiling water. Recirculate the wort until it is clear, then run off.

Use sufficient sparge water to collect about 5.6 gallons (21 L) of wort. Boil wort for 60 minutes, adding hops and Irish moss at times indicated. Chill wort, then rack to fermenter. If needed, add water to make 5.0 gallons (19 L). Aerate the wort thoroughly and pitch the sediment from the yeast starter. Ferment at 68°F (20°C). After fermentation stops, keg or bottle and carbonate to 2.0 volumes of CO_2. Alternately, ferment and dispense from a cask.

MALT EXTRACT OPTION

You can make a version of this without the mild ale malt by adding 3 pounds 4 ounces (1.5 kg) of dried malt extract to the recipe. Omit the mild ale malt and reduce the amount of 2-row pale ale malt to 1 pound 6 ounces (620 g). Put the crushed grains in a nylon steeping bag and "steep" in 4.1 quarts (3.9 L) of water in your brew pot for 45 minutes. Hold the temperature at 154°F (68°C) during this time.

After the "steep" (really a small mash), lift the grain bag out and place in a large colander. Place the colander over your brew pot and rinse grains with 2.0 quarts (1.9 L) of water at 170°F (77°C). Stir in roughly a third of the malt extract and add water to make 3.0 gallons (11 L) of wort. Boil wort for 60 minutes, adding hops and Irish moss at times indicated. Stir in remaining malt extract in the final 10 minutes of the boil.

CASK ALE

In the past, most British pubs served ale from casks. The beer was brewed, and then transferred to a sealed cask with some priming sugar for carbonation. Once the beer was carbonated, it was hand-pumped from the cask, using a device called a beer engine. The beer was lightly carbonated and had to have been fresh, as the keg allowed air in as beer was pumped from it.

This practice of conditioning and serving ale has seen a revival since the emergence of CAMRA (the Campaign for Real Ale), which began in the 1970s and has been increasingly influential since then. Homebrewers can mimic this style of serving by brewing their beer as normal, then racking the beer to a pin—a 5.4-gallon (20-L) cask—and letting it carbonate.

The brewer can also add dry hops and refining agents, if desired. Once carbonated, the cask is tapped and beer can be served by gravity, or via a beer engine. Only a few homebrew shops carry the equipment to dispense real ale, but they can be found with an Internet search.

RECIPE OPTIONS AND NOTES

This recipe contains roughly 12 percent mild ale malt. This malt can sometimes be hard to find. If you can't find any mild ale malt, replace it with an equal amount of either Munich malt (8–10°L) or U.K. 2-row pale malt (3°L). These changes will produce somewhat different tasting beers, but—if brewed well—all will be brown ales and taste good.

STRAIGHT OUTTA MORDOR PORTER
ENGLISH PORTER

English porter is a dark ale with a moderate amount of roasted malt character, balanced by a moderate amount of hop bitterness. The dark color usually comes from darkly roasted grains, especially chocolate malt, but may also partially come from dark sugars added in the kettle. Brown malt is often found in those recipes emulating a London-style porter. Other specialty malts, especially crystal malts, may be evident.

English porter is a moderate strength beer with medium body. The best versions are well-balanced and very drinkable. The American version of porter is generally stronger, shows more roasted grain character and more bitterness.

5.0 GALLONS (19 L) AT 4.4% ABV
OG = 1.046, FG = 1.011
31 IBU, 29 SRM

+ Wyeast 1028 (London Ale), White Labs WLP013 (London Ale) or Danstar Windsor yeast
+ A 1.1-qt. (1.0-L) yeast starter is recommended
+ 6 lb. 2 oz. (2.8 kg) English pale ale malt
+ 1.0 lb. (450 g) brown malt (50°L)
+ 6.0 oz. (170 g) crystal malt (40°L)
+ 12 oz. (340 g) crystal malt (60°L)
+ 4.0 oz. (110 g) roasted barley (300°L)
+ 8.0 oz. (230 g) chocolate malt (350°L)
+ 1.0 oz. (28 g) First Gold hops at 8% alpha acids, boiled for 60 minutes (30 IBU)
+ 0.25 oz. (7.1 g) Fuggles hops at 5% alpha acids, boiled for 5 minutes (1 IBU)
+ 0.25 oz. (7.1 g) Fuggles hops at 5% alpha acids, boiled for 0 minutes (0 IBU)
+ 0.75 tsp. Irish moss, boiled for 15 minutes
+ 4.0 oz. (110 g) corn sugar, to prime to 2.2 volumes of CO_2

If you are using one of the liquid yeasts, make your yeast starter two to three days ahead of time. Heat 11 quarts (11 L) of brewing liquor to 163°F (73°C) and mash in grains. To do this, use two large scoops of equal size, such as beer pitchers. Add one "scoop" of water, followed by one "scoop" of grains. Stir once and repeat until grains are used up. Check mash temperature and add remaining water until you hit 152°F (67°C). Mash at 152°F (67°C) for 45 minutes, stirring every 15 minutes, if you can do so without losing too much heat from your mash tun. Heat or add boiling water to mash out to 168°F (76°C).

Recirculate wort until clear, and then run off. Sparge steadily over 90 minutes to collect about 5.9 gallons (22 L) of wort. Boil wort for 60 minutes, adding hops and Irish moss at times indicated. Chill wort, then rack to fermenter. Aerate wort thoroughly and pitch sediment from yeast starter. Ferment at 68°F (20°C). After fermentation stops, keg or bottle and carbonate to 2.2 volumes of CO_2.

MALT EXTRACT OPTION

Add 3.5 pounds (1.6 kg) of light dried malt extract to the recipe. Reduce the amount of 2-row pale ale malt to just 2.0 ounces (57 g). "Steep" the crushed grains in 4.1 quarts (3.9 L) of water at 152°F (67°C) for 60 minutes. ("Steep" is in quotes because technically this is a partial mash.) Place the grain bag in a colander over your brew pot and rinse the grains with 2.0 quarts (1.9 L) of 170°F (77°C) water. Add roughly one-third of the malt extract to this wort. Add water to bring brew pot volume to 3.0 gallons (11 L). Boil for 60 minutes, adding hops and Irish moss at times indicated. Add the remaining malt extract in the final 15 minutes of the boil.

MASH-IN OPTIONS

In any mash, crushed grains are soaked in hot water. The grains and water can be mixed in a few different ways. For example, the brewer could add the grains to his mash tun and then add water. In practice, this is not a good option as it requires a lot of stirring and the crushed malt can form "malt balls"—masses of dried malt that clump together and resist taking on water. Stirring the grains into the hot strike water is a much better idea. However, this requires that you have the correct volume of water in your mash tun. The best idea, I think, is to add both the water and the grains at (roughly) the same time. If you take two equally sized scoops and alternate between adding a scoop of water, followed by a scoop of grain, you will gradually mash in to a thickness around 1.0 quart per pound (2.1 L/kg).

As you approach being completely mashed in, you can check if you are close to your desired mash temperature. If not, you can adjust the temperature of the last bit of strike water as you finish scooping water and grains and add water to thin the mash out to your target mash thickness. This is frequently 1.25 quarts per pound (2.6 L/kg). Stir the mash once after each addition of water and grain. Then, after all the water and grain has been added, the amount of stirring required to mix the two should be minimal.

Equal volumes of water and crushed malt yield a mash thickness around 1.0 qt. (2.1 L/kg).

COLBY HOUSE PORTER
ROBUST PORTER

Porters vary in character from fairly mild ales with a "soft," chocolate-like roast character to beers with a bit of a "bite" from a lot of roasted grains and relatively high hopping levels. The more aggressive porters can be called robust porters. This is my "house ale," a robust porter I've brewed over 40 times. I don't think I've ever brewed it exactly the same way twice, but the recipe always hovers around a basic idea.

This porter has a fairly strong roast character, and a firm hop bitterness (from the "minty" hop Northern Brewer). In all other respects, it's balanced and makes an awesome "everyday" beer—at least as far as my taste buds are concerned. The aroma is a blend of roasted grains, "earthy" Fuggles hops and a light fruitiness from the yeast strain.

5.0 GALLONS (19 L) AT 5.0% ABV
OG = 1.053, FG = 1.014
45 IBU, 36 SRM

+ Wyeast 1968 (London ESB) yeast or White Labs WLP002 (English Ale) yeast
+ A 1.3-qt. (1.2-L) yeast starter is recommended
+ 6 lb. 8 oz. (3.0 kg) 2-row U.K. pale ale malt
+ 1.0 lb. (450 g) Munich malt
+ 1.0 lb. (450 g) crystal malt (40°L)
+ 7.0 oz. (200 g) chocolate malt
+ 6.0 oz. (170 g) black patent malt
+ 3.0 oz. (85 g) roasted barley (500°L)
+ 1.2 oz. Northern Brewer hops at 9% alpha acids, boiled for 60 minutes (40 IBU)
+ 0.50 oz. (14 g) Fuggles hops at 5% alpha acids, boiled for 15 minutes (4.6 IBU)
+ 0.50 oz. (14 g) Fuggles hops at 5% alpha acids, boiled for 0 minutes (0 IBU)
+ 1.0 tsp. Irish moss, boiled for 15 minutes
+ 12 fl. oz. (360 ml) molasses, boiled for 10 minutes
+ 5.0 oz. (140 g) corn sugar, to prime to 2.5 volumes of CO_2

Make your yeast starter two to three days ahead of time. Heat 12 quarts (11 L) of brewing liquor to 163°F (73°C) and mash in grains. Mash at 152°F (67°C) for 60 minutes. Stir every 15 minutes if you can manage it. Heat mash or add boiling water to mash out to 168°F (76°C). Recirculate wort until clear, and then run off. Sparge to collect about 6.2 gallons (23 L) of wort. Boil wort for 60 minutes, adding hops and Irish moss at the times indicated.

(continued)

RECIPE OPTIONS AND NOTES

I used to add a stick of brewers licorice (about 4 inches [10 cm] long) late in the boil every time I brewed this. This added an interesting anise-like flavor to the beer, and especially to the aftertaste. I've stopped since the flavor wasn't that strong and the beer tastes great without it. But, it's still a reasonable option.

You can add sparge water in "pulses" to simplify continuous (or fly) sparging.

Add molasses in the final 10 minutes of the boil. Chill wort, and then rack to fermenter. Aerate wort thoroughly and pitch sediment from yeast starter. Ferment at 68°F (20°C). After fermentation stops, keg or bottle and carbonate to 2.5 volumes of CO_2.

MALT EXTRACT OPTION

This is a partial mash in which 4.0 pounds (1.8 kg) of grains are mashed, and the roasted grains are steeped separately. The best way to approach this is to use a countertop partial mash (page 36), but additionally steep the dark grains as described here. Add 2 pounds 10 ounces (1.2 kg) light dried malt extract to the recipe. Lower the amount of 2-row pale malt to 2.0 pounds (910 g). Mash the crushed malts—with the exception of the three dark roasted grains—in 5.5 quarts (5.2 L) of water. The mash temperature should be 152°F (67°C). Hold this temperature for 60 minutes.

Collect about 2.6 gallons (9.8 L) of wort from the mash. Place the dark grains in a nylon steeping bag and let them steep in the wort as it is run off from the mash. Make sure the dark grains steep at least 30 minutes before proceeding. Once all the wort is collected, remove the steeping bag and stir in roughly a third of the malt extract. Add water to make (at least) 3.5 gallons (13 L) of wort. Boil for 60 minutes, adding hops and Irish moss at the times indicated. Stir in molasses and remaining malt extract in the last 10 minutes of the boil.

PULSED SPARGING

Some homebrewers shy away from continuous (or fly) sparging because of the perceived complexity or because of the "extra" equipment required (the sparge arm). There is, however, a way to simplify continuous sparging and I use it on all my beers. Instead of worrying about precisely matching the inflow of sparge water with the outflow of wort from the lauter tun, I simply add an "extra" pitcher of sparge water on top of the grain bed, wait until I've collected a pitcher's worth of wort and then add the next pitcher of sparge water. I don't need my sparge arm when I do this. And, adding a "pitcher for a pitcher" means I don't have to worry about fine-tuning the flow rate out of the lauter tun.

The only drawback is that I need to actively add water to the mash tun every 5 minutes or so. As such, I can't go off and do other things while lautering. I call this method pulsed sparging, although it's really just a slight variant of fly sparging and probably doesn't really need a name of its own. Still, it's simple and works great.

OPERON STOUT
SWEET STOUT

Sweet stout is a very descriptive name. Sweet stouts are generally regular-strength beers with some lactose added in the kettle. Brewers yeast does not ferment lactose, so the sugar carries over into the beer. Lactose is roughly one-sixth as sweet as table sugar, but 1 pound (half a kilo) in a 5.0 gallon (19-L) batch leaves a definite sweetness.

Sweet stouts have less roast aroma and flavor than other stouts and are usually lightly hopped. They are usually fermented with a clean ale yeast strain. The best sweet stouts manage to be sweet without being cloying.

5.0 GALLONS (19 L) AT 4.2% ABV
OG = 1.053, FG = 1.020
28 IBU, 36 SRM

+ Wyeast 1084 (Irish Ale) or White Labs WLP004 (Irish Ale) yeast
+ A 1.3-qt. (1.2-L) yeast starter is recommended
+ 7.0 lb. (3.2 kg) U.S. 2-row pale malt
+ 6.0 oz. (170 g) caramel malt (40°L)
+ 10 oz. (280 g) caramel malt (60°L)
+ 14 oz. (400 g) black malt (500°L)
+ 1.0 lb. (450 g) lactose
+ 1.5 oz. (43 g) East Kent Goldings hops at 5% alpha acids, boiled for 60 minutes (28 IBU)
+ 0.50 tsp. Irish moss, boiled for 15 minutes
+ 4.25 oz. (120 g) corn sugar, for priming to 2.4 volumes CO_2

Make your yeast starter two to three days ahead of time. Mash in by heating 12 quarts (11 L) of brewing liquor to 164°F (73°C) and combine with malts. Mash at 153°F (67°C) for 60 minutes, stirring every 15 minutes if possible. Mash out to 168°F (76°C), either by adding heat or boiling water. Recirculate the wort until it is clear, then run off. Sparge until you have collected about 5.8 gallons (22 L) of wort.

Boil wort for 60 minutes, adding hops and Irish moss at the times indicated. Add the lactose in the final 10 minutes of the boil. (You may need to add water during the boil to ensure you don't dip below 5.0 gallons [19 L].) Chill the wort and transfer it to your fermenter. Aerate the wort thoroughly and pitch the sediment from the yeast starter. Ferment at 68°F (20°C). After fermentation stops, keg or bottle and carbonate to 2.4 volumes of CO_2.

(continued)

MALT EXTRACT OPTION

Add 3 pounds 6 ounces (1.5 kg) of light dried extract to the ingredients. Reduce the amount of pale malt to 1 pound 2 ounces (510 g). "Steep" the crushed grains in 4.1 quarts (3.9 L) of water at 153°F (67°C) for 60 minutes. ("Steep" is in quotes because technically this is a partial mash.) Place the grain bag in a colander over your brew pot and rinse the grains with 2.0 quarts (1.9 L) of 170°F (77°C) water. Add roughly one-third of the malt extract to this wort. Add water to bring brew pot volume to 3.0 gallons (11 L). Boil for 60 minutes, adding hops and Irish moss at times indicated. Add the remaining malt extract and lactose in the final 15 minutes of the boil.

LACTOSE AND SWEET STOUTS

In brewing, most sugars added to the kettle are 100 percent fermentable. They add alcohol to the finished beer, without raising the final gravity (FG)—or adding color in the case of clear sugars like glucose and sucrose. In contrast, lactose is not fermentable by brewers yeast. It is not converted to lactose and carries over into the finished beer where it adds sweetness. It also raises the final gravity of the beer. Lactose is not as sweet as sucrose, glucose or fructose (the most common sugars used for sweetening).

However, it is easy to add enough to affect the character of the beer. Commercial sweet stouts may use lactose, or they may add sucrose to finished beer, and then pasteurize the product. Since pasteurization kills any microorganisms, including any brewers yeast, the sugar does not get fermented.

RECIPE OPTIONS AND NOTES

You can spice up this recipe with a little vanilla. One to two vanilla beans, sliced and added in secondary, can give some vanilla flavor that will work well with the sweetness of the beer. You might want to start with one vanilla bean and taste the beer a few days later to see if you want to add the second.

GROOVY GRANOLA STOUT
OATMEAL STOUT

As with barley, oats were historically grown as much for animal feed as they were for human consumption (or beer production). In beer, they lend the characteristic flavor of oats, and a creamy or silky mouthfeel. The flavor from the oats isn't strong, however, although this can be accentuated by toasting them.

Oats usually comprise between 5 and 20 percent of the grist in an oatmeal stout. Below 5 percent, they add little to the beer. Over 20 percent, and the beer may acquire a grainy astringency. A good oatmeal stout has a slight sweetness to complement the silky mouthfeel and moderate roasted grain flavors.

5.0 GALLONS (19 L) AT 5.4% ABV
OG = 1.057, FG = 1.015
30 IBU, 33 SRM

+ Wyeast 1968 (London ESB) or White Labs WLP002 (English Ale) yeast
+ A 1.6-qt. (1.5-L) yeast starter is recommended
+ 7 lb. 2 oz. (3.2 kg) pale ale malt (3°L)
+ 1 lb. 8 oz. (680 g) flaked oats
+ 1.0 lb. (450 g) Munich malt (3°L)
+ 12 oz. (340 g) crystal malt (40°L)
+ 6.0 oz. (170 g) chocolate malt (350°L)
+ 5.0 oz. (140 g) roasted barley (300°L)
+ 5.0 oz. (140 g) roasted barley (500°L)
+ 1.0 oz. (28 g) First Gold hops at 8% alpha acids, boiled for 60 minutes (30 IBU)
+ 0.25 oz. (7.1 g) Kent Goldings hops at 5% alpha acids, boiled for 0 minutes (0 IBU)
+ 0.50 tsp. Irish moss, boiled for 15 minutes
+ 4.25 oz. (120 g) corn sugar, to prime for 2.3 volumes of CO_2

Make your yeast starter two to three days ahead of time. Heat 14 quarts (13 L) of brewing liquor to 165°F (74°C) and mash in flaked oats and crushed malts. You do not need to crush the flaked oats or do anything to prepare them to be mashed. Just add them with or after the crushed malts. Mash at 154°F (68°C) for 45 minutes, stirring every 15 minutes if you can do so without losing too much heat from your mash tun. Heat or add boiling water to mash out to 168°F (76°C). Recirculate wort until clear, and then run off.

Sparge steadily over 90 minutes to collect about 7.3 gallons (28 L) of wort. Boil wort for 90 minutes, or however long it takes to reduce wort volume to 5.0 gallons (19 L). Add hops and Irish moss at the times indicated. Chill wort, then rack to fermenter. Aerate wort thoroughly and pitch sediment from yeast starter. Ferment at 68°F (20°C). Keg or add priming sugar and bottle. Carbonate to 2.3 volumes of CO_2.

(continued)

RECIPE OPTIONS AND NOTES

One option, advocated by Jamil Zainasheff, is to toast the flaked oats lightly. This gives them an oatmeal-cookie-like quality. To do this, preheat your oven to 350°F (180°C) and spread the flaked oats out on a cookie sheet. Place the oats in the oven for just a few minutes, until you start smelling toasted oat aroma and the flakes have maybe picked up a tiny bit of color. To get the right amount of roasting for your taste, buy more oats than you need for the batch and do a trial run roasting the excess oats. Start a timer and take samples every couple minutes and stop roasting before you've gone too far.

Another option is to swap some dark crystal malt or malts (over 90°L) for some or all the crystal malt (40°L). This will add some raisin-like notes to the beer, as well as a darker caramel flavor.

Malts and grains are best stored in a cool, dry place.

FLAKED ADJUNCTS

A number of brewing grains are available as flaked adjuncts. These include barley, wheat, rye, oats, maize (corn) and rice. Flaked grains are unmalted grains that are heated and extruded through a roller. This flattens them and the heat also gelatinizes the starches in the grains. As such, they can be stirred directly into the mash. In some cases—for example, that of corn and rice—a cereal mash is needed to use the raw grains. Because they are not malted, flaked adjuncts add comparatively little color and flavor to the wort.

MACGOWAN'S STOUT
FOREIGN EXPORT STOUT

Foreign export stout is a moderately strong stout with a pronounced roasted-grain character and high hop bitterness. Most are fairly well attenuated from their fermentation with a neutral ale strain. Although the level of bitterness is high, there is relatively little late hopping. A relatively high level of carbonation keeps the beer from seeming too full-bodied.

5.0 GALLONS (19 L) AT 6.4% ABV
OG = 1.064, FG = 1.015
60 IBU, 40 SRM

+ Wyeast 1084 (Irish Ale) or White Labs WLP004 (Irish Ale) yeast
+ A 1.9-qt. (1.8-L) yeast starter is recommended
+ 10 lb. 8 oz. (4.8 kg) U.K. 2-row pale malt (3°L)
+ 1.0 lb. (450 g) flaked barley
+ 1 lb. 2 oz. (510 g) roasted barley (500°L)
+ 2.0 oz. (57 g) Challenger hops at 8% alpha acids, boiled for 60 minutes (60 IBU)
+ 0.50 oz. (14 g) Fuggles hops at 5% alpha acids, boiled for 0 minutes (0 IBU)
+ 0.75 tsp. Irish moss, boiled for 15 minutes
+ 5.0 oz. (140 g) corn sugar, to prime to 2.5 volumes of CO_2

Make your yeast starter two to three days ahead of time. Heat 16 quarts (15 L) of brewing liquor to 161°F (72°C) and mash in the crushed pale malt and flaked barley. Then, stir the (crushed) roasted barley into the top layers of the grain bed. Mash at 150°F (66°C) for 60 minutes, stirring every 15 minutes if possible. Heat or add boiling water to raise the temperature to 168°F (76°C) for a mash out.

Recirculate the wort until it's clear, then collect your wort. If you fully sparge the grain bed, you can collect about 8.2 gallons (31 L) of wort. Boil wort to reduce it to 5.0 gallons (19 L). Add the hops and Irish moss at times indicated. Chill the wort, and then rack it to the fermenter. Aerate wort thoroughly and pitch sediment from yeast starter. Ferment at 68°F (20°C). After fermentation stops, keg or bottle and carbonate to 2.5 volumes of CO_2.

(continued)

Dark roasted grains can mingle with the pale malts in your grist. Or, they can be separated.

MALT EXTRACT OPTION

Add 5 pounds 10 ounces (2.6 kg) of light dried malt extract to the recipe. Reduce the amount of 2-row pale ale malt to 14 ounces (390 g). "Steep" the crushed grains in 4.1 quarts (3.9 L) of water at 150°F (66°C) for 60 minutes. ("Steep" is in quotes because technically this is a partial mash.) Place the grain bag in a colander over your brew pot and rinse the grains with 2.0 quarts (1.9 L) of 170°F (77°C) water. Add roughly one-third of the malt extract to this wort. Add water to bring brew pot volume to 3.5 gallons (13 L). Boil for 60 minutes, adding hops and Irish moss at times indicated. Add the remaining malt extract in the final 15 minutes of the boil.

DARK GRAINS IN THE MASH

Dark grains can simply be mixed with the other grains being mashed when brewing a dark beer. However, some brewers feel that beers with dark grains—and especially roasted barley—make a grain bed more difficult to lauter. For that reason, they mash in with the base malts and kilned specialty grains (such as crystal malts), and then stir the dark roasted grains into the top layers of the grain bed. In some cases, the brewer may even wait until near the end of the mash to stir the dark grains in. In most cases, this isn't needed. However, if you have problems lautering your dark beers, this will help.

YANG PORTER
BLACK IPA BLENDER

This beer can be a porter, if you'd like, but it's really meant to be a beer to blend with an American IPA to make a black IPA. Dark, dry and very hoppy, this beer—when blended 1:1 with an American IPA—will produce a black IPA. If you have a specific homebrewed American IPA in mind, you can substitute its hop schedule for the one here. Note that you don't need to brew a full 5.0-gallon (19 L) batch of this. If you have 5.0 gallons (19 L) of American IPA, you can brew 2.5 gallons (9.5 L) of this and enjoy 5.0 gallons (19 L) of blended black IPA and 2.5 gallons (9.5 L) of pale IPA.

5.0 GALLONS (19 L) AT 7.3% ABV
OG = 1.071, FG = 1.014
66 IBU, 40+ SRM

+ Wyeast 1056 (American Ale) or White Labs WLP001 (California Ale) yeast
+ A 2.4-qt. (2.3-L) yeast starter is recommended
+ 9.0 lb. (4.1 kg) U.S. 2-row pale malt
+ 1 lb. 8 oz. (680 g) Munich malt (10°L)
+ 8.0 oz. (230 g) caramel malt (40°L)
+ 3.0 oz. (85 g) chocolate malt (350°L)
+ 5.0 oz. (140 g) roasted barley (500°L)
+ 14 oz. (400 g) black malt (500°L)
+ 1.0 lb. (450 g) cane sugar
+ 0.80 oz. (23 g) Northern Brewer hops at 9% alpha acids, boiled for 60 minutes (27 IBU)
+ 0.60 oz. (17 g) Magnum hops at 12% alpha acids, boiled for 60 minutes (28 IBU)
+ 0.50 oz. (14 g) Centennial hops at 10% alpha acids, boiled for 10 minutes (6.7 IBU)
+ 0.50 oz. (14 g) Centennial hops at 10% alpha acids, boiled for 5 minutes (3.7 IBU)
+ 0.75 oz. (21 g) Cascade hops at 5% alpha acids, boiled for 0 minutes (0 IBU)
+ 0.75 oz. (21 g) Amarillo hops at 5% alpha acids, boiled for 0 minutes (0 IBU)
+ 1.25 oz. (35 g) Cascade hops (dry hops)
+ 1.25 oz. (35 g) Amarillo hops (dry hops)
+ 1.0 tsp. Irish moss, boiled for 15 minutes
+ 5.0 oz. (140 g) corn sugar, to prime to 2.5 volumes of CO_2

(continued)

Make your yeast starter two to three days ahead of time. Heat 16 quarts (15 L) of brewing liquor to 161°F (72°C) and mash in grains. Mash at 150°F (66°C) for 60 minutes, stirring every 15 minutes if you can. Heat or add boiling water to mash out to 168°F (76°C). Recirculate wort until clear, and then run off.

Sparge to collect about 8.0 gallons (30 L) of wort. Boil wort to reduce to 5.0 gallons (19 L), adding hops and Irish moss at times indicated. Stir in the sugar in the final 10 minutes of boil. Chill wort, then rack to fermenter. Aerate wort thoroughly and pitch sediment from yeast starter. Ferment at 68°F (20°C). Dry hop in secondary for 7–10 days. Keg or bottle and carbonate to 2.5 volumes of CO_2. Blend 1:1 with a pale American IPA for a black IPA. Or, explore other blend ratios. (Or, enjoy the beer by itself as a dry, hoppy porter.) Keg or add priming sugar and bottle.

MALT EXTRACT OPTION

Add 5 pounds 7 ounces (2.5 kg) of light dried malt extract to the ingredient list. Omit pale malt. Lower the amount of Munich malt to 1 pound 2 ounces (510 g). "Steep" the crushed grains in 4.1 quarts (3.9 L) of water at 150°F (66°C) for 60 minutes. ("Steep" is in quotes because technically this is a partial mash.) Place the grain bag in a colander over your brew pot and rinse the grains with 2.0 quarts (1.9 L) of 170°F (77°C) water. Add roughly one-third of the malt extract to this wort. Add water to bring brew pot volume to 3.5 gallons (13 L). Boil for 60 minutes, adding hops and Irish moss at the times indicated. Add the sugar and remaining malt extract in the final 15 minutes of the boil.

BLENDING

Winemakers frequently blend different wines to make a pleasing final product. In contrast, blending is relatively rare in brewing. But there are a few well-known examples of blended beer. Gueuze is a blended lambic, combining three-year-old, two-year-old and one-year-old lambics. Newcastle Brown Ale is made by blending an aged, fairly strong old ale with a younger, weaker amber ale. And occasionally you will see blended beers that are a collaboration between two breweries. (And of course, the big brewers "blend" water with malt liquor to make American Pilsner and international lagers. They also blend batches for consistency.)

If you brew two different, but compatible beers, you can have at least three beers to enjoy—the two beers separately and a blended beer. And, if there is more than one blending ratio that yields decent beer, then you have even more to enjoy.

BALTIC WAY PORTER
BALTIC PORTER

Baltic porter is a strong dark beer. Although dark in color, it does not have as much roasted-grain character as most stouts or American porters. The beer is richly malty, often with fruity notes that are from dark crystal malts. It can be made with either lager yeast or clean ale yeast and should not show prominent fruity esters. A smooth, clean taste—without a strong alcohol flavor—is the hallmark of the best examples of this style.

5.0 GALLONS (19 L) AT 8.0% ABV
OG = 1.083, FG = 1.021
27 IBU, 29 SRM

+ Wyeast 1056 (American Ale) or White Labs WLP001 (California Ale) yeast
+ A 3.4-qt. (3.2-L) yeast starter is recommended
+ 15 lb. (6.8 kg) Vienna malt
+ 1.0 lb. (450 g) Munich malt (10°L)
+ 8.0 oz. (230 g) Special B malt (150°L)
+ 4.0 oz. (110 g) chocolate malt (350°L)
+ 5.0. (140 g) Carafa Special II (430°L)
+ 0.50 oz. (14 g) Magnum hops at 14.5% alpha acids, boiled for 60 minutes (27 IBU)
+ 0.75 tsp. Irish moss, boiled for 15 minutes
+ 4.5 oz. (130 g) corn sugar, to prime for 2.4 volumes CO_2

Make your yeast starter two to three days ahead of time. Heat 21 quarts (20 L) of brewing liquor to 160°F (71°C) and mash in crushed malts. Mash at 149°F (65°C) for 60 minutes, stirring every 15 minutes if you can do so without losing too much heat from your mash tun. Heat or add boiling water to mash out to 168°F (76°C).

Recirculate wort until clear, and then run off. Sparge steadily over 90 minutes to collect your wort. You can collect up to 11 gallons (42 L) of wort without oversparging. Boil wort until its volume is reduced to 5.0 gallons (19 L). Add hops and Irish moss at times indicated. Chill wort, then rack to fermenter. Aerate wort thoroughly and pitch sediment from yeast starter. Ferment at 68°F (20°C). Carbonate to 2.4 volumes of CO_2. Keg or add priming sugar and bottle.

MALT EXTRACT OPTION

Add 7 pounds 10 ounces (3.5 kg) of light dried malt extract to the recipe. Lower the amount of Vienna malt to 15 ounces (430 g). In your brew pot, steep the 3.0 pounds (1.4 kg) total of crushed grains in 4.1 quarts (3.9 L) of water at 149°F (65°C) for 60 minutes. (This is really a mash, so follow the temperature and volume guidelines closely.)

(continued)

RECIPE OPTIONS AND NOTES

Most commercial Baltic porters are lagers. However, a few are ales and homebrewers are more likely to make this beer as an ale. If you'd like to make this beer as a lager, use Wyeast 2124 (Bohemian Lager) or White Labs WLP830 (German Lager) yeast to ferment the wort. A 6.8-quart (6.4-L) yeast starter is recommended to raise the proper amount of yeast. Ferment at 55°F (13°C), but let the temperature rise to 60°F (16°C) near the end of fermentation. Hold at that temperature for three days.

After steeping, place the grain bag in a large colander over your brew pot. Rinse the grains with 2.0 quarts (1.9 L) of 170°F (77°C) water. Add roughly a quarter of the malt extract to the wort collected and adjust the wort volume with water to make at least 3.5 gallons (13 L) of wort. Boil for 60 minutes, adding hops and Irish moss at times indicated. Add the remaining malt extract in the final 10 minutes of the boil.

AVOIDING A LONG BOIL

The bigger the beer, the larger the grain bed. And the larger the grain bed, the more wort you can collect from it without oversparging. However, collecting more wort requires boiling it down to your target post-boil volume. In some cases, a homebrewer's setup will not allow him or her to collect the full volume of wort possible. In other cases, he or she will not want to spend the time to boil the wort down to size. In these cases, the brewer's extract efficiency will suffer and their original gravity (OG) will be lower than planned. However, there are a couple of options to adjust for this.

The first is to add more base malt to compensate for the decrease in your extract efficiency. Figuring out how much malt to add is tricky, but a quick rule of thumb for 5.0-gallon (19-L) batches of strong beer is to add roughly 3.0 pounds (1.4 kg) of base malt for every 1.0 gallon (3.84 L) of wort you could have collected, but didn't. Sometimes, however, this ends up overfilling your mash tun. In any case, you can always add malt extract near the end of the boil to correct a low OG.

To do this, take your specific gravity near the end of the boil. Then stir in malt extract gradually and take a new gravity reading for each little bit you stir in. For a 5.0-gallon (19-L) batch, adding 8.0 ounces (230 g) of dried malt extract will raise the specific gravity by 5 "gravity points." Be sure to stir in the malt extract well. For best results, take some wort from your kettle and dissolve the extract in a small pot. Then add the dissolved extract back into the kettle. You will still need to stir well to prevent the thick, cooler mix from sinking to the bottom of the kettle and scorching.

IMPERIAL SMOKED PORTER
(BY DAN IRONSIDE)

This is Dan Ironside's recipe for imperial smoked porter. His imperial porter is a scaled-up robust porter. The word "imperial" in a beer name indicates a bigger version of that type of beer. The beer is, as Dan puts it, for "smoke bomb lovers." He recommends letting this age at least a couple of months so it will turn into a nice fireside sipper.

5.0 GALLONS (19 L) AT 8.4% ABV
OG = 1.089, FG = 1.024
52 IBU, 45 SRM

+ Wyeast 1728 (Scottish Ale) or White Labs WLP028 (Edinburgh Scottish Ale) yeast
+ A 3.9-qt. (3.7-L) yeast starter is recommended
+ 8 lb. 10 oz. (3.9 kg) German rauchmalz (smoked malt)
+ 5 lb. 5 oz. (2.4 kg) U.S. 2-row pale malt
+ 1.0 lb. (450 g) Munich malt (6°L)
+ 1 lb. 8 oz. (680 g) caramel malt (40°L)
+ 12 oz. (340 g) U.K. chocolate malt (475°L)
+ 8.0 oz. (230 g) U.K. black malt
+ 1.0 oz. (28 g) German Magnum hops at 14% alpha acids, boiled for 60 minutes (52 IBU)
+ 1 tsp. Irish moss, boiled for 15 minutes
+ 0.50 tsp. yeast nutrients, boiled for 10 minutes
+ 3.75 oz. (106 g) corn sugar, to prime to 2.2 volumes of CO_2

Make your yeast starter two to three days ahead of time. Heat 22 quarts (21 L) of brewing liquor to 160°F (71°C) and mash in grains. Mash at 149°F (65°C) for 60 minutes, stirring every 15 minutes if you can. Mash out to 168°F (76°C), if possible. Recirculate wort until clear, and then run off. Completely sparging the grain bed will allow you to collect about 11.5 gallons (43.5 L) of wort.

Boil wort to reduce to 5.0 gallons (19 L), or slightly more, adding hops, Irish moss and yeast nutrients at times indicated. Chill wort, then rack to fermenter. Aerate wort thoroughly and pitch sediment from yeast starter. Pitch yeast at 57°F (14°C), but allow the fermentation temperature to rise to 64°F (18°C). After fermentation stops, keg or bottle and carbonate to 2.2 volumes of CO_2.

(continued)

Avoiding a stuck fermentation is easy if you pitch enough yeast.

STUCK FERMENTATIONS

Sometimes a fermentation will quit prematurely, leaving your beer under-attenuated. This happens most often when the brewer does not pitch enough yeast when fermenting a big beer. The best way to deal with a stuck fermentation is to avoid it. If you make a properly sized yeast starter every time you brew, you will likely never have to encounter a stuck fermentation. If you do, however, here are some ways of dealing with it.

First, check that the fermentation is really stuck, and not just finished. Big beers finish at higher final gravities (FG). Check the expected FG from the recipe and the apparent attenuation range listed for your yeast strain. (The latter can be found on the manufacturer's website.) If your fermentation stopped at a final gravity near the recipe's stated FG or at level of attenuation within the yeast strain's range, it's done, not stuck.

If you do experience a stuck fermentation, stir the beer gently to rouse the yeast and raise the temperature to the top end of the yeast strain's recommended fermentation temperature range. You can even let the temperature climb a few degrees above the top end of the range if you cool it back down into the range when the fermentation renews. In most cases—especially when the fermentation is almost complete—this should do the trick. If it doesn't, or if the fermentation starts briefly, then sticks again, do not repeat.

If the fermentation sticks far from your intended FG, you should pitch more yeast. Make a yeast starter adequate for your volume of beer at its current specific gravity. Pitch the yeast and make sure the temperature is in the top half of the yeast strain's recommended range. Adding a small amount of yeast nutrients—up to a quarter teaspoon per 5.0 gallons (19 L)—when you add the yeast can also be a good idea. It's not always possible to save a stuck fermentation, which is why avoiding one is always the best course.

Dan Ironside is a member of the Austin ZEALOTS, the homebrew club I belong to—and the author of Idiot's Guide to Homebrewing *(2015, Alpha Books). He also has a website,* The Apartment Homebrewer *(theapthomebrewer.com).*

CTHULHU 13°
BELGIAN QUADRUPEL (DARK STRONG ALE)

A Belgian quadrupel, or Belgian dark strong ale, is stronger and darker than a Belgian tripel. Dark does not necessarily mean brown, as in a porter or stout. It is typically brewed from a highly fermentable wort to yield a high degree of attenuation and a correspondingly low final gravity (FG), given its high original gravity.

The beer is complex and malty, with the fermentation character playing a large role in the final impression of the beer. It is not strongly bitter, but contains enough bitterness to balance the sweetness. If you pitch an adequate amount of yeast, and run a good fermentation, this will condition remarkably quickly (within a few months). However, it also has the potential to age well, too.

5.0 GALLONS (19 L) AT 10% ABV
OG = 1.092, FG = 1.014
28 IBU, 21 SRM

+ Wyeast 3787 (Trappist High Gravity) or White Labs WLP530 (Abbey Ale) yeast
+ A 4.2-qt. (4.0-L) yeast starter is recommended
+ 8 lb. 4 oz. (3.7 kg) Belgian Pils malt
+ 2.0 lb. (910 g) Munich malt (8°L)
+ 12 oz. (340 g) wheat malt
+ 13 oz. (370 g) crystal malt (60°L)
+ 9.0 oz. (260 g) Belgian special B malt (150°L)
+ 3.0 oz. (85 g) chocolate malt (350°L)
+ 3.0 lb. (1.4 kg) cane sugar
+ 1.25 oz. (35 g) Styrian Goldings hops at 6% alpha acids, boiled for 60 minutes (28 IBU)
+ 1.0 tsp. Irish moss, boiled for 15 minutes
+ 0.50 tsp. yeast nutrients, boiled for 10 minutes
+ 5.75 oz. (160 g) corn sugar, to prime to 2.7 volumes of CO_2

Make your yeast starter two to three days ahead of time. Aerate the yeast starter again the night before you brew the beer. Heat 16 quarts (15 L) of brewing liquor to 159°F (71°C) and mash in grains. Mash at 148°F (64°C) for 60–90 minutes, stirring every 15 minutes if you can. Heat mash to 168°F (76°C) for a mash out. Recirculate the wort until it is clear, then begin running it off. Fully sparging the grain bed will allow you to collect about 8.2 gallons (31 L) of wort.

(continued)

RECIPE OPTIONS AND NOTES

You have a lot of options when brewing a beer like this. Although this beer is meant to have a complex malt character, the simplest Belgian beers of this style are brewed with mostly base malt and a small amount of either dark malts or dark sugars. If you want to reduce the amount of crystal malts, and replace the color by adding more dark malts or dark sugars (including dark candi sugar), you can do so.

Much of the complexity of this beer comes from the fermentation, so a simpler grist is not necessarily a drawback. Reducing the amount of crystal malts and increasing the amount of sugar in the recipe will allow you to obtain higher attenuation, if you're interested in that.

Boil wort to reduce volume to just over 5.0 gallons (19 L), adding hops and Irish moss at times indicated. Add sugar and yeast nutrients in the final 10 minutes of the boil. Chill wort, then rack to fermenter. Aerate wort thoroughly and pitch sediment from yeast starter. If fermentation has not started within 8 hours, aerate the wort a second time. Begin fermentation at 68°F (20°C) and hold it there until after high kräusen (the most vigorous part of fermentation). Then, allow the temperature to rise. Do not let the temperature exceed 75°F (24°C). After fermentation stops, keg or bottle and carbonate to 2.7 volumes of CO_2.

MALT EXTRACT OPTION

This option calls for mashing 4.0 pounds (1.8 kg) of grains. See the procedure for a countertop partial mash page 36 for an easy way to do this. Add 5.0 pounds (2.3 kg) light dried malt extract to the recipe. Omit the Pils malt. Reduce the amount of Munich malt to 1 pound 11 ounces (770 g). Mash the grains at 148°F (64°C) for 60 minutes. Collect about 2.6 gallons (9.9 L) of wort from the mash. Add roughly one-third of the malt extract to this wort. Add water to bring the brew pot volume to at least 3.5 gallons (13 L). Boil for 60 minutes, adding hops and Irish moss at times indicated. Add the sugar, yeast nutrients and remaining malt extract in the final 15 minutes of the boil.

YEAST HEALTH FOR BIG BEERS

Fermenting strong beers can be stressful to the yeast. In addition to pitching an adequate amount of yeast, the brewer should make every effort to ensure they are healthy. In very big beers, aerating the wort a second time prior to the beginning of fermentation can help. If the wort is aerated well, but fermentation has not started after 8 hours, the brewer can aerate the wort a second time. If fermentation is already active at this point, there is no need for a second shot of aeration. Likewise, the brewer should never aerate the wort after high kräusen. This can lead to excessive diacetyl in the wort that the yeast cannot reabsorb.

When preparing to ferment a big beer, the brewer can also aerate his yeast starter more than once. A second shot of aeration the day before the yeast is pitched can help the yeast build stronger cell walls and multiply to larger numbers. You can, in fact, aerate a yeast starter intermittently while it is fermenting. If you do, however, pitch only the yeast sediment from the starter. The starter beer is likely to be heavily laden with diacetyl.

Adding yeast nutrients to big beer fermentations never hurts. This is especially true if a fair amount of simple sugars are added in the kettle. The sugars are fuel for the yeast, but they don't contain amino acids, vitamins and minerals, as wort from malted grains does. Adding yeast nutrients makes the wort more nutritious for the yeast and—if everything else is in order—they will respond by delivering an ordered fermentation.

ROCHE LIMIT STOUT
IMPERIAL STOUT

This is a huge stout. It's big. It's roasty. It's bitter. It's basically an American-style stout pushed to the limit. However, if you make the recommended size yeast starter and run a good fermentation, it conditions fairly quickly and hides its alcohol amazingly well. Although this ale will age well, I think it's at its best when still young—a couple months after fermentation is complete.

The aroma of the Centennial and Cascade hops mixed with the aroma from the dark grains is fantastic. The longer it ages, the more the hop aroma fades. If you age it, a complex fruity, dark malt character—with a Sherry-like edge—grows over time. And I know from experience that it continues to evolve for at least three years.

5.0 GALLONS (19 L) AT 9.9% ABV
OG = 1.100, FG = 1.023
70 IBU, 40+ SRM

+ Wyeast 1056 (American Ale), White Labs WLP001 (California Ale) or Fermentis Safale U.S.-05 yeast
+ A 5.1-qt. (4.8-L) yeast starter is recommended
+ 17 lb. (7.7 kg) U.S. 2-row pale malt
+ 6.0 oz. (170 g) caramel malt (90°L)
+ 10 oz. (280 g) crystal malt (120°L)
+ 6.0 oz. (170 g) chocolate malt (350°L)
+ 10 oz. (280 g) black malt (500°L)
+ 12 oz. (340 g) roasted barley (500°L)
+ 1.25 oz. (35 g) Columbus hops at 15% alpha acids, boiled for 60 minutes (70 IBU)
+ 1.0 oz. (28 g) Centennial hops at 10% alpha acids, boiled for 0 minutes (0 IBU)
+ 1.0 oz. (28 g) Cascade hops at 5% alpha acids, boiled for 0 minutes (0 IBU)
+ 0.50 oz. (14 g) Centennial hops (dry hops)
+ 1.5 oz. (43 g) Cascade hops (dry hops)
+ 1.0 tsp. Irish moss, boiled for 15 minutes
+ 0.50 tsp. yeast nutrients, boiled for 10 minutes
+ 4.5 oz. (130 g) corn sugar, for priming to 2.4 volumes CO_2

(continued)

Make your yeast starter two to three days ahead of time. Heat 24 quarts (23 L) of brewing liquor to 159°F (71°C) and mash in grains. If you have a 10-gallon (38-L) mash tun, it will be almost full to the rim. Mash at 148°F (64°C) for 60–90 minutes, stirring every 15 minutes if possible. Heat to mash out to 168°F (76°C). Recirculate the wort until clear, then run off and collect wort. Fully sparging the grain bed will yield 13 gallons (48 L) of wort. This is at least a 5-hour boil, so you'll probably want to consider collecting less wort and supplementing your grist with malt extract. Boil wort to reduce volume to just over 5.0 gallons (19 L), adding hops, Irish moss and yeast nutrients at times indicated. Chill the wort, then rack to fermenter. Aerate wort thoroughly and pitch sediment from yeast starter.

Ferment at 68°F (20°C). If the fermentation becomes sluggish near the end, allow the temperature to rise—up to 75°F (24°C). Dry hops for seven to 10 days in secondary. Keg or bottle and carbonate to 2.4 volumes of CO_2. You may want to add "a pinch" of fresh yeast if you bottle condition. About ¼ teaspoon dried U.S.-05 would be a good choice. This beer will condition quickly, given its age. Check on it two months after kegging or bottling, and every couple weeks after that if it isn't ready. This can age well for at least three years (and probably longer), but the hop aromas will be almost gone after a year or so.

MALT EXTRACT OPTION

This option calls for mashing 4.0 pounds (1.8 kg) of grains. See the procedure for a countertop partial mash on page 36 for an easy way to do this. Add 8.75 pounds (4.0 kg) of light dried malt extract to the ingredient list. Reduce the amount of pale malt to 1 pound 14 ounces (850 g). Mash the grains at 148°F (64°C) for 60 minutes. Collect about 2.6 gallons (9.9 L) of wort from the mash. Add roughly one-quarter of the malt extract to this wort. Add water to bring the brew pot volume to at least 4.0 gallons (15 L). Boil for 60 minutes, adding hops and Irish moss at times indicated. Add the remaining malt extract in the final 30 minutes of the boil. This is a lot of malt extract, so add a little at a time starting at the 30-minute-to-go mark.

AGING BEERS

Most beer is meant to be consumed fresh. Average-strength beers remain fresh for about 8 months, give or take. A few beers, however, have the potential to age well beyond that point. Strong beers have a better chance of aging than average-strength beers. But simply being strong is not a guarantee a beer will age well. Likewise, dark beers have the potential to age better than pale beers, but a strong dark beer is not guaranteed to age well. Sour beers also can age well, although some can age poorly, too.

One characteristic in beer that fairs poorly with age is hop aroma. Hoppy beers lose their floral, hoppy aroma when aged for extensive periods of time. And often, the underlying malt does not yield an interesting aged beer.

If you choose to age any of your homebrews, follow these guidelines. Ideally, store the beers cool (50–60°F [10–16°C]). If they are capped, store them upright. If they are corked, store them lying on their side. Isolate them from light and vibration and label when each beer was brewed. Ideally, if you are aging homebrew, age at least a few bottles from candidate batches. Sample them occasionally and get ready to drink them up once they seem to have peaked.

3

AMBER ALES: SUMPTUOUS SPECIALTY MALTS

This section gives the recipes for 10 amber ales. They range from an OG 1.033 (3.1 percent ABV) mild ale to an OG 1.087 (8.1 percent ABV) English barleywine—with bitters, Scottish ales, an American amber ale, an altbier and others in between. The color of these beers ranges from 12 SRM to 20 SRM.

If you are treating your water, you should aim to have at least 100 ppm calcium (Ca^{+2}) ions, and between 90 ppm and 190 ppm bicarbonate (HCO_3^-), with the lower end being for beers around 12 SRM and the upper end for beers around 20 SRM. When the boil starts, you may want add 50 ppm more calcium. As with the dark ales, you do not have to adjust your water chemistry to match your beer's SRM exactly. Being in the ballpark is all you need.

If you are making your water by adding minerals to 5.0 gallons (19 L) of distilled or RO water, start by adding 3–6 grams of sodium bicarbonate ($NaHCO_3$, baking soda), with the low end of the range corresponding to beers around 12 SRM and the high end corresponding to beer around 20 SRM. Then choose a calcium addition depending on how much you want to accentuate the hops. For a balanced beer, add 4 grams of calcium chloride ($CaCl_2{*}2H_2O$) and 4 grams of calcium sulfate ($CaSO_4{*}2H_2O$, gypsum).

For a beer in which the hops are to be accentuated, add 8 grams of calcium sulfate ($CaSO_4{*}2H_2O$, gypsum). You will need to prepare more than 5.0 gallons (19 L) of brewing liquor for the all-grain versions of these beers. For the extract versions, you only need to prepare brewing liquor (water with the correct mineral additions) of the grains you steep or mash. Use distilled water, RO water or naturally soft water for diluting the malt extract.

If you have a water report that describes what is in your water, you can use brewing software to plan your mineral additions. Remember to treat your water to remove any chlorine compounds, if present (as they are in all municipal water sources).

MARSHALL AMP MILD
MILD ALE

Mild ale is—get this—a mildly flavored ale. Most modern milds are dark milds, and are low-gravity, moderately malty ales. Dark milds are not strongly roasty and all milds have little discernable hop character. They are a low-gravity session beer for people who don't like the bitterness found in British bitters, porters, brown ales or stouts.

This recipe uses the no-sparge version of wort collection. The grains are mashed as usual, and then a large amount of water is added to boost the temperature to the mash out temperature. Then, the wort is run off without rinsing the grain bed with any sparge water. You could argue, however, that the large volume of water added for the mash out is—effectively—sparge water.

5.0 GALLONS (19 L) AT 3.1% ABV
OG = 1.033, FG = 1.008
14 IBU, 14 SRM

+ Wyeast 1968 (London ESB) or White Labs WLP002 (English Ale) yeast
+ No yeast starter required if yeast is fresh
+ 4.0 lb. (1.8 kg) English pale ale malt
+ 1 lb. 8 oz. (680 g) mild ale malt
+ 12 oz. (340 g) crystal malt (60°L)
+ 2.0 oz. (57 g) black patent malt
+ 0.75 oz. (21 g) Kent Goldings hops at 5% alpha acids, boiled for 60 minutes (14 IBU)
+ 0.25 oz. (7.1 g) Kent Goldings hops at 5% alpha acids, boiled for 60 minutes (0 IBU)
+ 1.0 tsp. Irish moss, boiled for 15 minutes
+ 4.25 oz. (120 g) corn sugar, to prime for 2.3 volumes of CO_2

If your yeast is fresh, you don't need a yeast starter. If you are unsure of the health of your yeast, make a 1.1-quart (1.0-L) yeast starter two to three days ahead of time. Heat 8.0 quarts (7.6 L) of brewing liquor to 163°F (73°C) and mash in grains. Mash at 152°F (67°C) for 45 minutes, stirring every 15 minutes, if you can do so without losing too much heat from your mash tun. Add 12 quarts (11 L) of 179°F (82°C) water to mash out to 168°F (76°C). Stir this water in then let the mash sit for about 5 minutes for the grain bed to settle out. This should result in about 4.0 gallons (15 L) of wort in your mash tun, depending on how much water the grains absorbed.

(continued)

RECIPE OPTIONS AND NOTES

The yeast strains recommended for this beer have an apparent attenuation range that tops out at about 70 percent, which is relatively low among ale strains. This can be a good thing when brewing a low-gravity beer, as the FG will be high enough to leave the beer with a reasonable amount of body. On the other hand, an almost bone-dry session beer isn't a bad thing either. For a dry version of this beer, ferment with Danstar Nottingham yeast. This yeast is relatively neutral, as English ale strains go, but can exhibit levels of apparent attenuation over 85 percent.

Recirculate the wort until clear, and then run it off. Since you will not be sparging, you can run the wort off as fast as you can manage. Add water to make 6.0 gallons (23 L), or however much pre-boil wort will yield 5.0 gallons (19 L) after a 60-minute boil. Boil wort for 60 minutes, adding hops and Irish moss at times indicated. Chill wort, then rack to fermenter. Aerate wort thoroughly and pitch yeast. Ferment at 68°F (20°C). Keg or add priming sugar and bottle. Carbonate to 2.3 volumes of CO_2.

MALT EXTRACT OPTION

Add 2.0 pounds (910 g) of light dried malt extract to the recipe. Lower the amount of 2-row pale ale malt to 10 ounces (280 g). "Steep" the crushed grains in 2.0 gallons (7.6 L) of water at 152°F (67°C) for 60 minutes. ("Steep" is in quotes because technically this is a partial mash.) Place the grain bag in a colander over your brew pot and rinse the grains with 1.0 gallon (3.8 L) of 170°F (77°C) water.

Add roughly half of the malt extract to this wort, and add water to bring brew pot volume to 3.0 gallons (11 L). Boil for 60 minutes, adding hops and Irish moss at times indicated. Add the remaining malt extract in the final 15 minutes of the boil. Chill wort. Transfer to fermenter, and top up to 5.0 gallons (19 L) with cool water.

NO-SPARGE WORT COLLECTION

No-sparge wort collection is a way to save a little time in your brew day. It works best with lower gravity beer, as you need to add a lot of water to your mash tun. There are several variations to no-sparge brewing. The simplest is to mash the grains in a fairly thin mash—up to 2.5 quarts/pound of grain (5.2 L/kg)—then drain the mash tun. Since you are not continuously sparging, you can run the wort off as fast as you can manage. After this, you would add water to make reasonable pre-boil wort volumes and proceed to the boil.

A second way involves mashing the grains, then adding a large volume of water for the mash out. This mash out water effectively doubles as sparge water. The easiest way to do this is to mash the grains at a mash thickness of 1.5 quarts/pound (3.1 L/kg). Mash out using that same volume of water. The temperature of this mash out water (in Fahrenheit) should be T = 336 – T (strike water). In Celsius, it's T = 169 – T (strike water). This approximation only works if your volume of strike water and mash out water is equal. And notice that you don't use the mash temperature in the calculation, it's the temperature of the strike water—the water you added at mash-in—and that is usually 10–12°F (~5–6°C) higher than your mash temperature. If you follow this procedure, you should collect the right amount of wort given the size of your grain bed and have your mash out temperature near 168°F (76°C).

This recipe uses a third method where the initial mash is 1.25 quarts/pound (2.6 L/kg), a common mash thickness for a single infusion mash, and a larger amount of mash out water is used. If you try no-sparge brewing with other recipes, be sure to figure out the total amount of water you will need to add to your mash tun and be sure it will fit.

SPHAGNUM SIXTY
SCOTTISH LIGHT

Scottish light is a low-gravity, malt-focused ale. Scottish ales are malty, but with less crystal malt flavor than British pale ales. They are usually fermented at temperatures lower than most ales, and are thus relatively "clean" with regards to fermentation character. They are hopped just enough to maintain balance and are highly quaffable session ales.

Although low in gravity (and alcohol), a Scottish light still has plenty of malt character and should not seem "thin" (although you will not mistake it for a big beer). A low level of carbonation, compared to American pale ales, contributes to the body of the beer.

5.0 GALLONS (19 L) AT 3.2% ABV
OG = 1.034, FG = 1.009
14 IBU, 17 SRM

+ Wyeast 1084 (Irish Ale) or White Labs WLP004 (Irish Ale) yeast
+ A 1.1-qt. (1.0-L) yeast starter is recommended
+ 4 lb. 8 oz. (2.0 kg) U.K. 2-row pale ale malt
+ 1 lb. 4 oz. (570 g) Munich malt (10°L)
+ 6.0 oz. (170 g) amber malt (30°L)
+ 4.0 oz. (110 g) crystal malt (90°L)
+ 3.5 oz. (99 g) roasted barley (500°L)
+ 0.50 oz. (14 g) First Gold hops at 7.5% alpha acids, boiled for 60 minutes (14 IBU)
+ 0.25 oz. (7.1 g) East Kent Goldings hops at 5% alpha acids, boiled for 0 minutes (0 IBU)
+ 1.0 tsp. Irish moss, boiled for 15 minutes
+ 4.0 oz. (110 g) corn sugar, to prime for 2.2 volumes CO_2

Make your yeast starter two to three days ahead of time. Heat 8.2 quarts (7.8 L) of brewing liquor to 165°F (74°C) and mash in grains. Mash at 154°F (68°C) for 45 minutes, stirring every 15 minutes if you can. Heat or add boiling water to mash out to 168°F (76°C). Recirculate wort until clear, and then run off.

Sparge to collect about 4.3 gallons (16 L) of wort. Add water to make around 6.0 gallons (23 L) of pre-boil wort. Boil wort for 60 minutes, adding hops and Irish moss at times indicated. Chill wort, then rack to fermenter. Aerate wort thoroughly and pitch sediment from yeast starter. Ferment at 63°F (17°C). After fermentation stops, keg or bottle and carbonate to 2.3 volumes of CO_2.

(continued)

MALT EXTRACT OPTION

Add 2 pounds 2 ounces (960 g) of light dried malt extract to the recipe. Reduce the amount of 2-row pale ale malt to 14.5 ounces (410 g). "Steep" the crushed grains in 4.1 quarts (3.9 L) of water at 154°F (68°C) for 45 minutes. ("Steep" is in quotes because technically this is a partial mash.)

Place the grain bag in a colander over your brew pot and rinse the grains with 2.0 quarts (1.9 L) of 170°F (77°C) water. Add roughly one-half of the malt extract to this wort. Add water to bring brew pot volume to at least 2.5 gallons (9.5 L). Boil for 60 minutes, adding hops and Irish moss at times indicated. Add the remaining malt extract in the final 15 minutes of the boil.

DOUBLE-SIZE BATCH

Whenever you brew a low-gravity ale, you should consider making a double batch. If the grist is small enough, you can easily double the amount of grain and still have it fit in an ordinary homebrew mash tun. (These are usually around 10 gallons [38 L].) Likewise, you can boil all the wort you collect in a 10-gallon (38-L) kettle. However, as you are boiling less volume than your batch size, you will need to add water in the fermenter to make this up. (In a way, it's like making a beer from malt extract.)

To double your batch size for this recipe, double the amount of all the ingredients. Mash the grains and collect around 8.6 gallons (33 L) of wort. Boil the wort for 60 minutes to reduce the volume to around 7.5 gallons (28 L). Cool and rack equal amounts of wort to two homebrew-sized fermenters. Add water in each to make 5.0 gallons (19 L). Aerate, pitch the yeast and—voilà! You will now have 10 gallons (38 L) for roughly the same amount of effort of brewing 5.0 gallons (19 L).

EVENING IN EDINBURGH
SCOTTISH HEAVY

Scottish ales are malty amber ales with a hint of roast character. The Scottish heavy (sometimes called a 70/- ale) is only heavy in relation to the Scottish light. It is a fairly low-gravity, "pub strength" ale for session drinking. The word "heavy" in the name can sometimes lead to some confusion with the strong Scottish beer called Wee Heavy.

The best Scottish ales are malty, without the caramel flavor and pronounced bitterness of similar British pale ales. They also lack the fruity esters of many English ales. Scottish ales are fermented cool and meant to have a very clean aroma. As such, pitching at a higher rate than comparable ales will help you brew the best Scottish heavy.

5.0 GALLONS (19 L) AT 3.7% ABV
OG = 1.040, FG = 1.011
18 IBU, 14 SRM

+ Wyeast 1728 (Scottish Ale) or White Labs WLP028 (Edinburgh) yeast
+ A 1.6-qt. (1.5-L) yeast starter is recommended
+ 5 lb. 12 oz. (2.6 kg) Scottish pale ale malt
+ 1.5 lb. (680 g) Munich malt (10°L)
+ 5.0 oz. (140 g) crystal malt (60°L)
+ 2.5 oz. (71 g) roasted barley (500°L)
+ 0.60 oz. (17 g) First Gold hops at 8% alpha acids, boiled for 60 minutes (18 IBU)
+ 0.25 oz. Kent Goldings hops at 5% alpha acids, boiled for 0 minutes (0 IBU)
+ 1.0 tsp. Irish moss, boiled for 15 minutes
+ 4.0 oz. (110 g) corn sugar, to prime for 2.3 volumes CO_2

Make your yeast starter two to three days ahead of time. Heat 10 quarts (9.5 L) of brewing liquor to 164°F (73°C) and mash in crushed grains. Mash at 153°F (67°C) for 60 minutes, stirring every 15 minutes if feasible. Mash out to 168°F (76°C) by adding direct heat or boiling water. Recirculate wort until clear, and then run off. Sparge to collect about 5.0 gallons (19 L) of wort.

Add water to yield a pre-boil volume that will yield 5.0 gallons (19 L) of wort after a 90-minute boil—about 6.5 gallons (25 L) for most homebrew burners. Boil wort for 90 minutes. Add hops and Irish moss at times indicated. Chill wort, then rack to fermenter. Aerate wort thoroughly and pitch sediment from yeast starter. Ferment at 60°F (16°C). Keg or add priming sugar and bottle. Carbonate to 2.3 volumes of CO_2.

(continued)

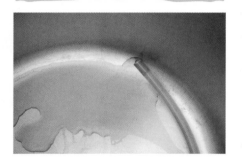

MALT EXTRACT OPTION

Add 2 pounds 14 ounces (1.3 kg) of light dried malt extract to the recipe. Lower the amount of pale ale malt to 1.0 pound (450 g). In your brew pot, steep the 3.0 pounds (1.4 kg) total of crushed grains in 4.1 quarts (3.9 L) of water at 153°F (67°C) for 60 minutes. (This is really a mash, so follow the temperature and volume guidelines closely.) After steeping, place the grain bag in a large colander over your brew pot. Rinse the grains with 2.0 quarts (1.9 L) of 170°F (77°C) water. Add roughly one-third of the malt extract to the wort collected and adjust the wort volume with water to make 3.0 gallons (11 L) of wort. Boil for 60 minutes, adding hops and Irish moss at times indicated. Add remaining malt extract in the final 10 minutes of boil.

HOW MUCH WORT SHOULD YOU COLLECT?

In brewing an all-grain beer, the grains are mashed, and then the liquid wort is separated from the spent grain solids. Usually, the grain bed is rinsed with hot water (called sparge water) to obtain sugars that would be left behind if only the first wort were collected. The first wort is the undiluted wort that flows from the lauter tun before sparge water has been added. But, how much wort should you collect?

Wort collection is a compromise between rinsing as much sugar from the grains as possible, without extracting excess tannins. Plus, the more wort you collect, the longer you have to boil it to reduce the volume to your batch size. In continuous sparging, the longer the grain bed is sparged, the fewer sugars remain, and the more soluble tannins become. For this reason, most brewers stop collecting wort when the pH of the final runnings climbs above 5.8 or when their specific gravity falls below 1.008–1.010. (In those ranges, tannins are very soluble.)

Generally, homebrewers can collect about 0.65 gallons per pound of grain (5.4 L/ kg) before they reach this point. (This varies, however, so it's best to use that figure as a guideline, but still measure either the pH or specific gravity of your final runnings.) Brewers who batch sparge can mash at 1.25 quarts/pound (2.6 L/kg), and add sparge water twice—to reach the same level in the lauter tun—to yield three batches of wort without oversparging. Another way of looking at this is they can add two doses of sparge water, both approximately 60 percent of the volume of their strike water (depending on how much water the grain absorbs) and not oversparge.

In the case of low-gravity beers, you will need to add water to the wort to make a reasonable pre-boil volume. In the case of very strong beers, you will need to boil the wort for an extended amount of time, or decide to leave some sugars behind in the grain bed.

There is an optional volume of wort to collect from every grain bed.

RHEINTURM ALT
ALTBIER

The "alt" in "altbier" is German for old. This refers to the fact that it is brewed in the "old way," i.e., as an ale instead of a lager. These well-balanced, copper-colored ales continued to be brewed in northern Germany after the emergence of lager beers. The malt character of these beers may have a grainy or nutty character, and this is balanced by a firm bitterness.

Altbier is typically fermented at temperatures in the low ale range, or intermediate between the ale and lager range. Extended cold conditioning (compared to other ales) gives alts a smoothness not found in most other ale styles.

5.0 GALLONS (19 L) AT 4.8% ABV
OG = 1.050, FG = 1.012
35 IBU, 14 SRM

+ White Labs WLP036 (Düsseldorf Alt) or Wyeast 1007 (German Ale) yeast
+ A 2.4-qt. (2.3-L) yeast starter is recommended
+ 3 lb. 14 oz. (1.8 kg) Pilsner malt
+ 3 lb. 8 oz. (1.6 kg) Munich malt (8°L)
+ 2 lb. 4 oz. (1.0 kg) dark Munich malt (10°L)
+ 4.0 oz. (110 g) CaraMunich malt (60°L)
+ 2.0 oz. (57 g) Carafa III Special (dehusked) malt
+ 0.42 oz. (12 g) Magnum hops at 14% alpha acids, boiled for 60 minutes (22 IBU)
+ 1.0 oz. (28 g) Saaz hops at 3.5% alpha acids, boiled for 60 minutes (13 IBU)
+ 0.33 oz. (9.4 g) Saaz hops at 3.5% alpha acids, boiled for 0 minutes (0 IBU)
+ 4.5 oz. (130 g) corn sugar, to prime bottles for 2.5 volumes of CO_2

Make your yeast starter two to three days ahead of time. Heat 13 quarts (12 L) of brewing liquor to 163°F (73°C) and mash in grains. Mash at 152°F (67°C) for 60 minutes, stirring every 15 minutes, if you can do so without losing too much heat from your mash tun. Heat or add boiling water to mash out to 168°F (20°C). Recirculate wort until clear, and then run off.

Sparge to collect about 6.5 gallons (25 L) of wort. Vigorously boil wort for 90 minutes, to yield a post-boil volume just over 5.0 gallons (19 L). Add hops at times indicated. Chill wort, then rack to fermenter. Aerate wort thoroughly and pitch sediment from yeast starter. Ferment at 62°F (17°C). This beer will benefit from cold conditioning after fermentation. If possible, hold beer at 50°F (10°C) for two weeks, then lower to normal lagering temperatures (30–40°F/-1.1–4.4°C), and hold for at least another two weeks. Rack to keg or bottling bucket and carbonate to 2.5 volumes of CO_2.

(continued)

MALT EXTRACT OPTION

Add 4.75 pounds (2.2 kg) of Munich liquid malt extract (which is typically made from a 50:50 blend of Munich and Pilsner malt). Reduce the amount of Munich malt to 3 ounces (85 g). Reduce the amount of Pilsner malt to 3.0 ounces (85 g). "Steep" the crushed grains in 2.0 gallons (7.6 L) of water at 152°F (67°C) for 60 minutes. ("Steep" is in quotes because technically this is a partial mash.) Place the grain bag in a colander over your brew pot and rinse the grains with 1.0 gallon (3.8 L) of 170°F (77°C) water.

Add roughly half of the malt extract to this wort, and add water to bring brew pot volume to 3.0 gallons (11 L). Boil for 60 minutes, adding hops at times indicated. Add the remaining malt extract in the final 15 minutes of the boil. Chill wort. Transfer to fermenter, and top up to 5.0 gallons (19 L) with cool water.

CONTINUOUS SPARGING

Sparging refers to rinsing the grain bed with hot water. The aim is to collect the sugars that did not flow out of the lauter tun with the first wort. In continuous sparging, a steady stream of sparge water is sprinkled on top of the grain bed while the wort is being run off. The rate of sparge water input matches the rate of wort runoff, so the liquid level remains steady—for homebrewers, often an inch or two (2.5–5.0 cm) above the grain bed. Among homebrewers, continuous sparging is also known as fly sparging.

In homebrewing, sparge water may be applied through a sprinkler-like device called a sparge arm. The sparge arm may be fed by gravity or a pump. If the wort is run off too fast, the grain bed can contract and slow the flow of wort. As wort collection continues, the brewer may need to adjust the flow rate from the lauter tun (or to the lauter tun) to keep the flow rates equal. It takes some practice to do this flawlessly. However, if you get it to work, continuous sparging is—at least in theory—the method of lautering that can produce the highest level of extract efficiency. (It's also the method most commercial brewers use.)

EIGHTY BOB ALE
SCOTTISH EXPORT

In the early 19th century, Scottish ales were graded by the price they commanded per hogshead. These prices were related to their strength. These included ales that were rated 60/- (60 shilling), 70/- and 80/- per hogshead. Higher-gravity ales, at higher per-barrel prices (up to 160/-), were also available.

Today, a typical Scottish ale that would have sold for 80/- per hogshead would most likely be called a Scottish export ale. Likewise, a 60/- ale would be called Scottish light and a 70/- ale would be called Scottish heavy, despite being in the OG 1.035–1.040 range. Beers labeled as Scottish ales are typically malty, sometimes with toasty or roasted notes. Although similar in color and strength to English bitters, Scottish ales are far less bitter and show less caramel character.

5.0 GALLONS (19 L) AT 5.5% ABV
OG = 1.056, FG = 1.014
18 IBU, 16 SRM

+ Wyeast 1728 (Scottish Ale) or White Labs WLP028 (Edinburgh) yeast
+ A 2.1-qt. (2.0-L) yeast starter is recommended
+ 7.5 lb. (3.4 kg) Scottish pale ale malt
+ 2.0 lb. (910 g) Munich malt (10°L)
+ 1.0 lb. (450 g) amber malt (30–35°L)
+ 6.0 oz. (170 g) crystal malt (60°L)
+ 2.0 oz. (57 g) roasted barley (500°L)
+ 0.60 oz. (17 g) First Gold hops at 8% alpha acids, boiled for 60 minutes (18 IBU)
+ 0.25 oz. Kent Goldings hops at 5% alpha acids, boiled for 0 minutes (0 IBU)
+ 1.0 tsp. Irish moss, boiled for 15 minutes
+ 4.5 oz. (130 g) corn sugar, to prime for 2.5 volumes CO_2

Make your yeast starter two to three days ahead of time. Heat 14 quarts (13 L) of brewing liquor to 163°F (73°C) and mash in grains. Mash at 152°F (67°C) for 60 minutes, stirring every 15 minutes if you can do so without losing too much heat from your mash tun. Heat or add boiling water to mash out to 168°F (76°C). Recirculate wort until clear, and then run off.

Sparge to collect about 7.0 gallons (27 L) of wort. Vigorously boil to yield a post-boil volume of just over 5.0 gallons (19 L). Add hops and Irish moss at times indicated. Chill wort, then rack to fermenter. Aerate wort thoroughly and pitch sediment from yeast starter. Ferment at 60°F (16°C). Keg or add priming sugar and bottle. Carbonate to 2.5 volumes of CO_2.

(continued)

In the early days of modern homebrewing, many sources claimed that Scottish ales had a smoky character. Because Scotland produces peated (smoked) malts for whiskey production, many brewers incorrectly thought that this was the source. So for awhile it was *de rigueur* to include a small amount of peated malt in homebrewed Scottish ales. These days, this is heavily frowned upon, as peated malt is not the source of any smoky character in Scottish ale.

Although not historically accurate, a Scottish ale with some smoked malt character can be very tasty. Peated malt is very intense. Just an ounce or two (28–57 g) in a 5.0-gallon (19-L) recipe will give a noticeable smoke character. German rauchmalz (smoked malt) is much less intense. If you want to make a smoked Scottish ale, you could swap this for some or all of the pale ale malt. One pound (450 g) in a 5.0-gallon (19-L) recipe will yield a light smoke character. Replacing all the pale malt with rauchmalz will yield a level of smoke character similar to the more intense German rauchbiers (smoked beers).

MALT EXTRACT OPTION

Add 4 pounds 2 ounces (1.9 kg) of light dried malt extract to the recipe. Lower the amount of pale ale malt to 8.0 ounces (230 g). This recipe requires a fairly large partial mash to be brewed with extract. Mash the 4.0 pounds (1.8 kg) total of crushed grains in 5.5 quarts (5.2 L) of water at 152°F (67°C) for 60 minutes. This is easiest if you follow the general instructions for a countertop partial mash, as seen in the porter recipe on page 36.

Add roughly a quarter of the malt extract to the wort collected and adjust the wort volume with water to make 3.0 gallons (11 L) of wort. Boil for 60 minutes, adding hops at times indicated. Add remaining malt extract in the final 10 minutes of boil.

PROGRESSIVE MASH OUT

After mashing, it's best to heat the mash to 168–170°F (76–77°C) for a mash out. Mashing out lowers the viscosity of the wort, which makes lautering easier. And, it can increase your extract efficiency (slightly). Some homebrewers cannot add direct heat to their mash/lauter tuns and need to mash out via adding boiling water to the mash. This works well unless the mash tun is too small to receive the volume of boiling water required. For brewers who use continuous sparging, there is a workaround for this.

If you heat your sparge water to 190–200°F (88–93°C), and begin sparging the grain bed, the grain bed temperature will slowly start to rise. You can slowly swap the grain bed temperature up from mash temperature to mash out temperature. You can monitor the top of the grain bed—which will be the hottest—until the temperature rises to 168°F (76°C), then cool your sparge water to this temperature. Cool it simply by stirring in cooler water.

You can use this method if you skip the mash out entirely or if adding boiling water did not raise the mash temperature all the way to 168–170°F (76–77°C). Be careful not to exceed 170°F (77°C) near the end of lautering, as you will extract excess tannins and produce an astringent beer. I've never heard of this being used in a commercial brewery, but it works in a homebrew scale.

UNCHAINED AMBER
WEST COAST AMBER ALE (RED IPA)

This is a hoppy amber ale, in the style of many amber ales brewed on the West Coast of the U.S. You could also call it a red IPA. This beer is bitter, with the citrusy, grapefruit-like aroma of Cascade and Amarillo hops from dry hopping. Unlike pale IPAs, however, this beer has a substantial degree of caramel malt flavor. The caramel malts also lend body to the beer, so it is not as dry as a typical IPA.

5.0 GALLONS (19 L) AT 5.9% ABV
OG = 1.061, FG = 1.015
61 IBU, 14 SRM

+ Wyeast 1272 (American Ale II) or White Labs WLP051 (California V Ale) yeast
+ A 1.6-qt. (1.6-L) yeast starter is recommended
+ 10 lb. (4.5 kg) U.S. 2-row pale malt
+ 1.0 lb. (450 g) caramel malt (40°L)
+ 8.0 oz. (230 g) caramel malt (60°L)
+ 5.0 oz. (140 g) Victory malt (25°L)
+ 1.0 oz. (28 g) black malt (500°L)
+ 1.5 oz. (43 g) Northern Brewer hops at 9% alpha acids, boiled for 60 minutes (51 IBU)
+ 1.0 oz. (28 g) Cascade hops at 5% alpha acids, boiled for 10 minutes (6.7 IBU)
+ 1.0 oz. (28 g) Willamette hops at 5% alpha acids, boiled for 5 minutes (3.7 IBU)
+ 1.0 oz. (28 g) Cascade hops (dry hops)
+ 1.0 oz. (28 g) Amarillo hops (dry hops)
+ 1.0 tsp. Irish moss, boiled for 15 minutes
+ 5.0 oz. (140 g) corn sugar, to prime bottles for 2.5 volumes of CO_2

Make your yeast starter two to three days ahead of time. Heat 15 quarts (14 L) of strike water to 163°F (73°C). Mash crushed malts at 152°F (67°C) for 60 minutes, stirring every 15 minutes if possible. Mash out to 168°F (76°C). You can do this by adding direct heat or add boiling water to the mash tun. Recirculate wort until it is clear, and then begin wort collection.

Sparge to collect about 7.7 gallons (29 L) of wort. Boil wort until wort volume is reduced to 5.0 gallons (19 L). This will likely take between a little less than two hours to three hours, depending on your evaporation rate. Add hops and Irish moss at times indicated. Chill wort, then rack to fermenter. Aerate wort thoroughly and pitch sediment from yeast starter. Ferment at 68°F (20°C). Dry hop in secondary for seven to 10 days. Keg or add priming sugar and bottle. Carbonate to 2.5 volumes of CO_2.

(continued)

RECIPE OPTIONS AND NOTES

You can make this beer into a rye IPA—or something similar—by swapping 10 ounces to 3.0 pounds (280 g to 1.4 kg) of rye malt for pale malt. This corresponds to (roughly) 5–25 percent of the grain bill. This will give the beer the characteristic "snap" of rye, but may make the beer harder to lauter at higher percentages.

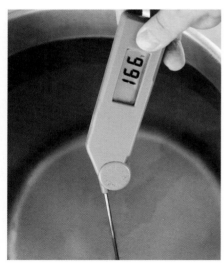

Your sparge water may need to be hotter than 170°F (77°C) to maintain a grain bed temperature of 170°F (77°C).

MALT EXTRACT OPTION

Add 5.0 pounds (2.3 kg) of light dried malt extract to the recipe. Lower the amount of pale malt to 1 pound 2 ounces (510 g). In your brew pot, steep the 3.0 pounds (1.4 kg) total of crushed grains in 4.1 quarts (3.9 L) of water at 152°F (67°C) for 60 minutes. (This is really a mash, so follow the temperature and volume guidelines closely.) After steeping, place the grain bag in a large colander over your brew pot. Rinse the grains with 2.0 quarts (1.9 L) of 170°F (77°C) water.

Add roughly a quarter of the malt extract to the wort collected and adjust the wort volume with water to make at least 3.0 gallons (11 L) of wort. Boil for 60 minutes, adding hops and Irish moss at times indicated. Add the remaining malt extract in the final 10 minutes of the boil.

HOW HOT SHOULD YOUR SPARGE WATER BE?

When a brewer uses continuous sparging, he or she gradually rinses the sugars from the spent grains. The hotter the water, the more effective it is at dissolving sugar. However, near the end of wort collection—when the sugar level is low and the pH is rising—excessively hot water extracts excess tannins from the grain husks. Brewing scientists have experimented and found that water around 168–170°F (76–77°C) works well for sparging—it's hot enough to dissolve sugars, but not so hot as to yield too many tannins late during wort collection.

On a homebrew scale, lauter tuns tend to drop in temperature during use. If you sparge with 168–170°F (76–77°C) water, the temperature of your grain bed may fall well below this as it loses heat to the environment. (And, of course, some homebrewers skip the mash out step. So, their grain beds are not at 168–170°F [76–77°C] to begin with.) Although using 168–170°F (76–77°C) sparge water works fine, you are better off heating your sparge water to the temperature required to keep your grain bed in the 168–170°F (76–77°C) range. This will take some experimentation on your part, but you can start by measuring the temperature of your grain bed when using 168–170°F (76–77°C) sparge water and see how it changes over the course of wort collection.

The next time you brew, increase the sparge water temperature by a few degrees and see what effect it has. Continue adjusting until you find a temperature that works. Monitor the top of the grain bed, and when it reaches 168–170°F (76–77°C), cool the sparge water to that temperature so you don't overshoot. You can cool your sparge water by adding cool water.

If you batch sparge, find the temperature of sparge water that yields a 168–170°F (76–77°C) grain bed for each batch collected.

WALDO LAKE AMBER (BY DENNY CONN)

AMBER ALE

Denny Conn says, "I know some crazy people, but one of the craziest is my good friend Mel Lemay. Every year, she runs the Where's Waldo 100K Ultramarathon around Waldo Lake in the Oregon Cascade Mountain Range. Waldo Lake, 5,400-odd-feet (1.6-kilometers) up in the Cascade Mountains, is the second-largest non-alkali lake in Oregon. The race starts at an elevation of 5,120 feet (1.5 kilometers), and goes to over 7,800 feet (2.4 kilometers) at points. There's a total of over 11,000 feet (3.3 kilometers) of elevation change over the course of the race. You have to be crazy to do that! Several of us go camping at the lake to give moral support when she runs and I developed this recipe to her tastes so she'd have something to look forward to at the end of the race. It's a smooth amber ale . . . not too hoppy, but with enough bitterness and hop flavor that the rest of us enjoy it, too. The Magnum hops give it a smooth, mellow bitterness, with flavor from the first wort hop Cascades and a wonderful nose from the Centennial. The CaraRed gives it a nice malt flavor I've never gotten any other way. And the Wyeast 1450 (Denny's favorite) smooths out the mouthfeel to complement the flavor. You certainly don't have to be crazy to enjoy this beer, but it sure doesn't hurt!"

5.0 GALLONS (19 L) AT 6.2% ABV
OG = 1.063, FG = 1.014
42 IBU, 12 SRM

+ Wyeast 1450 (Denny's favorite) yeast
+ A 1.9-qt. (1.8-L) yeast starter is recommended
+ 7 lb. 12 oz. (3.5 kg) 2-row pale malt
+ 3 lb. 11 oz. (1.7 kg) Munich malt
+ 1 lb. 13 oz. (820 g) CaraRed malt
+ 7.3 oz. (210 g) melanoidin malt
+ 1.25 oz. (35 g) Cascade hops at 6.5% alpha acids, added to mash (7 IBU)
+ 0.70 oz. (20 g) Magnum hops at 14.5% alpha acids, boiled for 60 minutes (35 IBU)
+ 1.0 oz. (28 g) Amarillo hops at 9% alpha acids, boiled for 0 minutes (0 IBU)
+ 1 tablet Whirlfloc, boiled for 15 minutes
+ 5.0 oz. (140 g) corn sugar, to prime bottles for 2.5 volumes of CO_2

Make your yeast starter two to three days ahead of time. Denny Conn says, "I would recommend to the novice batch sparger to use 1.5–1.65 quarts/pound on this. After mash runoff, measure how much wort you have in the kettle. Subtract that from the amount you want to boil. The answer you get is how much sparge water to use. After doing it that way a few times, you should have enough info about your system and process to be able to calculate sparge amounts in the future."

(continued)

So, two to three days after making your yeast starter, heat 21 quarts (20 L) of strike water to 164°F (73°C) to mash in to 153°F (67°C). Mash for 60 minutes, then mash out, recirculate and run off first wort. Estimate the amount of wort in your kettle (it should be around 3.1 gallons [12 L]). Add 12–20 quarts (11–19 L) of sparge water and recirculate again. Run off second wort. Boil wort to reduce volume to just over 5.0 gallons (19 L). Add hops and whirlfloc at times indicated. Ferment at 68°F (20°C). Keg or bottle and carbonate to 2.5 volumes CO_2.

MALT EXTRACT OPTION

You can get pretty close to Denny's all-grain recipe by adding 7 pounds 6 ounces (3.4 kg) of liquid Munich malt extract to the recipe. Reduce the amount of 2-row pale malt to 8.0 ounces (230 g). "Steep" the crushed grains in 4.1 quarts (3.9 L) of water at 153°F (67°C) for 60 minutes. ("Steep" is in quotes because technically this is a partial mash.) Place the grain bag in a colander over your brew pot and rinse the grains with 2.0 quarts (1.9 L) of 170°F (77°C) water. Add roughly one-third of the malt extract to this wort. Add water to bring brew pot volume to 3.0 gallons (11 L). Do not let boil volume fall below 2.5 gallons (9.5 L) during the boil. Top up with boiling water, if needed. Boil for 60 minutes, adding hops and whirlfloc at times indicated. Add the remaining malt extract in the final 15 minutes of the boil.

BATCH SPARGING

Batch sparging is a straightforward method of lautering. Instead of continuously applying sparge water and simultaneously collecting wort at the same rate, the wort is collected in batches. The simplest way to batch sparge would be to mash your grains, then mash out. Recirculate the wort and run off the first wort. You are just draining the available wort, not adding sparge water, so you can run off as quickly as you'd like. Next, you would add hot sparge water—hot enough to keep the grain bed temperature around 168°F (75°C). The volume of sparge water should bring the liquid level to where it was during the mash. This will take less water than before because now the grains have absorbed some water. Recirculate and run off the second batch of wort. If your initial mash thickness was around 1.25 quarts/pound (2.1 L/kg), you can even collect a third batch of wort. Once the wort is collected, heat it to a boil and proceed as you would for any beer.

Many homebrewers use a variation on the above method that lets them collect two equal volume batches of wort. Basically, they mash the grains at their preferred mash thickness, and then add some water to the lauter tun before the first wort is run off. By calculation or trial and error, they collect half their pre-boil wort volume as first wort with a little water added and the second half as sparged wort. You can estimate how much water the grain will absorb by multiplying the weight (in pounds) times 0.15 gallons per pound. (Or you can multiply the weight in kilograms by 1.2 L/kg.) To estimate how much water to add before collecting the first wort, subtract the volume of water absorbed by the grain from the volume of strike water. This is the amount of first wort present after the mash. Divide your intended pre-boil wort volume by two and subtract the volume of first wort from it. This is how much water to add before collecting the first batch. Add a volume of sparge water equal to half of your intended pre-boil wort volume to collect the second batch.

Denny Conn is the coauthor, along with Drew Beechum, of Experimental Homebrewing *(2014, Quarto Publishing). He is the homebrewer who popularized batch sparging.*

The lauter tun is refilled with water after the first wort has been drained.

OLD GLACIER ALE

OLD ALE

Old ale is strong, aged beer. It's usually malty, with a complex fruity aroma. This aroma may have Sherry-like notes due to oxidation during aging. Properly aged examples usually show little hop aroma, even if it was initially highly hopped. The finish may vary from somewhat sweet to fairly dry. This is a great beer to sip on a stormy winter night.

5.0 GALLONS (19 L) AT 7.7% ABV
OG = 1.074, FG = 1.015
37 IBU, 15 SRM

+ Wyeast 1275 (Thames Valley Ale) or White Labs WLP023 (Burton Ale) yeast
+ A 2.9-qt. (2.8-L) yeast starter is recommended
+ 11 lb. (5.0 kg) U.K. pale ale malt (3°L)
+ 8.0 oz. (230 g) crystal malt (60°L)
+ 4.0 oz. (110 g) crystal malt (75°L)
+ 3.0 oz. (85 g) chocolate malt (350°L)
+ 1 lb. 4 oz. (570 g) cane sugar
+ 1.0 oz. (28 g) Target hops at 10% alpha acids, boiled for 60 minutes (Z IBU)
+ 1.0 oz. (28 g) East Kent Goldings hops at 5% alpha acids, boiled for 0 minutes (0 IBU)
+ 1.0 tsp. Irish moss, boiled for 15 minutes
+ 4.5 oz. (130 g) corn sugar, to prime bottles for 2.3 volumes of CO_2

Make your yeast starter two to three days ahead of time. Heat 15 quarts (14 L) of brewing liquor to 161°F (72°C) and mash in grains. Mash at 150°F (66°C) for 60 minutes, stirring every 15 minutes if you can. Heat mash out to 168°F (76°C). Recirculate the wort until it is clear, then run off. Sparge to collect about 7.8 gallons (29 L) of wort.

Boil wort to reduce to just over 5.0 gallons (19 L), adding hops and Irish moss at times indicated. Stir in sugar in final 10 minutes of boil. Chill wort, then rack to fermenter. Aerate wort thoroughly and pitch sediment from yeast starter. Ferment at 70°F (21°C). After fermentation stops, rack to a secondary fermenter (preferably one with little headspace). Age for eight months before packaging. Preferably, do this in a cool location—50–60°F (10–16°C). Be sure to check on the airlock periodically so it doesn't dry out. Although the beer may benefit from a small amount of oxidation, do not purposely do anything to aerate the beer or expose it to oxygen. Keg or add priming sugar and bottle and carbonate to 2.3 volumes of CO_2.

(continued)

RECIPE OPTIONS AND NOTES

You can replace 4.0–8.0 ounces (110–230 g) of crystal malt (60°L) with biscuit malt for a light to moderate biscuit flavor in the beer. This will also lighten the color of the beer and lessen the caramel flavor.

A spark plug gap tool can allow you to measure your grain mill gap.

MALT EXTRACT OPTION

Add 5 pounds 4 ounces (2.4 kg) of light dried malt extract to the recipe. Reduce the amount of 2-row pale ale malt to 2 pounds 1 ounce (930 g). "Steep" the crushed grains in 4.1 quarts (3.9 L) of water at 152°F (67°C) for 60 minutes. ("Steep" is in quotes because technically this is a partial mash.) Place the grain bag in a colander over your brew pot and rinse the grains with 2.0 quarts (1.9 L) of 170°F (77°C) water. Add roughly one-third of the malt extract to this wort. Add water to bring brew pot volume to at least 3.5 gallons (13 L). Boil for 60 minutes, adding hops and Irish moss at times indicated. Add sugar and the remaining malt extract in the final 15 minutes of the boil.

EXTRACT EFFICIENCY

When you mash grains and collect the wort from them, your actions determine how much of the sugars you extract from the grains. A brewer who routinely achieves a higher extract efficiency will have to use less malt to achieve the same original gravity. If you want to improve your extract efficiency, there are several variables that make a difference.

The more finely the malt is crushed, the better your extract efficiency. However, finer crushes also make grain beds that are more difficult to lauter. So, a brewer needs to find a compromise between crushing finely enough and leaving big enough pieces of grain husk to set up a filter in the grain bed. They can do this by adjusting the gap between the roller on their mill. Most brewers find a mill gap between 0.035 and 0.050 inches (0.89 and 1.3 mm) to work well.

The more wort you collect, the better your extract efficiency. However, beyond a certain point, continuing to collect wort only yields extremely low-gravity, highly tannic wort. From a standpoint of extract efficiency, most brewers find that collecting wort until the pH of final runnings rises above 5.8 (or the specific gravity falls below 1.008) is optimal.

The hotter your sparge water, the higher your extract efficiency (due to sugars being more soluble in hotter water). However, if your sparge water is too hot, you can extract excessive tannins from the grain bed. Sparging with water hot enough to maintain your grain bed temperature at 170°F (77°C) is a good compromise.

Stirring the mash also increases your extract efficiency. If you can stir your mash without losing temperature, you should do so.

LITTLE WILLY'S WEE HEAVY
WEE HEAVY

A Wee Heavy is a strong, malty Scottish ale. Wee Heavies are full-bodied beers, generally with more caramel flavor than other Scottish ales.

5.0 GALLONS (19 L) AT 8.1% ABV
OG = 1.084, FG = 1.021
23 IBU, 15 SRM

+ Wyeast 1084 (Irish Ale) or White Labs WLP004 (Irish Ale) yeast
+ A 3.5-qt. (3.3-L) yeast starter is recommended
+ 14 lb. 12 oz. (6.7 kg) Scottish 2-row pale ale malt (3°L)
+ 8.0 oz. (230 g) amber malt (36°L)
+ 8.0 oz. (230 g) crystal malt (30°L)
+ 2.0 oz. (57 g) roasted barley (500°L)
+ 1.25 oz. (35 g) East Kent Goldings hops at 5% alpha acids, boiled for 60 minutes (23 IBU)
+ 1.0 tsp. Irish moss, boiled for 15 minutes
+ 4.0 oz. (110 g) corn sugar, to prime bottles for 2.3 volumes of CO_2

Make your yeast starter two to three days ahead of time. Heat 20 quarts (19 L) of brewing liquor to 161°F (72°C) and mash in grains. Mash at 150°F (66°C) for 60 minutes, stirring every 15 minutes if you can. Heat mash to 168°F (76°C) for a mash out. Recirculate wort until clear, and then run off. A fully sparged grain bed will yield about 10 gallons (38 L) of wort. (You may want to collect less volume and add malt extract to make up the difference.)

Boil wort to reduce volume to just over 5.0 gallons (19 L), adding hops and Irish moss at times indicated. Chill wort, then rack to fermenter. Aerate wort thoroughly and pitch sediment from yeast starter. Ferment at 62°F (17°C). After fermentation stops, keg or add priming sugar and bottle and carbonate to 2.3 volumes of CO_2.

MALT EXTRACT OPTION

Add 7 pounds 10 ounces (3.5 kg) of light dried malt extract to the ingredients. Reduce the amount of 2-row pale ale malt to 1 pound 14 ounces (850 g). "Steep" the crushed grains in 4.1 quarts (3.9 L) of water at 152°F (67°C) for 60 minutes. ("Steep" is in quotes because technically this is a partial mash.) Place the grain bag in a colander over your brew pot and rinse the grains with 2.0 quarts (1.9 L) of 170°F (77°C) water. Add roughly one-third of the malt extract to this wort. Add water to bring brew pot volume to 3.5 gallons (131 L). Boil for 60 minutes, adding hops and Irish moss at times indicated. Add the remaining malt extract in the final 15 minutes of the boil.

In the early days of homebrewing, many homebrewers relied on wort caramelization to add extra color and caramel flavor to their wee heavies. This process is not traditional, but can add an interesting twist to your beer. One way this is done is to divert 2–3 quarts (~2–3 L) of first wort to a small pot and boil it vigorously as you collect the rest of your wort. Stir frequently to avoid scorching. Reduce the volume until you have reached a level of color and caramel flavor that you find appealing. Then, combine the caramelized wort with the rest of your wort and finish brewing as you normally would.

RED TRIANGLE BARLEY WINE

ENGLISH BARLEYWINE

English ales form a continuum from ordinary bitter through much stronger ales, such as old ales. At the top of the heap, however, is barleywine. English barleywine is a strong ale with a complex malt character. It is rich and full-bodied and often served in smaller volumes from a glass that helps the drinker enjoy the aroma (such as a snifter). English barleywines are generally heavily hopped, although not to the degree that American barleywines are. This barleywine has malt sweetness and a hint of caramel upfront, with a firm hop bitterness in the aftertaste.

5.0 GALLONS (19 L) AT 8.1% ABV
OG = 1.087, FG = 1.024
40 IBU, 12 SRM

+ Wyeast 1968 (London ESB) or White Labs WLP002 (English Ale) yeast
+ A 3.8-qt. (3.6-L) yeast starter is recommended
+ 15 lb. 12 oz. (7.1 kg) U.K. pale ale malt (3°L)
+ 8.0 oz. (230 g) crystal malt (60°L)
+ 4.0 oz. (110 g) crystal malt (90°L)
+ 1.25 oz. (35 g) Northdown hops at 8.6% alpha acids, boiled for 60 minutes (40 IBU)
+ 1.25 oz. (35 g) East Kent Goldings hops at 5% alpha acids, boiled for 0 minutes (0 IBU)
+ 1.5 oz. (43 g) Fuggles hops (dry hops)
+ 1.0 tsp. Irish moss, boiled for 15 minutes
+ 4.5 oz. (130 g) corn sugar, to prime bottles for 2.4 volumes of CO_2

Make your yeast starter two to three days ahead of time. Heat 21 quarts (20 L) of brewing liquor to 161°F (72°C) and mash in grains. Mash at 150°F (66°C) for 60 minutes, stirring every 15 minutes if you can. Heat mash to 168°F (76°C) for a mash out. Recirculate wort until it is clear, then run off. If you fully sparge your grain bed, you can collect up to 11 gallons (41 L) of wort. You can, of course, collect less and add malt extract to make up for any loss in extract efficiency.

Boil wort to reduce its volume to just over 5.0 gallons (19 L), adding hops and Irish moss at times indicated. Chill wort, then rack to fermenter. Aerate wort thoroughly and pitch sediment from yeast starter. Ferment at 68°F (20°C). Dry hop for seven to 10 days in secondary, and then age for approximately four months. Make sure the secondary fermenter has little headspace (or flush the headspace with CO_2 before affixing the fermentation lock). Ideally, condition the beer at 50–55°F (10–13°C) and watch that the fermentation lock does not dry out during this period. After aging, keg or add priming sugar and bottle and carbonate to 2.4 volumes of CO_2.

MALT EXTRACT OPTION

Add 8.0 pounds (3.6 kg) of light dried malt extract to the recipe. Reduce the amount of 2-row pale ale malt to 2 pounds 4 ounces (1.0 kg). "Steep" the crushed grains in 4.1 quarts (3.9 L) of water at 152°F (67°C) for 60 minutes. ("Steep" is in quotes because technically this is a partial mash.) Place the grain bag in a colander over your brew pot and rinse the grains with 2.0 quarts (1.9 L) of 170°F (77°C) water. Add roughly one-fourth of the malt extract to this wort. Add water to bring brew pot volume to 3.5 gallons (131 L). Boil for 60 minutes, adding hops and Irish moss at times indicated. Add the remaining malt extract in the final 30 minutes of the boil. There is a lot of malt extract so add it in little doses throughout the final 30 minutes of the boil.

SMALLER BATCHES FOR BIG BEERS

Brewing a big beer can potentially cause a variety of problems. Depending on how big the beer is, the grist may be larger than the homebrewer's mash tun can handle. Or, the brewer's kettle may not be large enough to hold the full pre-boil wort volume. Plus, making the large yeast starter required can sometimes be a hassle. And, the cost of brewing a big beer can get prohibitive—especially if the brewer is using a lot of malt extract or the beer is both big and hoppy.

It's worthwhile considering if scaling down your batch volume might lead to a smoother brew day. There are 3.0-gallon (11-L) and 2.0-gallon (7.6-L) carboys that you can use for aging smaller batches. A 1.0-gallon (3.8-L) glass jug will also work. If you can tolerate generating less beer, brewing a smaller volume of the biggest beers can sometimes lead to more enjoyable brew days.

4

PALE ALES: FROM WELL-BALANCED TO HOP HEAVEN

The section gives the recipes for 20 pale ales. They range from an OG 1.037 (3.5 percent ABV) ordinary bitter to an OG 1.122 (12 percent ABV) imperial barleywine—with pale ales, IPAs and others in between. The color of these beers ranges from 3 SRM to 10 SRM.

If you are treating your water, you should aim to have at least 100 ppm calcium (Ca^{+2}) ions, and between 0 ppm and 60 ppm bicarbonate (HCO_3^-), with the lower end for beers around 3 SRM and the upper end for beers around 10 SRM. (When the boil starts, you may want add 50 ppm more calcium.) As with the darker ales, you do not have to adjust your water chemistry to match your beer's SRM exactly. Being in the ballpark is all you need.

If you are making your water by adding minerals to 5.0 gallons (19 L) of distilled or RO water, start by adding 0 to 2 grams of sodium bicarbonate ($NaHCO_3$, baking soda), with no addition corresponding to beers around 3 SRM and the high-end corresponding to beer around 10 SRM. Then choose a calcium addition depending on how much you want to accentuate the hops. For a balanced beer, add 4 grams of calcium chloride ($CaCl_2*2H_2O$) and 4 grams of calcium sulfate ($CaSO_4*2H_2O$, gypsum). For a beer in which the hops are to be accentuated, add 8 grams of calcium sulfate ($CaSO_4*2H_2O$, gypsum). You will need to prepare more than 5.0 gallons (19 L) of brewing liquor for the all-grain versions of these beers.

For the extract versions, you only need to prepare brewing liquor (water with the correct mineral additions) of the grains you steep or mash. Use distilled water, RO water or naturally soft water for diluting the malt extract.

If you have a water report that describes what is in your water, you can use brewing software to plan your mineral additions. Remember to treat your water to remove any chlorine compounds, if present (as they are in all municipal water sources).

ON THE SLATE ORDINARY
ORDINARY BITTER

"Ordinary bitter" is not a name that a modern marketing person would come up with. It comes from the fact that many British brewers brew more than one bitter. The higher gravity of those two would be called the best bitter, while the lower-gravity version would be called just bitter, or ordinary bitter. These low-gravity beers were traditionally brewed to be served from a cask, and served via gravity or hand pump. Like all bitters, ordinary bitter is a pale ale, flavored with crystal malt, and hopped enough to be distinctly bitter. As they were traditionally served from a cask, they were not highly carbonated.

5.0 GALLONS (19 L) AT 3.5% ABV
OG = 1.037, FG = 1.009
32 IBU, 8.0 SRM

+ Wyeast 1968 (London ESB) or White Labs WLP002 (English Ale) yeast
+ With a fresh pack/tube of yeast, you do not need a yeast starter
+ 5 lb. 8 oz. (2.6 kg) U.K. pale ale malt (3°L)
+ 4.0 oz. (113 g) biscuit malt
+ 6.0 oz. (170 g) crystal malt (60°L)
+ 2.0 oz. (57 g) crystal malt (90°L)
+ 12 oz. (340 g) flaked maize
+ 1.0 oz. (28 g) First Gold hops at 8% alpha acids, boiled for 60 minutes (30 IBU)
+ 0.66 oz. (19 g) Kent Goldings hops at 5% alpha acids, boiled for 5 minutes (2.5 IBU)
+ 0.66 oz. (19 g) Fuggles hops at 5% alpha acids, at knockout (0 IBU)
+ 0.33 oz. (9.4 g) Fuggles hops (dry hops)
+ 1.0 tsp. Irish moss, boiled for 15 minutes
+ 4.0 oz. (110 g) corn sugar, to prime bottles for 2.2 volumes of CO_2

Make your yeast starter two to three days ahead of time. Heat 11 quarts (10 L) of brewing liquor to 163°F (73°C) and mash in grains and maize. Mash at 152°F (67°C) for 60 minutes, stirring every 15 minutes, if you can do so without losing too much heat from your mash tun. Heat or add boiling water to mash out to 168°F (76°C). Recirculate wort until clear, and then run off.

Sparge steadily over 90 minutes to collect about 5.6 gallons (21 L) of wort. Add water to make 6.0 gallons (23 L). Boil wort for 60 minutes. Add hops and Irish moss at times indicated. Chill wort, then rack to fermenter. Aerate wort thoroughly and pitch sediment from yeast starter. Ferment at 68°F (20°C). After fermentation stops, let beer settle for two to three days, then rack to secondary fermenter with dry hops. Dry hop for five to six days, then rack to keg or bottling bucket. Carbonate to 2.2 volumes of CO_2.

(continued)

MALT EXTRACT OPTION

Add 2.0 pounds (910 g) of light dried malt extract and 7.0 ounces (200 g) of cane sugar to the recipe. Omit the flaked maize and reduce amount of pale ale malt to 2.25 pounds (1.0 kg). "Steep" the crushed grains in 2.0 gallons (7.6 L) of water at 152°F (67°C) for 60 minutes. ("Steep" is in quotes because technically this is a partial mash.) Place the grain bag in a colander over your brew pot and rinse the grains with 1.0 gallon (3.8 L) of 170°F (77°C) water.

Add roughly half of the malt extract to this wort, and add water to bring brew pot volume to 3.0 gallons (11 L). Boil for 60 minutes, adding hops and Irish moss at times indicated. Add sugar and the remaining malt extract in the final 15 minutes of the boil. Chill wort. Transfer to fermenter. Top up to 5.0 gallons (19 L) with cool water.

SPEED BREW

Sometimes you may be low on homebrew and want to have some beer fast. If you are looking to minimize your grain-to-glass time and get a beer ready in a hurry, here are some tips:

First of all, choose a low-gravity or moderate-gravity ale, something under a specific gravity of 1.048. Strong ales or lagers take longer to ferment and condition than session ales or "everyday" ales.

Make sure to pitch an adequate amount of yeast, or even slightly overpitch. Aerate the wort well, and run the fermentation in the upper half of the yeast strain's recommended fermentation temperature range. A session ale can easily ferment to completion in three to four days, if everything goes well. Do not, however, rush to package the beer as soon as the fermentation stops.

Separating the beer from the yeast too soon can leave residual diacetyl in the beer. Give the beer one day after fermentation ends to condition, then rack to a keg or bottle the beer. In some cases, if you keg the beer, you can be drinking beer after only six days (assuming you carbonate the keg by shaking and giving the beer a day or two to let the carbonation even out). If you bottle condition, store the bottles warm—70–80°F (21–27°C)—and test one a week later to see if they are ready.

GRIMACING CURMUDGEON IPA
SESSION IPA

This is a session IPA made with American hops with interesting—and some would say aggressive—characteristics. Simcoe—one of the dry hops—has a pleasant aroma with pine-like elements to it. Nugget is a spicy hop, usually used just for bittering. Columbus, which is also usually used just for bittering, is a strongly flavored hop that gives this beer a sharp "kick."

The beer is fairly dry, with just a hint of caramel in the malt profile. At 4.3 percent ABV, it's a real session beer. But given the hops used, it's a session beer for those who like their beer aggressively bitter. (See the other session IPA recipe, on page 25, for a recipe with a milder hop character.)

5.0 GALLONS (19 L) AT 4.3% ABV
OG = 1.043, FG = 1.010
56 IBU, 5.0 SRM

+ Wyeast 1056 (American Ale) or White Labs WLP001 (California Ale) yeast
+ A 1.1-qt. (1.0-L) yeast starter is recommended
+ 8.0 lb. (3.6 kg) U.S. 2-row pale malt
+ 5.0 oz. (140 g) caramel malt (40°L)
+ 1.0 oz. (28 g) Columbus hops at 15% alpha acids, boiled for 60 minutes (56 IBU)
+ 1.0 oz. (28 g) Nugget hops at 13% alpha acids, boiled for 0 minutes (0 IBU)
+ 1.0 oz. (28 g) Columbus hops at 15% alpha acids, boiled for 0 minutes (0 IBU)
+ 1.0 oz. (28 g) Simcoe hops (dry hops)
+ 1.0 oz. (28 g) Columbus hops (dry hops)
+ 1.0 tsp. Irish moss, boiled for 15 minutes
+ 5.0 oz. (140 g) corn sugar, to prime bottles for 2.5 volumes of CO_2

Make your yeast starter two to three days ahead of time. Heat 11 quarts (12 L) of strike water to 161°F (72°C). Mash the malts at 150°F (66°C) for 60 minutes. Stir the mash every 15 minutes, if that is possible. Add direct heat or boiling water to boost the mash temperature to 168°F (76°C) for a mash out. Recirculate the wort until it is clear. Then, run off the first wort and sparge to collect about 5.4 gallons (20 L) of pre-boil wort.

Add water to bring pre-boil volume up to 6.0 gallons (23 L). Boil wort for 60 minutes, adding hops and Irish moss at times indicated. Chill wort, then rack to fermenter. Aerate the wort thoroughly and the pitch sediment from your yeast starter. Ferment at 68°F (20°C). Dry hop for seven to 10 days in secondary. After fermentation stops, keg or add priming sugar and bottle and carbonate to 2.5 volumes of CO_2.

(continued)

Pellet hops are the most commonly used form of hops in homebrewing.

You can wet Irish moss in water before adding it to your kettle.

MALT EXTRACT OPTION

Add 3 pounds 1 ounce (1.4 kg) of light dried malt extract to the recipe. Reduce the amount of 2-row pale malt to 2 pounds 11 ounces (1.2 kg). "Steep" the crushed grains in 4.1 quarts (3.9 L) of water at 150°F (66°C) for 60 minutes. (This is actually a partial mash, so follow volumes and temperatures as close as you can.) Place the grain bag in a colander over your brew pot and rinse the grains with 2.0 quarts (1.9 L) of 170°F (77°C) water. Add roughly one-third of the malt extract to this wort. Add water to bring brew pot volume to 3.0 gallons (11 L). Boil for 60 minutes, adding hops and Irish moss at times indicated. Add the remaining malt extract in the final 15 minutes of the boil.

SINGLE HOP BEERS

There are numerous hop varieties for homebrewers to explore. And new hop varieties are released every year. One way to evaluate a hop you've never worked with before is to make a single hop beer. Single hop beers generally have a malt background of mostly pale malt. In fact, frequently only a single malt is used. These beers are called SMASH beers, meaning Single Malt, Single Hops. They are usually formulated as a moderate-strength pale ale.

A session IPA or SMASH beer is a good beer in which to test hop varieties as the malt character is not going to overshadow the hops. For low-alpha hop varieties, you may want to bitter the beer with a neutral high-alpha hops, then use the hops you're investigating for the late hops. When you taste the beer, you may want to taste other beers you've brewed, or commercial beers for which you know the hops used, for comparison. You can also try blending beers to see which hop combinations are pleasing.

If you plan to use the hop only in a certain kind of beer, a session IPA or SMASH beer might not be the best thing to brew. For example, if you're evaluating a hop to use in your porter, make a single hop beer from your usual porter recipe. The malt background can affect how the hop is perceived. For example, "minty" hops may seem more pleasant against a dark, roasted malt background than in a pale beer.

BLETCHLEY'S BEST BOMBE BITTER
BEST BITTER

Bitter is a style of pale, hoppy English ale that comes in a variety of strengths. The current BCP guidelines describe these, in ascending order, as ordinary bitter, best bitter and strong bitter. Given their low alcoholic strength, ordinary or best bitters are the ale of choice for many English beer drinkers when they plan to enjoy several rounds at the pub. Best bitters typically show some caramel flavor and some may also show notes of biscuit. As the name implies, the beers are bitter—although not to the level of modern IPAs. Also, for many breweries, their best bitter is the highest quality ale in their portfolio.

5.0 GALLONS (19 L) AT 4.1% ABV
OG = 1.045, FG = 1.013
39 IBU, 10 SRM

+ Wyeast 1968 (London ESB) or White Labs WLP002 (English Ale) yeast
+ A 1.1-qt. (1.0-L) yeast starter is recommended
+ 7 lb. 8 oz. (3.4 kg) English pale ale malt (3 °L)
+ 14 oz. (400 g) crystal malt (60°L)
+ 4.0 oz. (110 g) biscuit malt
+ 1.3 oz. (35 g) First Gold hops, at 8% alpha acids, boiled for 60 minutes (37 IBU)
+ 0.33 oz. (9.4 g) Fuggles hops, at 5% alpha acids, boiled for 5 minutes (1.2 IBU)
+ 0.33 oz. (9.4 g) Fuggles hops, at 5% alpha acids, boiled for 0 minutes (0 IBU)
+ 0.50 oz. (14 g) Fuggles hops (dry hops)
+ 1.0 tsp. Irish moss, boiled for 15 minutes
+ 4.25 oz. (120 g) corn sugar, to prime bottles for 2.3 volumes of CO_2

Make your yeast starter two to three days ahead of time. Heat 11 quarts (10 L) of brewing liquor to 163°F (73°C) and mash in grains. Mash at 152°F (67°C) for 60 minutes, stirring every 15 minutes if you can. Heat or add boiling water to mash out to 168°F (76°C). Recirculate wort until clear, and then run off. Sparge to collect about 5.6 gallons (21 L) of wort.

Boil wort for 60 minutes, to reduce to just over 5.0 gallons (19 L). You may need to add some water to the kettle to do this. Add hops and Irish moss at times indicated. Chill wort, then rack to fermenter. Aerate wort thoroughly and pitch sediment from yeast starter. Ferment at 68°F (20°C). After fermentation stops, let beer settle for a couple days, then rack to secondary fermenter with dry hops. Dry hop for five to six days, then rack to keg or bottling bucket. Carbonate to 2.3 volumes of CO_2.

(continued)

EXTRACT OPTION

Add 3 pounds 5 ounces (1.5 kg) of light dried malt extract to the recipe and reduce the amount of 2-row pale ale malt to 1 pound 14 ounces (850 g). "Steep" the crushed grains in 2.0 gallons (7.6 L) of water at 152°F (67°C) for 60 minutes. ("Steep" is in quotes because technically this is a partial mash.) Place the grain bag in a colander over your brew pot and rinse the grains with 1.0 gallon (3.8 L) of 170°F (77°C) water. Add roughly a third of the malt extract to this wort, and add water to bring brew pot volume to 3.0 gallons (11 L). Boil for 60 minutes, adding hops and Irish moss at times indicated. Add the remaining malt extract in the final 15 minutes of the boil. Chill wort. Transfer to fermenter, and top up to 5.0 gallons (19 L) with cool water.

SINGLE INFUSION MASH

The single infusion mash is historically associated with British brewing, but currently common in all brewing traditions. In single infusion mashing, crushed malt is mixed with hot water and allowed to stand at a single temperature. In other mash programs, two or more rests at different temperatures may be employed. Almost all the brewing malt produced today is suitable for infusion mashing and this is a basic all-grain technique that can work well when brewing most all-grain beers.

Single infusion mashes are usually in the 148–162°F (64–72°C) range. The temperature of the mash affects the fermentability of the wort produced. Wort made from mashes near the lower end of this range is (relatively) highly fermentable. Wort produced from a mash near the top end of this range is less fermentable.

Single infusion mashes are usually conducted at a mash thickness between 1.0 quart/pound and 2.5 quarts/pound (2.1–5.2 L/kg). Among homebrewers, 1.25 quarts/pound (2.6 L/kg) is a common mash thickness for single infusion mashes. If all goes well, and your brewing liquor is suited to the type of beer you are brewing, the mash pH should fall in the 5.2–5.6 range, with the lower half of that range being preferable.

Although there is only one mash rest in a single infusion mash, many brewers will raise the temperature of the mash to 168°F (76°C) at the end for a mash out. This step lowers the viscosity of the wort and makes lautering easier.

A mash at this temperature will produce a wort with an intermediate level of fermentability.

THYLACINE ALE
AUSTRALIAN SPARKLING ALE

Australian sparkling ale is light in color, dry and highly carbonated. It's a highly refreshing beer and a showcase for Australian ingredients. Pride of Ringwood hops have a distinctive flavor and aroma, and this recipe uses them both for bittering and a small late hop addition. The Coopers ale yeast is highly attenuative, with a fruity aroma. The beer is not boldly malty or aggressively hoppy, but all the elements of the beer should come together in balance to create a very thirst-quenching beer for a hot summer day.

5.0 GALLONS (19 L) AT 5.1% ABV
OG = 1.047, FG = 1.007
26 IBU, 4.1 SRM

+ Coopers Brewing Yeast (15 g sachet)
+ A 1.1-qt. (1.0-L) yeast starter is recommended
+ 7.0 lb. (3.2 kg) 2-row pale malt
+ 4.0 oz. (110 g) caramel malt (30°L)
+ 1.0 lb. (450 g) cane sugar
+ 0.75 oz. (21 g) Pride of Ringwood hops at 8.5% alpha acids, boiled for 60 minutes (24 IBU)
+ 0.33 oz. (9.4 g) Pride of Ringwood hops at 8.5% alpha acids, boiled for 5 minutes (2.1 IBU)
+ 1.0 tsp. Irish moss, boiled for 15 minutes
+ 0.50 tsp. yeast nutrients, boiled for 15 minutes
+ 5.5 oz. (160 g) corn sugar, to prime bottles for 2.7 volumes of CO_2

Make your yeast starter two to three days ahead of time. Heat 9.0 quarts (8.6 L) of brewing liquor to 151°F (66°C) in your kettle. Mash in to 140°F (60°C) in the kettle (not your mash tun) and hold for 15 minutes. Heat mash to 152°F (67°C) and hold for 45 minutes. Stir the mash almost constantly while heating. Heat the mash again to 168°F (76°C) for a mash out. Scoop mash over to mash/lauter tun for lautering. Recirculate wort until clear, and then run off.

Sparge to collect about 4.7 gallons (18 L) of wort. Add water to make 6.0 gallons (23 L) and boil wort for 60 minutes, adding hops and Irish moss at times indicated. Stir in sugar during final 10 minutes of the boil. Chill the wort, then rack to fermenter. Aerate wort thoroughly and pitch sediment from yeast starter. Ferment at 70°F (21°C). After fermentation stops, keg or bottle and carbonate to 2.7 volumes of CO_2.

MALT EXTRACT OPTION

Add 2.5 pounds (1.1 kg) of light dried malt extract to the recipe. Reduce the amount of 2-row pale ale malt to 2 pounds 12 ounces (1.3 kg). "Steep" the crushed grains in 4.1 quarts (3.9 L) of water at 148°F (65°C) for 60 minutes. (Technically, this is a partial mash so follow volume and temperature as closely as you can manage.) Place the grain bag in a colander over your brew pot and rinse the grains with 2.0 quarts (1.9 L) of 170°F (77°C) water. Add roughly one-third of the malt extract to this wort. Add water to bring brew pot volume to 3.0 gallons (11 L). Boil for 60 minutes, adding hops and Irish moss at times indicated. Add sugar and the remaining malt extract in the final 15 minutes of the boil.

ATTENUATION

Some beers are full-bodied, and perhaps sweet. Others are thinner and drier. Part of this sensation is determined by how well attenuated the beer is. Attenuation is a measure of what percentage of the available sugars the yeast consume. If you are looking to brew a dry beer, with a low final gravity (FG), there are a number of variables that affect the fermentability of your wort.

Worts made from only base malts tend to be more fermentable than worts made from grists with a high percentage of specialty malts (such as crystal malts). Also, wort made with a high percentage of simple sugars—sucrose, glucose or fructose—are more fermentable than worts made entirely from mashing malted grains.

In a single infusion mash, the mash temperature affects fermentability. Mashing at the low end of the saccharification range—148–150°F (64–66°C)—produces a more fermentable wort that will finish at a lower FG. Mashing at the high end of the saccharification range —158–162°F (70–72°C)—produces a less fermentable wort that will finish at a higher FG. Intermediate mash temperatures will yield results between these two. A step mash, with a 15-minute or longer rest in the 140–145°F (60–63°C) range, will produce an even more fermentable wort than any single infusion mash.

Finally, some yeast strains are more attenuative than others. If you are looking to brew a dry beer, choose a yeast strain with a high rate of apparent attenuation. (Data on yeast strain attenuation is given on both Wyeast Laboratories and White Labs Yeast websites.)

So, if you're looking to brew a dry, crisp beer, use only a small amount of specialty malts (or none) at all in your grist. Consider formulating the recipe so 5–30 percent of the fermentables come from simple sugars. Mash low in the saccharification range, or do a step mash. And finally, pick a yeast that will consume a higher percentage of the wort sugars (i.e., exhibit a high degree of apparent attenuation). And obviously, for a more full-bodied beer, do the opposite.

RECIPE OPTIONS AND NOTES

If you don't like the fruity esters from Coopers Brewing Yeast, you can ferment this beer with Danstar Nottingham yeast. Nottingham has a high degree of apparent attenuation, as suits this beer, but has cleaner fermentation characteristics.

Recirculation of the wort clarifies it before the boil.

HËAVY METÄL KÖLSCH
KÖLSCH

Great beer does not require a complex recipe. This Kölsch is brewed using only Pilsner malt, with a single hop addition for bittering. The light malt character and comparatively low hopping rate produce a balanced beer. The cool fermentation and short cold conditioning period give the beer a smooth, almost lager-like, character. Choose quality ingredients that are fresh when brewing this beer, as this beer does not rely on strong flavors. It succeeds when the sweetish flavor of Pilsner malt is accentuated by the lightly spicy flavor of Tettnanger hops.

5.0 GALLONS (19 L) AT 4.8% ABV
OG = 1.048, FG = 1.011
25 IBU, 3.0 SRM

+ Wyeast 2565 (Kölsch) or White Labs WLP029 (German Ale/Kölsch) yeast
+ A 1.6-qt. (1.5-L) yeast starter is recommended
+ 9.0 lb. (4.1 kg) Pilsner malt
+ 1.5 oz. (43 g) Tettnanger hops at 4.5% alpha acids, boiled for 60 minutes (25 IBU)
+ 4.75 oz. (130 g) corn sugar, to prime bottles for 2.5 volumes of CO_2

Make your yeast starter two to three days ahead of time. Heat 12 quarts (11 L) of brewing liquor to 163°F (73°C) and mash in grains. Mash at 152°F (67°C) for 60 minutes, stirring every 15 minutes if you can. Heat or add boiling water to mash out to 168°F (76°C). Recirculate wort until clear, and then run off wort. Sparge to collect about 5.9 gallons (22 L) of wort.

Boil wort for 60 minutes, adding hops at the beginning of the boil. Chill wort, then rack to fermenter. Aerate wort thoroughly and pitch sediment from yeast starter. Ferment at 65°F (18°C). After fermentation stops, cold condition—at 50–55°F (10–13°C)—for two to three weeks. Then, keg or bottle and carbonate to 2.5 volumes of CO_2.

MALT EXTRACT OPTION

Add 4 pounds 6 ounces (2.0 kg) of liquid Pilsner malt extract to the recipe. Reduce the amount of Pilsner malt to 3.0 pounds (1.4 kg). "Steep" the crushed grains in 4.1 quarts (3.9 L) of water at 152°F (67°C) for 60 minutes. ("Steep" is in quotes because technically this is a partial mash.) Place the grain bag in a colander over your brew pot and rinse the grains with 2.0 quarts (1.9 L) of 170°F (77°C) water. Add roughly one-third of the malt extract to this wort. Add water to bring brew pot volume to at least 3.5 gallons (13 L). Boil for 60 minutes, adding hops at times indicated. Add the remaining malt extract in the final 15 minutes of the boil.

(continued)

Noble hops are a good choice for most European lager beers.

NOBLE HOPS

This recipe uses Tettnanger hops, which are one of the noble hops. There are no official criteria for what makes a hop noble, but most brewers would list Saaz, Tettnanger, Hallertau Mittelfrüher and Hallertau Hersbrucker as noble hops. Some would also include Spalter. (And some English brewers would also add East Kent Goldings.) Noble hops are low-alpha hops with a refined hop aroma. They are widely used in the best German and Czech lagers.

Noble hops have relatively high levels of humulene—the hop oil that many brewers prize as the most delicate and pleasant. The English hops Fuggle and East Kent Goldings also have high levels of humulene. The American hop Mt. Hood also has a high percentage of this oil.

BREADBASKET WHEAT
AMERICAN WHEAT

American wheat beers are pale, moderate-strength ales brewed with a sizable proportion of wheat in the grist. Unlike German wheat beers, they do not show the banana, clove and bubblegum flavors derived from the specialized yeast strains used to brew those beers. Instead, they are most often brewed with a neutral ale yeast strain, although some commercial examples use lager yeast.

The wheat in the grist, often a combination of malted wheat and raw wheat, often gives the beer a hazy appearance with the characteristic "zing" of wheat. The beer's haze may be enhanced by the presence of yeast in the beer. The level of hop character varies considerably, but many are intended to be well-balanced and easy drinking. Some examples have a slightly tart edge.

5.0 GALLONS (19 L) AT 4.7% ABV
OG = 1.049, FG = 1.012
24 IBU, 3.9 SRM

+ Wyeast 1056 (American Ale), White Labs WLP001 (California Ale) or Fermentis U.S.-05 yeast
+ A 1.1-qt. (1.0-L) yeast starter is recommended with liquid yeast
+ 5 lb. 8 oz. (2.5 kg) U.S. 2-row pale malt
+ 3 lb. 8 oz. (1.6 kg) white wheat malt
+ 6.0 oz. (170 g) torrified wheat
+ 1.0 oz. (28 g) Mt. Hood hops at 6% alpha acids, boiled for 60 minutes (22 IBU)
+ 0.33 oz. (9.3 g) Willamette hops at 5% alpha acids, boiled for 10 minutes (2 IBU)
+ 0.33 oz. (9.3 g) Willamette hops at 5% alpha acids, boiled for 0 minutes (0 IBU)
+ 4.75 oz. (135 g) corn sugar, to prime bottles for 2.5 volumes of CO_2

If you are using one of the liquid yeasts, make your yeast starter two to three days ahead of time. Heat 12 quarts (11 L) of brewing liquor to 161°F (72°C) and mash in grains. Mash at 150°F (66°C) for 60 minutes, stirring every 15 minutes, if you can do so without losing too much heat from your mash tun. Heat or add boiling water to mash out to 168°F (76°C). Recirculate wort until clear, and then run off.

Sparge to collect about 6.1 gallons (23 L) of wort. Boil wort for 60 minutes, adding hops at times indicated. Reduce wort volume to just over 5.0 gallons (19 L). Chill wort, then rack to fermenter. Aerate wort thoroughly and pitch sediment from yeast starter. Ferment at 66°F (19°C). After fermentation stops, keg or bottle and carbonate to 2.5 volumes of CO_2.

(continued)

RECIPE OPTIONS AND NOTES

This recipe uses torrified wheat in addition to the wheat malt. Flaked wheat can be used in place of the torrified wheat. So can pretty much any form of raw wheat. Another option is to substitute rye malt for some of the wheat malt and brew a beer that shows a combination of wheat and rye character. Or, you could entirely replace the wheat malt with rye malt for a beer that tasted strongly of rye. (And likewise, raw rye could be substituted for some or all of the torrified wheat.) Rye can get sticky in the mash. If it exceeds 20 percent of the mash, it may become difficult to lauter.

Rye malt or flaked rye can be used instead of, or in addition to, the wheat in this recipe.

MALT EXTRACT OPTION

Add 3 pounds 2 ounces (1.4 kg) of light dried malt extract to the recipe. Lower the amount of pale malt to 2 pounds 13 ounces (1.3 kg). Lower the amount of wheat malt to 13 ounces (370 g). This recipe requires a fairly large partial mash to use the raw (torrified) wheat. Mash the 4.0 pounds (1.8 kg) total of crushed grains in 5.5 quarts (5.2 L) of water at 150°F (66°C) for 60 minutes. This is easiest if you follow the general instructions for a countertop partial mash, as seen in the porter recipe on page 36.

Add roughly a quarter of the malt extract to the wort collected and adjust the wort volume with water to make 3 gallons (11 L) of wort. Boil for 60 minutes, adding hops at times indicated. Add remaining malt extract in the final 10 minutes of boil.

WHEAT MALT

Wheat malt can be made from either red wheat or white wheat. Red wheat does not lend beer a red color, as a crystal malt would, but has phenolic compound in the bran that makes the malt look slightly reddish-brown. German hefeweizens are generally made from red wheat malt, while most Belgian beers made with wheat favor white wheat. American wheat beers are most often made with white wheat.

Wheat beers are generally hazy due to the high protein content in wheat as compared to barley. Many brewers will try different wheat malts from different maltsters until they find one that gives them a stable haze that they like. In addition, many brewers mix wheat malt with a bit of raw wheat (wheat flakes or torrified wheat) in their recipes to give the beer a pleasing flavor and appearance.

ICE FISHING ALE
CREAM ALE

Cream ale is a light ale adaptation of an American Pilsner. It's brewed with the same ingredients and has a very similar balance and overall character, but generally has slightly more malt and hop character. Despite having the word "cream" in the title, it is not brewed using any dairy products and there is nothing particularly creamy about it.

Cream ale is usually fermented with an ale strain, but lager strains can be used. Likewise, it is usually packaged shortly after primary fermentation is complete, but a short period of cold conditioning can be employed. This lightly flavored, highly carbonated ale is thirst quenching and can be a welcome beverage after any strenuous outdoor activity … or ice fishing.

5.0 GALLONS (19 L) AT 5.1% ABV
OG = 1.051, FG = 1.011
19 IBU, 3.5 SRM

+ Wyeast 1056 (American Ale) or White Labs WLP001 (California Ale) yeast
+ A 1.6-qt. (1.5-L) yeast starter is recommended
+ 4.0 lb. (1.8 kg) U.S. 2-row pale malt
+ 4.0 lb. (1.8 kg) U.S. 6-row pale malt
+ 2.0 lb. (910 g) flaked maize
+ 0.55 oz. (16 g) Brewers Gold hops at 9% alpha acids, boiled for 60 minutes (19 IBU)
+ 1.0 tsp. Irish moss, boiled for 15 minutes
+ 5.0 oz. (140 g) corn sugar, to prime bottles for 2.6 volumes of CO_2

Make your yeast starter two to three days ahead of time. Heat 13 quarts (12 L) of brewing liquor to 161°F (72°C) and mash in crushed malts and flaked maize. Mash at 150°F (66°C) for 60 minutes, stirring every 15 minutes if you can do so without losing too much heat from your mash tun. Heat or add boiling water to mash out to 168°F (76°C). Recirculate wort until clear, and then run off.

Sparge to collect about 6.5 gallons (25 L) of wort. Boil wort for 90 minutes. Add hops and Irish moss at times indicated. Chill wort, then rack to fermenter. Aerate wort thoroughly and pitch sediment from yeast starter. Ferment at 66°F (19°C). Keg or add priming sugar and bottle. Carbonate to 2.6 volumes of CO_2.

(continued)

MALT EXTRACT OPTION

Add 2 pounds 14 ounces (1.3 kg) of light dried malt extract to the recipe. Lower the amount of 2-row pale malt to 1.5 pounds (680 g). Also lower the amount of 6-row pale malt to 1.5 pounds (680 g). Replace the flaked maize with 1 pound 6 ounces (620 g) of corn sugar. In your brew pot, steep the 3.0 pounds (1.4 kg) total of crushed grains in 4.1 quarts (3.9 L) of water at 150°F (66°C) for 60 minutes. (This is really a mash, so follow the temperature and volume guidelines closely.)

After steeping, place the grain bag in a large colander over your brew pot. Rinse the grains with 2.0 quarts (1.9 L) of 170°F (77°C) water. Add roughly a third of the malt extract to the wort collected and adjust the wort volume with water to make 3.0 gallons (11 L) of wort. Boil for 60 minutes, adding hops and Irish moss at times indicated. Add the remaining malt extract and the corn sugar in the final 10 minutes of the boil.

CEREAL MASH

Flaked maize or flaked rice can be stirred directly into a mash. These flakes have been extruded through hot rollers so their starches have all been gelatinized. If you add them to the mash, the starches will dissolve and the enzymes from the grain can go to work on them. If you brew from raw corn or rice, however, the gelatinization temperatures of their starches is greater than that of the mash. As such, you need to gelatinize the starches in these cereals before mashing them. For that, you'll need to use a cereal mash.

A cereal mash is a mix of the cereal(s) you plan to mash and 10–20 percent barley malt. It is mixed to roughly the consistency of porridge. Brewer's corn grits and plain rice are two common cereals used in brewing. The cereal mash is boiled, to gelatinize the starches in the corn or rice, and then stirred into the main mash. For a cream ale, you can start the main mash at 140–145°F (60–63°C). In a separate (heatable) vessel, mash in the cereal mash to roughly the same temperature, then heat it to around 158°F (70°C) and hold for 5 minutes. This will give the enzymes from the barley malt a little time to work on any starch that is gelatinized at that point.

Then, heat the cereal mash to a boil. You will need to stir the cereal mash almost constantly. You may also need to add water if it gets too thick. Boil for 30 minutes, and then stir the cereal mash into the main mash. This should raise the temperature of the combined mash. Adjust the mash temperature so it is 150–152°F (66–67°C) and mash for at least another 45 minutes.

PATRICK HENRY PALE ALE
AMERICAN PALE ALE

American-style pale ale is, arguably, the beer that kick-started the craft beer movement in the United States. American pale ales are based on their English cousins. Early American pale ales, including Sierra Nevada Pale Ale and New Albion Ale, introduced beer drinkers to a full-bodied beer with the flavor and aroma of American hops. In both these cases, Cascade was the signature hop.

The malt character of an American pale ale comes from U.S. 2-row malt, with support from crystal or caramel malts. American pale ales are generally lighter in color than their English counterparts, as well as being more hoppy and more highly carbonated.

5.0 GALLONS (19 L) AT ABV 5.3% ABV
OG = 1.052, FG = 1.011
44 IBU, 11 SRM

+ Wyeast 1056 (American Ale), White Labs WLP001 (California Ale), or Fermentis U.S.-05 yeast
+ A 1.6-qt. (1.5-L) yeast starter for liquid yeasts
+ 9 lb. 8 oz. (4.3 kg) U.S. 2-row pale malt
+ 8.0 oz. (220 g) crystal malt (40°L)
+ 3.0 oz. (84 g) crystal malt (60°L)
+ 0.375 oz. (11 g) Simcoe hops at 13% alpha acids, boiled for 60 minutes (13 IBU)
+ 0.50 oz. (14 g) Centennial hops at 10% alpha acids, boiled for 30 minutes (14 IBU)
+ 0.625 oz. (18 g) Cascade hops at 7% alpha acids, boiled for 15 minutes (9 IBU)
+ 0.25 oz. (7.1 g) Amarillo hops at 8% alpha acids, boiled for 15 minutes (3.7 IBU)
+ 0.625 oz. (18 g) Cascade hops at 7% alpha acids, boiled for 0 minutes (0 IBUs)
+ 0.25 oz. (7.1 g) Amarillo hops at 8% alpha acids, boiled for 0 minutes (0 IBUs)
+ 0.75 oz. (21 g) Cascade hops (dry hops)
+ 0.50 oz. (14 g) Amarillo hops (dry hops)
+ 1.0 tsp. Irish moss, boiled for 15 minutes
+ 0.25 tsp. yeast nutrients, boiled for 15 minutes
+ 5.0 oz. (140 g) corn sugar, to prime bottles for 2.5 volumes of CO_2

If you are using one of the liquid yeasts, make your yeast starter two to three days ahead of time. Mash in by heating 13 quarts (12 L) of brewing liquor to 163°F (73°C) and combining with crushed grains. The temperature should settle in to 152°F (67°C). Hold mash at 152°F (67°C) for 60 minutes. If you can stir the mash without losing heat, do so every 10 minutes or so. Heat the mash or add boiling water to mash out to 168°F (76°C). Let mash sit for 5 minutes, then recirculate the wort until it runs clear, or for 20 minutes. Then, collect your wort.

(continued)

Sparge to collect about 7.0 gallons (27 L) of pre-boil wort. Keep the sparge water heated so that grain bed temperature remains at 168°F (76°C). Vigorously boil the wort for 90 minutes, to yield a post-boil volume just over 5.0 gallons (19 L). Add hops, Irish moss and yeast nutrients at times indicated. If hops cling to the side of your kettle, above the boiling wort, knock them back in with your brewing paddle. Chill the wort to 68°F (20°C), then rack to your fermenter.

Aerate the wort thoroughly and pitch the sediment from your yeast starter. Ferment the beer at 68°F (20°C). After fermentation stops, let the beer settle for two to three days, then rack to secondary fermenter with dry hops. For best results, dry hop in a carboy with as little headspace as possible. Dry hop for five to six days, then rack to keg or bottling bucket for bottling. Carbonate to 2.5 volumes of CO_2.

MALT EXTRACT OPTION

Replace the 9 pounds 8 ounces (4.3 kg) of U.S. 2-row pale malt with 1 pound 5 ounces (590 g) of U.S. 2-row pale malt. Add 4.25 pounds (1.9 kg) of light dried malt extract to the recipe. Place crushed grains in a steeping bag. In your brew pot, steep crushed grains in 3.0 quarts (2.8 L) of water at 152°F (67°C). Hold this temperature for 60 minutes. Remove grains and add water to "grain tea" to make 3.0 gallons (11 L) of wort. Add roughly half of the malt extract and bring to a boil. Boil wort for 60 minutes, adding hops, Irish moss and yeast nutrients at times indicated. Stir in remaining malt extract during the final 10 minutes of the boil. Chill the wort and transfer to your fermenter.

DRY HOPPING

Dry hopping is the practice of adding hops to beer that has finished fermenting. Dry hopping with fresh, aromatic hops lends a wonderful aroma that you can't get no matter how many hops you add late in the boil or whirlpool. Brewers frequently dry hop with whole hops, but pellets can also be used. As the hops remain in contact with the beer, their oils are dissolved. Contact time should be at least a few days, and is commonly around a week to 10 days. Extended dry hopping times add little aroma and can lend a grassy character to the beer. Because heat is required to isomerize alpha acids into iso-alpha acids (the primary molecules that confer hop bitterness), dry hopping does not increase the bitterness of the beer. It does, however, increase the overall hop character, which can make the beer seem more bitter. Dry hopping is usually done at the same temperature as the fermentation.

Heavily dry hopped beer can be hazy, as tannins are also extracted as the hops steep. Also, as air is entrained between the bracteoles of the cones, dry hopping can add oxygen to the beer and make it go stale early. To avoid this, you can flush the hops with CO_2 before using them (for example, by placing them in a keg and filling it with CO_2). Although dry hops are not sanitized before adding them to the beer, dry hopping does not cause contaminated beer. The alcohol content and fairly low pH of the beer suppresses the growth of contaminants.

Brewers can place their dry hops in a nylon (or other mesh) bag, and then place the bag in their secondary fermenter or keg. They can tie a length of (unflavored) dental floss to the bag and seal the fermenter or keg with the floss hanging outside. (Dental floss is thin enough that a rubber stopper or keg O-ring will still seal the vessel.) When the contact time is over, the bag can be removed by pulling on the dental floss.

Hops will float, so sometimes a sanitized, nonreactive weight is placed in the bag to weigh it down. A stainless steel fitting or small glass object can be used, as long as it can be cleaned and sanitized. If you dry hop in a keg, be sure to purge the headspace after removing the dry hops.

STELLER'S JAY PA
AMERICAN PALE ALE (II)

There are a wide variety of hops available to homebrewers these days, and brewing a hoppy American pale ale is a great way to discover their characteristics. This pale ale is bittered with Magnum, a neutral hop with a high level of alpha acids. The late hops and dry hops are all Cascade—the classic "American" hop. This gives the beer the quintessential "citrusy American" hop flavor and aroma. (See the recipe options for another hopping option.) A light caramel flavor colors the malt character and the beer finishes moderately dry. Overall, this is well-balanced "go-to" pale ale for everyday drinking.

5.0 GALLONS (19 L) AT 5.2% ABV
OG = 1.052, FG = 1.012
45 IBU, 6.9 SRM

+ Wyeast 1056 (American Ale), White Labs WLP001 (California Ale), or Fermentis U.S.-05 yeast
+ A 1.4-qt. (1.3-L) yeast starter is recommended
+ 9 b. 8 oz. (4.3 kg) U.S. 2-row pale malt
+ 11 oz. (310 g) caramel malt (40°L)
+ 0.75 oz. (21 g) Magnum hops at 14.5% alpha acids, boiled for 60 minutes (41 IBU)
+ 1.25 oz. (35 g) Cascade hops at 5% alpha acids, boiled for 5 minutes (4.7 IBU)
+ 0.50 oz. (14 g) Cascade hops at 5% alpha acids, boiled for 0 minutes (0 IBU)
+ 1.5 oz. (43 g) Cascade hops (dry hops)
+ 1.0 tsp. Irish moss, boiled for 15 minutes
+ 5.0 oz. (140 g) corn sugar, to prime bottles for 2.5 volumes of CO_2

If you are using one of the liquid yeasts, make your yeast starter two to three days ahead of time. Heat 13 quarts (12 L) of brewing liquor to 163°F (73°C) and mash in crushed malts. Mash at 152°F (67°C) for 60 minutes, stirring every 15 minutes if you can do so without losing too much heat from your mash tun. Heat or add boiling water to mash out to 168°F (76°C). Recirculate wort until clear, and then run off.

Sparge to collect about 6.6 gallons (25 L) of wort. Boil wort for 90 minutes, until the wort volume reduced to just over 5.0 gallons (19 L). Add hops and Irish moss at times indicated. Chill wort, then rack to fermenter. Aerate wort thoroughly and pitch sediment from yeast starter. Ferment at 68°F (20°C). Dry hop in secondary for seven to 10 days. Keg or add priming sugar and bottle. Carbonate to 2.5 volumes of CO_2.

Boiling hops converts their alpha acids into isomerized alpha acids, the main bittering agent in beer.

This recipe, and the American pale ale recipe that precedes it, showcase American hops with a citrus-like flavor and aroma. You can brew essentially the same pale ale, except featuring American hops with a "piney" character by changing the hop bill. To do this, swap the Magnum hops for Chinook hops. Replace the 1.25 ounces (35 g) of Cascade hops added in the last 5 minutes of the boil with 1.0 ounce (28 g) of Simcoe hops. And lastly, swap the hops added at knockout and dry hops with Ahtanum hops. Alternately, you can blend the two hop bills to make a pale ale with both citrus and pine notes.

MALT EXTRACT OPTION

Add 4 pounds 2 ounces (1.9 kg) of light dried malt extract to the recipe. Lower the amount of pale malt to 2 pounds 5 ounces (1.1 kg). In your brew pot, steep the 3.0 pounds (1.4 kg) total of crushed grains in 4.1 quarts (3.9 L) of water at 152°F (67°C) for 60 minutes. (This is really a mash, so follow the temperature and volume guidelines closely.)

After steeping, place the grain bag in a large colander over your brew pot. Rinse the grains with 2.0 quarts (1.9 L) of 170°F (77°C) water. Add roughly a third of the malt extract to the wort collected and adjust the wort volume with water to make 3.0 gallons (11 L) of wort. Boil for 60 minutes, adding hops and Irish moss at times indicated. Add remaining malt extract in the final 10 minutes of the boil.

GOLD RUSH STEAMER
CALIFORNIA COMMON

California Common, or steam beer, is a pale beer that is similar to an American pale ale. Most homebrew versions are based on Anchor Steam, the beer that revived the style. The beer is pale, with the aroma of hops that were available in the Gold Rush area. In practice, this has come to mean Northern Brewer hops.

This recipe mixes Northern Brewer and Cluster—another American hop with a long history—with the modern hop Willamette as a late hop. American hops with a citrus character, such as Cascade and Centennial, aren't used in versions of this beer that strive to taste authentic. This beer is fermented at temperatures between typical ale and lager fermentation temperatures, using a lager strain that performs well at higher temperatures.

5.0 GALLONS (19 L) AT 5.5% ABV
OG = 1.055, FG = 1.013
41 IBU, 9.1 SRM

+ Wyeast 2112 (California Lager) or White Labs WLP810 (San Francisco Lager) yeast
+ A 3.0-qt. (2.8-L) yeast starter is recommended
+ 9 lb. 10 oz. (4.4 kg) U.S. pale ale malt (3°L)
+ 13 oz. (370 g) caramel malt (40°L)
+ 3.0 oz. (85 g) caramel malt (60°L)
+ 0.88 oz. (25 g) Northern Brewer hops at 8% alpha acids, boiled for 60 minutes (26 IBU)
+ 0.50 oz. (14 g) Northern Brewer hops at 8% alpha acids, boiled for 15 minutes (7.5 IBU)
+ 0.50 oz. (14 g) Cluster hops at 7% alpha acids, boiled for 10 minutes (4.7 IBU)
+ 0.75 oz. (21 g) Willamette hops at 5% alpha acids, boiled for 5 minutes (2.8 IBU)
+ 1.0 tsp. Irish moss, boiled for 15 minutes
+ 4.75 oz. (130 g) corn sugar, to prime bottles for 2.5 volumes of CO_2

Make your yeast starter two to three days ahead of time. Heat 14 quarts (13 L) of brewing liquor to 163°F (73°C) and mash in grains. Mash at 152°F (67°C) for 60 minutes, stirring every 15 minutes if you can. Heat or add boiling water to mash out to 168°F (76°C). Recirculate wort until clear, and then run off.

Sparge to collect about 6.8 gallons (26 L) of wort. Boil wort for 90 minutes, to reduce volume to just over 5.0 gallons (19 L), adding hops and Irish moss at times indicated. Chill wort, then rack to fermenter. Aerate wort thoroughly and pitch sediment from yeast starter. Ferment at 64°F (18°C). After fermentation stops, let the beer condition at 64°F (18°C) for about a week. Then, keg or add priming sugar and bottle and carbonate to 2.5 volumes of CO_2.

MALT EXTRACT OPTION

Add 4 pounds 7 ounces (2.0 kg) of light dried malt extract to the recipe. Reduce the amount of 2-row pale ale malt to 2.0 pounds (910 g). "Steep" the crushed grains in 4.1 quarts (3.9 L) of water at 152°F (67°C) for 60 minutes. ("Steep" is in quotes because technically this is a partial mash.) Place the grain bag in a colander over your brew pot and rinse the grains with 2.0 quarts (1.9 L) of 170°F (77°C) water. Add roughly one-third of the malt extract to this wort. Add water to bring brew pot volume to 3.0 gallons (11 L). Boil for 60 minutes, adding hops and Irish moss at times indicated. Add the remaining malt extract in the final 15 minutes of the boil.

BOIL PH

Hitting the proper mash pH range is important. In addition, hitting the proper boil pH is also important, but less appreciated in most homebrewing circles. After achieving a mash pH of 5.2–5.6, the pH should drop to 5.1–5.2 by the end of the boil. You can check your boil pH with a pH meter, but there is a visual cue that will let you know if your boil pH is OK. At a pH of 5.2, the hot break forms as big, fluffy flakes. Move away from pH 5.2 in either direction, and the flakes become smaller. If there is a problem with the boil pH, it is almost always that the pH is too high.

In most cases, adding about 50 ppm calcium ions to your boiling wort will lower the wort pH. And, you will be able to see a change in the hot break. Adding a teaspoon of either gypsum (calcium sulphate) or calcium chloride to 5.0 gallons (19 L) of boiling wort will raise the level of calcium ions by about 50 ppm. If this doesn't work, try adding another 50 ppm dose of calcium. If that doesn't work, adding more calcium will not help.

RECIPE OPTIONS AND NOTES

This recipe uses one modern hop, Willamette, for its pleasing floral properties. Replace the 0.75 ounce (21 g) of Willamette hops with 0.50 ounce (14 g) of Northern Brewer for a more authentic, period interpretation of the beer. (On the other hand, nobody will know that you used Willamette in your beer unless you tell them.)

Minerals such as calcium sulfate (gypsum), or calcium chloride can be added to brewing liquor—the water used to brew beer—to give it sufficient calcium. Calcium has many benefits in brewing liquor, including helping the mash drop to a proper pH.

WILDFIRE IPA
AMERICAN IPA

This is a very aromatic American IPA. Although the level of bitterness is in line with an American IPA, the level of late hopping is closer to that of a double IPA. The hop bill gets the best from seven classic American hops. The hop flavor is aggressive, with a bit of "bite" from some characterful hops. The floral aroma—with citrus and pine notes—almost jumps out of the glass. If you love uncompromisingly hoppy IPAs, this is the beer for you. This beer is fairly well attenuated, and carbonated enough to give the beer the impression of being a little drier than it actually is.

5.0 GALLONS (19 L) AT 6.4% ABV
OG = 1.065, FG = 1.015
66 IBU, 7.4 SRM

+ Wyeast 1056 (American Ale) or White Labs WLP001 (California Ale) yeast; A 2.1-qt. (2.0-L) yeast starter is recommended
+ 11 lb. (5.0 kg) U.S. 2-row pale malt
+ 1.0 lb. (450 g) Munich malt (10°L)
+ 10 oz. (280 g) caramel malt (30°L)
+ 0.50 oz. (14 g) Chinook hops at 13% alpha acids, boiled for 60 minutes (24 IBU)
+ 0.50 oz. (14 g) Columbus hops at 15% alpha acids, boiled for 60 minutes (28 IBU)
+ 0.50 oz. (14 g) Centennial hops at 10% alpha acids, boiled for 10 minutes (6.7 IBU)
+ 0.50 oz. (14 g) Simcoe hops at 13% alpha acids, boiled for 5 minutes (7.3 IBU)
+ 0.75 oz. (21 g) Cascade hops at 5% alpha acids, boiled for 0 minutes (0 IBU)
+ 0.75 oz. (21 g) Amarillo hops at 5% alpha acids, boiled for 0 minutes (0 IBU)
+ 1.25 oz. (35 g) Cascade hops (dry hops)
+ 1.25 oz. (35 g) Ahtanum hops (dry hops)
+ 1.0 tsp. Irish moss, boiled for 60 minutes
+ 5.25 oz. (150 g) corn sugar, to prime bottles for 2.6 volumes of CO_2

Make your yeast starter two to three days ahead of time. Heat 16 quarts (15 L) of brewing liquor to 161°F (72°C) and mash in crushed malts. Mash at 150°F (66°C) for 60 minutes, stirring every 15 minutes if you can. Heat or add boiling water to mash out to 168°F (76°C). Recirculate wort until clear, and then run off. Fully sparging the grain bed will yield up to 7.5 gallons (28 L) of wort.

Boil wort until wort volume is reduced to just over 5.0 gallons (19 L). If you've collected the full 8.2 gallons (31 L), this will likely take about 3 hours, depending on your evaporation rate. Add hops and Irish moss at times indicated. Chill wort, then rack to fermenter. Aerate wort thoroughly and pitch sediment from yeast starter. Ferment at 68°F (20°C). Dry hop in secondary for seven to 10 days. Keg or add priming sugar and bottle. Carbonate to 2.6 volumes of CO_2.

(continued)

MALT EXTRACT OPTION

Add 4.5 pounds (2.0 kg) of light dried malt extract to the recipe. Lower the amount of pale malt to just 6.0 ounces (170 g). In your brew pot, steep the 3.0 pounds (1.4 kg) total of crushed grains in 4.1 quarts (3.9 L) of water at 150°F (66°C) for 60 minutes. (This is really a mash, so follow the temperature and volume guidelines closely.)

After steeping, place the grain bag in a large colander over your brew pot. Rinse the grains with 2.0 quarts (1.9 L) of 170°F (77°C) water. Add roughly a quarter of the malt extract to the wort collected and adjust the wort volume with water to make at least 3.0 gallons (11 L) of wort. Boil for 60 minutes, adding hops and Irish moss at times indicated. Add the remaining malt extract in the final 10 minutes of the boil.

COHUMULONE

The bitterness in beer comes mostly from alpha acids. During the boil, the bitter alpha acids are rearranged into the substantially more bitter iso-alpha acids. The three most prevalent alpha acids in hops are humulone, adhumulone and cohumulone. Humulone is the most abundant of the three, but cohumulone attracts a lot of attention from brewers.

Brewers used to be convinced that cohumulone lent a harsher bitterness to beer than the other two alpha acids. However, this may have been because it is the most soluble of the three. As such, beers bittered with high cohumulone hops ended up being more bitter. Recent experiments have failed to show an association between cohumulone content and harshness.

In any case, in the past hop breeders strove to breed low cohumulone hop strains, even while some high-cohumulone hops—such as Cascade—remained very popular. In most noble hops—including Saaz and Tettnanger—the percentage of cohumulone (as a percentage of the total alpha acids) is less than 30 percent, with Hallertau varieties generally having less than 25 percent. In contrast, many of the American hops that are widely used in pale ales and IPAs—including Cascade, Centennial, Chinook, Columbus, Ahtanum and Willamette—have more than 30 percent, with Cascade sometimes pushing 40 percent. (On the other hand, Simcoe is a very low cohumulone hop, with 15–20 percent cohumulone. Likewise, Amarillo typically only has 20–24 percent.) Among English hops, Kent Goldings and Challenger are low in cohumulone (20–25 percent), with Fuggles and Northdown having slightly higher values (24–32 percent). Target and First Gold are both typically over 30 percent.

Each hop has a different character. And part of this character is due to the percentage of cohumulone it contains. However, don't be afraid to use a hop variety based solely on its cohumulone rating. There's no good evidence that the bitterness from cohumulone is harsher than other alpha acids.

Some hop varieties are—for whatever reasons—more "aggressive" than others. (Columbus, for example, has the reputation of being "pungent.") Don't shun these varieties, either. Some big, hoppy beers benefit from a little "bite" the same way that some food benefits from some fiery spices.

FEATHERED DINOSAUR IPA
AMERICAN IPA (II)

This is a straight-up American IPA with classic "citrusy" American hops. The amount of caramel malt is restrained and a small amount of sugar is added in the kettle to give this beer a dry finish and let the hops take center stage. The American yeast strain used to ferment this beer is clean and does not absorb as much hop bitterness as many other ale strains. An extra dose of sulfates in your water can accentuate the bitterness in this beer.

5.0 GALLONS (19 L) AT 7.1% ABV
OG = 1.068, FG = 1.013
66 IBU, 7.8 SRM

+ Wyeast 1056 (American Ale) or White Labs WLP001 (California Ale) yeast
+ A 2.2-qt. (2.1-L) yeast starter is recommended
+ 8.0 lb. (3.6 kg) U.S. 2-row pale malt
+ 2.0 lb. (910 g) Munich malt (10°L)
+ 10 oz. (280 g) caramel malt (30°L)
+ 1 lb. 8 oz. (680 g) cane sugar
+ 0.50 oz. (14 g) Magnum hops at 14.5% alpha acids, boiled for 60 minutes (27 IBU)
+ 0.50 oz. (14 g) Columbus hops at 15% alpha acids, boiled for 60 minutes (28 IBU)
+ 0.50 oz. (14 g) Centennial hops at 10% alpha acids, boiled for 10 minutes (6.7 IBU)
+ 0.50 oz. (14 g) Centennial hops at 10% alpha acids, boiled for 5 minutes (3.7 IBU)
+ 0.75 oz. (21 g) Cascade hops at 5% alpha acids, boiled for 0 minutes (0 IBU)
+ 0.25 oz. (7.1 g) Amarillo hops at 8% alpha acids, boiled for 0 minutes (0 IBU)
+ 1.5 oz. (35 g) Cascade hops (dry hops)
+ 0.50 oz. (14 g) Amarillo hops (dry hops)
+ 1.0 tsp. Irish moss, boiled for 15 minutes
+ 5.0 oz. (140 g) corn sugar, to prime bottles for 2.5 volumes of CO_2

Make your yeast starter two to three days ahead of time. Heat 14 quarts (13 L) of strike water to 161°F (72°C). Mash malts at 150°F (66°C) for 60 minutes, stirring every 15 minutes if you can. Heat or add boiling water to mash out to 168°F (76°C). Recirculate the wort until it is clear, then run off. Sparge to collect about 6.9 gallons (26 L) of wort. Boil wort for 90–120 minutes, to reduce wort volume to just over 5.0 gallons (19 L). Add hops and Irish moss at times indicated. Stir in sugar during the final 10 minutes of the boil. Chill wort, then rack to fermenter. Aerate wort thoroughly and pitch sediment from yeast starter. Ferment at 68°F (20°C). Dry hop for seven to 10 days in secondary. Keg or add priming sugar and bottle and carbonate to 2.5 volumes of CO_2.

(continued)

In an IPA, a concentration of 200 ppm (or more) of sulfate will enhance the hop bitterness.

MALT EXTRACT OPTION

Add 4 pounds 6 ounces (2.0 kg) of light dried malt extract to the recipe. Reduce the amount of 2-row pale malt to 6.0 ounces (170 g) "Steep" the crushed grains in 4.1 quarts (3.9 L) of water at 150°F (66°C) for 60 minutes. (Technically this is a partial mash, so follow the mash temperatures and volume closely.)

Place the grain bag in a colander over your brew pot and rinse the grains with 2.0 quarts (1.9 L) of 170°F (77°C) water. Add roughly one-third of the malt extract to this wort. Add water to bring brew pot volume to at least 3.5 gallons (13 L). Boil for 60 minutes, adding hops and Irish moss at times indicated. Add the sugar and remaining malt extract in the final 15 minutes of the boil.

SULFATE IN HOPPY BEERS

Water that has a fair amount of sulfates in it will accentuate the hop character of a hoppy beer. In order to bring out the hop character of an IPA, a brewer's water should have at least 200 ppm sulfate. Anywhere in the 200–400 ppm range should work fine. For a 5.0-gallon (19-L) volume of distilled water, you would need to add 0.25–0.50 ounce (7.1–14 g) of gypsum. This is approximately 3.5 to 7.0 teaspoons per 5.0 gallons (19 L). Before adding sulfate to your water via gypsum (calcium sulfate), you should check your water report and see how much is already present. In 5.0 gallons of water, every gram—roughly a half teaspoon—of gypsum adds approximately 30 ppm sulfate.

Some brewers also believe the chloride-to-sulfate ratio is important and advocate a 1:2 to 1:3 ratio of chloride ions to sulfate ions. Balanced beers are said to be best with a chloride-to-sulfate ratio around 1:1. If you are adding calcium to your brewing liquor, the ratio of the weight of calcium chloride to gypsum in your mineral additions will be fairly close to your chloride-to-sulfate ratio.

ZOMBIE HOTROD
BELGIAN IPA

Belgian IPAs are IPAs fermented with a yeast strain that lends "Belgian" notes to the flavor and aroma of the beer. Some Belgian IPAs are based on a recipe similar to a tripel. Others, such as this one, have a pale-ale-like base. European hops may be used, but the typical American hops used in pale ales and IPAs is more common. If you follow the pitching rate and fermentation temperature recommendations, this beer ferments mostly clean, with just a hint of esters and phenolic spiciness. Some Belgian IPAs are highly carbonated. Others, like this one, are carbonated to the level typical of American craft ales.

5.0 GALLONS (19 L) AT 6.8% ABV
OG = 1.068, FG = 1.015
66 IBU, 6.7 SRM

+ Wyeast 3787 (Trappist High Gravity) or White Labs WLP530 (Abbey Ale) yeast
+ A 2.2-qt. (2.1-L) yeast starter is recommended
+ 11 lb. (5.0 kg) Belgian pale malt (3°L)
+ 1.5 lb. (680 g) wheat malt
+ 5.0 oz. (140 g) biscuit malt (25°L)
+ 1.25 oz. (35 g) Citra hops at 12% alpha acids, boiled for 60 minutes (56 IBU)
+ 0.50 oz. (14 g) Centennial hops at 10% alpha acids, boiled for 10 minutes (6.7 IBU)
+ 0.75 oz. (21 g) Cascade hops at 5% alpha acids, boiled for 5 minutes (2.8 IBU)
+ 0.66 oz. (19 g) Centennial hops at 10% alpha acids, boiled for 0 minutes (0 IBU)
+ 0.66 oz. (19 g) Citra hops at 12% alpha acids, boiled for 0 minutes (0 IBU)
+ 1.0 oz. (28 g) Centennial hops (dry hops)
+ 0.50 oz. (14 g) Citra hops (dry hops)
+ 1.0 tsp. Irish moss, boiled for 15 minutes
+ 5.0 oz. (140 g) corn sugar, to prime bottles for 2.5 volumes of CO_2

Make your yeast starter two to three days ahead of time. Heat 16 quarts (15 L) of brewing liquor to 161°F (72°C) and mash in crushed malts. Mash at 150°F (66°C) for 60 minutes, stirring every 15 minutes, if you can do so without losing too much heat from your mash tun. Heat or add boiling water to mash out to 168°F (76°C). Recirculate wort until clear, and then run off.

Sparge steadily over 90 minutes to collect about 8.3 gallons (32 L) of wort. Boil wort until wort volume is reduced to 5.0 gallons (19 L). This will likely take at least a little over 2 hours, depending on your evaporation rate. Add hops and Irish moss at times indicated. Chill wort, then rack to fermenter. Aerate wort thoroughly and pitch sediment from yeast starter. Ferment at 68°F (20°C). Dry hop in secondary for seven to 10 days. Keg or add priming sugar and bottle. Carbonate to 2.6 volumes of CO_2.

(continued)

For yeast starters with a strong varietal character, higher fermentation temperatures accentuate the yeast's signature by-products.

MALT EXTRACT OPTION

Add 5 pounds 12 ounces (2.6 kg) of light dried malt extract to the recipe. Lower the amount of pale malt to 1 pound 3 ounces (540 g). In your brew pot, steep the 3.0 pounds (1.4 kg) total of crushed grains in 4.1 quarts (3.9 L) of water at 150°F (66°C) for 60 minutes. (This is really a mash, so follow the temperature and volume guidelines closely.) After steeping, place the grain bag in a large colander over your brew pot. Rinse the grains with 2.0 quarts (1.9 L) of 170°F (77°C) water. Add roughly a quarter of the malt extract to the wort collected and adjust the wort volume with water to make at least 3.0 gallons (11 L) of wort. Boil for 60 minutes, adding hops and Irish moss at times indicated. Add the remaining malt extract in the final 10 minutes of the boil.

MANIPULATING YEAST CHARACTER

Some yeast strains are fairly neutral. Others produce interesting flavors and aromas. For yeast strains that produce distinctive fruity esters or other interesting flavors—such as the clove from German hefeweizen yeast strains or a phenolic spice character as found in some Belgian strains—you can manipulate the intensity of these characteristics by how you conduct your fermentation.

Within the window of workable yeast fermentation temperatures, yeast produce more esters and other byproducts at higher temperatures. If you have an English or Belgian strain known for its fruity esters and you want to emphasize them, ferment near the top end of the yeast's fermentation range.

Fermentation by-products such as esters and phenols are produced in the greatest abundance when the yeast are replicating. Thus, if you encourage more "growth" from your yeast, they will produce more of their typical esters and phenols (if any). Pitching rate affects yeast performance and lower pitching rates—which require the yeast to replicate more before they reach fermentation density—encouraging the production of more fermentation by-products. Pitching three-quarters, or perhaps half, of the recommended amount of yeast will force the yeast to produce more esters and other flavors it is known for. Of course, there is only so far you can lower the pitching rate without risking a sluggish or stuck fermentation. Lower aeration rates, which stress the yeast a bit, also bring out the character in a yeast strain.

The yeast strain used in this recipe produces fairly clean ales when pitched at rates over the typical ale pitching rate and fermented in mid ale range—64–66°F (18–19°C). When fermented at slightly higher temperatures it produces a distinctive estery aroma with some peppery spice.

LOST PINES IPA
RYE IPA

This is an IPA with the characteristic "zing" of rye and piney American hops. The recipe uses around 20 percent rye—enough to give the beer the flavor of rye, but not so much as to cause serious issues when lautering.

5.0 GALLONS (19 L) AT 6.8% ABV
OG = 1.069, FG = 1.016
68 IBU, 7.4 SRM

+ Wyeast 1056 (American Ale) or White Labs WLP001 (California Ale) yeast
+ A 2.3-qt. (2.2-L) yeast starter is recommended
+ 10 lb. 8 oz. (4.8 kg) U.S. 2-row malt
+ 3.0 lb. (1.4 kg) rye malt
+ 8.0 oz. (230 g) caramel malt (40°L)
+ 1.25 oz. (35 g) Chinook hops at 13% alpha acids, boiled for 60 minutes (61 IBU)
+ 0.75 oz. (21 g) Simcoe hops at 13% alpha acids, boiled for 5 minutes (7.3 IBU)
+ 0.75 oz. (21 g) Ahtanum hops at 6% alpha acids, boiled for 0 minutes (0 IBU)
+ 0.50 oz. (14 g) Simcoe hops (dry hops)
+ 1.0 oz. (28 g) Ahtanum hops (dry hops)
+ 1.0 tsp. Irish moss, boiled for 15 minutes
+ 5.0 oz. (140 g) corn sugar, to prime bottles for 2.5 volumes of CO_2

Make your yeast starter two to three days ahead of time. Heat 18 quarts (17 L) of brewing liquor to 163°F (73°C) and mash in grains. Mash at 152°F (67°C) for 60 minutes, stirring every 15 minutes, if you can do so without losing too much heat from your mash tun. Heat or add boiling water to mash out to 168°F (76°C). Skipping the mash out will make lautering more difficult. Recirculate wort until clear, and then run off. You should be able to collect about 9.1 gallons (34 L) of wort from a fully sparged grain bed.

Keep your sparge water hot enough to maintain the grain bed temperature at 168°F (76°C). If you are fly sparging, collect the wort as slowly as you reasonably can. Boil the wort to reduce its volume to just over 5.0 gallons (19 L), adding hops and Irish moss at times indicated. Chill wort, then rack to fermenter. Aerate wort thoroughly and pitch sediment from yeast starter. Ferment at 68°F (20°C). Dry hop for seven to 10 days. After fermentation stops, keg or add priming sugar and bottle. Carbonate to 2.5 volumes of CO_2.

(continued)

RECIPE OPTIONS AND NOTES

Rye is used in making pumpernickel bread. The characteristic spice in pumpernickel is caraway seed. As such, adding some caraway to any rye beer can give it that anise-like flavor reminiscent of pumpernickel. In a 5.0-gallon (19-L) batch, try adding 0.50–0.75 ounce (14–21 g) caraway seed in the last couple minutes of the boil or at knockout.

Alternatively, try adding the same amount mixed in with the dry hops. You could also add much smaller amounts of cardamom, anise or fennel along with the caraway, as long as the total weight of the spices stays under 1.0 ounce (28 g). Recall that spices can be tricky, so use these amounts as a guideline, subject to your assessment of how potent the spices are. And remember, it's fairly easy to add spices to a beer—perhaps by making a tea or alcohol extract— but you can't take spices away. Err on the side of using less spice when you experiment. Other possibilities include adding some orange zest, as is found in some Scandinavian rye bread recipes, or swapping out 1.0 pound (450 g) of pale malt for 12 ounces (250 ml) of molasses.

Both malted rye (left) and flaked rye (right) are used in brewing.

MALT EXTRACT OPTION

Add 1 pound 6 ounces (740 g) of liquid rye malt extract and 4 pounds 6 ounces (2.1 kg) of light dried malt extract to the recipe. Reduce the amount of 2-row pale ale malt to 2 pounds 8 ounces (1.1 kg). "Steep" the crushed grains in 4.1 quarts (3.9 L) of water at 152°F (67°C) for 60 minutes. ("Steep" is in quotes because technically this is a partial mash.)

Place the grain bag in a colander over your brew pot and rinse the grains with 2.0 quarts (1.9 L) of 170°F (77°C) water. Add roughly two-thirds of the dried malt extract to this wort. Add water to bring brew pot volume to at least 3.5 gallons (13 L). Boil for 60 minutes, adding hops and Irish moss at times indicated. Add the rye malt extract and remaining dried malt extract in the final 15 minutes of the boil.

INFLATIONARY EPOCH IPA
IMPERIAL IPA

Imperial IPAs are bigger, hoppier versions of an IPA. For the boldest imperial IPAs, the sky is the limit when it comes to hops. There is a limit to iso-alpha acid solubility—as well as a limit to how much bitterness your tongue can sense—so a beer can only be so bitter. (And if an IPA really does have more than 70 IBUs, you probably couldn't perceive any more bitterness from a higher IBU rating.) However, piling on more hops does lead to a bigger hop aroma.

This imperial IPA is an explosion of American citrusy hops. The calculated IBUs are over 100, and this 5.0-gallon (19-L) recipe calls for a huge dose of late hops in the kettle—4.0 ounces (110 g) in the final 15 minutes—and 3.0 ounces (85 g) of dry hops. Although this is a big beer, it is not meant to be aged— drink it as soon as it is ready, when the hop aroma is at its peak.

5.0 GALLONS (19 L) AT 7.5% ABV
OG = 1.072, FG = 1.014
100+ IBU, 5.3 SRM

+ Wyeast 1056 (American Ale) or White Labs WLP001 (California Ale) yeast; A 2.6-qt. (2.5-L), yeast starter is recommended
+ 11 lb. (5.0 kg) 2-row pale malt
+ 5.0 oz. (140 kg) crystal malt (30°L)
+ 1 lb. 8 oz. (680 g) cane sugar
+ 1.25 oz. (35 g) Simcoe hops at 13% alpha acids, boiled for 60 minutes (61 IBU)
+ 1.0 oz. (28 g) Columbus hops at 15% alpha acids, boiled for 15 minutes (28 IBU)
+ 1.0 oz. (28 g) Centennial hops at 10% alpha acids, boiled for 10 minutes (13 IBU)
+ 1.0 oz. (28 g) Amarillo hops at 9% alpha acids, boiled for 5 minutes (6.7 IBU)
+ 1.0 oz. (28 g) Cascade hops at 5% alpha acids, boiled for 0 minutes (0 IBU)
+ 1.0 oz. (28 g) Centennial hops (dry hops)
+ 1.0 oz. (28 g) Amarillo hops (dry hops)
+ 1.0 oz. (28 g) Cascade hops (dry hops)
+ 1.0 tsp. Irish moss, boiled for 15 minutes
+ 5.0 oz. (140 g) corn sugar, to prime bottles for 2.5 volumes of CO_2

Make your yeast starter two to three days ahead of time. Heat 15 quarts (14 L) of brewing liquor to 161°F (72°C) and mash in crushed malts. Mash at 150°F (66°C) for 60 minutes, stirring every 15 minutes, if you can do so without losing too much heat from your mash tun. Heat or add boiling water to mash out to 168°F (76°C). Recirculate wort until clear, and then run off.

(continued)

Whole hops are commonly used when dry hopping.

Sparge to collect about 7.4 gallons (28 L) of wort. Boil wort for 90–150 minutes, until wort volume is reduced to just over 5.0 gallons (19 L). Add hops and Irish moss at times indicated. Stir in cane sugar in the final 10 minutes of boil. Chill wort, then let it sit (covered) for about 2 hours to let the hop debris settle and compact a bit. You may want to transfer the trub to sanitized mason jars and let it sit overnight; the wort will settle a bit more by the next day. You can pour any recovered wort into your fermenter. Rack to fermenter. Aerate wort thoroughly and pitch sediment from yeast starter. Ferment at 68°F (20°C). Dry hop in secondary for seven to 10 days. Keg or add priming sugar and bottle. Carbonate to 2.5 volumes of CO_2.

MALT EXTRACT OPTION

Add 4 pounds 12 ounces (2.2 kg) of light dried malt extract to the recipe. Lower the amount of pale malt to 2 pounds 11 ounces (1.2 kg). In your brew pot, steep the 3.0 pounds (1.4 kg) total of crushed grains in 4.1 quarts (3.9 L) of water at 150°F (66°C) for 60 minutes. (This is really a mash, so follow the temperature and volume guidelines closely.) After steeping, place the grain bag in a large colander over your brew pot. Rinse the grains with 2.0 quarts (1.9 L) of 170°F (77°C) water. Add roughly a quarter of the malt extract to the wort collected and adjust the wort volume with water to make at least 3.5 gallons (13 L) of wort. Boil for 60 minutes, adding hops and Irish moss at times indicated. Add the sugar and remaining malt extract in the final 10 minutes of the boil.

CONTINUOUS HOPPING

This recipe has four late hop additions to the kettle, at 15 minutes, 10 minutes, 5 minutes and 0 minutes remaining in the boil. As an option, you could combine these four hops in a bag or bowl and add them continuously throughout the last 15 minutes of the boil. (The commercial brewery Dogfish Head hops their 60-Minute IPA and 120-Minute IPA continually through the entire boil.) Starting with 15 minutes left if the boil, you could add the hops at a rate of roughly one-fifth of an ounce (5.8 g) per minute, then add the remaining hops—about 1.0 ounce (28 g)—at knockout. The result will not be radically different from adding the hops in four discrete doses, but mixing all the hops together will alter the flavor and aroma very slightly.

You can spread out the late hopping on any recipe by following this basic idea. Just take the total amount of hops added late in the boil and divide by the number of minutes left. You may want to leave any additions made at knockout out of that calculation, and add the full amount called for right then, but it's up to you.

WICKED WITCH GOLDEN ALE
BELGIAN STRONG GOLDEN ALE

The words "Belgian strong golden ale" tell you almost everything you need to know about this style of beer. It's "Belgian-y." It's strong. And it's light in color. The beer is also very dry, being made with just pale base malt and around 20 percent sugar. In this recipe, one dose of sugar is added in the kettle and another is added in the secondary fermenter. A relatively high level of hopping (as Belgian beers go) and prickly carbonation also enhances the dry character of this beer. The yeast strain yields an aroma with fruity esters, including pears, with just a hint of phenolic spiciness.

5.0 GALLONS (19 L) AT 8.3% ABV
OG = 1.075, FG = 1.011
30 IBU, 3.9 SRM

+ Wyeast 1388 (Belgian Strong Ale) or White Labs WLP570 (Belgian Golden Ale) yeast
+ A 2.6-qt. (2.5-L) yeast starter is recommended
+ 8.0 lb. (3.6 kg) Belgian Pils malt
+ 2.0 lb. (910 g) German Vienna malt (3°L)
+ 1 lb. 12 oz. (790 g) cane sugar (kettle)
+ 12 oz. (340 g) cane sugar (dosage)
+ 1.33 oz. (38 g) Styrian Goldings hops at 6% alpha acids, boiled for 60 minutes (30 IBU)
+ 0.50 oz. (14 g) Saaz hops at 3.5% alpha acids, boiled for 0 minutes (0 IBU)
+ 0.50 tsp. yeast nutrient, boiled for 15 minutes
+ 1.0 tsp. Irish moss, boiled for 15 minutes
+ 6.0 oz. (170 g) corn sugar, to prime bottles for 2.8 volumes of CO_2

Make your yeast starter two to three days ahead of time. Heat 13 quarts (12 L) of brewing liquor to 161°F (72°C) and mash in grains. Mash at 150°F (66°C) for 60 minutes, stirring every 15 minutes if you can do so. Heat or add boiling water to mash out to 168°F (76°C). Recirculate wort until clear, and then run off. Sparge to collect about 6.5 gallons (25 L) of wort.

Boil wort for 90 minutes, adding hops, Irish moss and yeast nutrients at times indicated. Stir in kettle sugar in final 10 minutes of boil. Reduce wort volume to 4.75 gallons (18 L)—about 1 quart (~1 L) below 5.0 gallons (19 L). (At this point, your wort will be around SG 1.072.) Chill wort, then rack to fermenter. Aerate wort thoroughly and pitch sediment from yeast starter. Ferment starting at 65°F (18°C). After high kräusen, let the fermentation temperature rise to as high as 80°F (27°C). Simmer dosage sugar in 1.0 quart (0.95 L) of water for 5 minutes, and then cool. Add the dosage sugar solution to a secondary fermenter and rack beer into it. After secondary fermentation subsides, keg or add priming sugar and bottle and carbonate to 2.8 volumes of CO_2.

(continued)

MALT EXTRACT OPTION

Add 5.0 pounds (2.3 kg) of liquid Pilsner malt extract to the recipe. Reduce the amount of Pilsner malt to 1.0 pound (450 g). "Steep" the crushed grains in 4.1 quarts (3.9 L) of water at 150°F (66°C) for 60 minutes. ("Steep" is in quotes because technically this is a partial mash.) Place the grain bag in a colander over your brew pot and rinse the grains with 2.0 quarts (1.9 L) of 170°F (77°C) water.

Add roughly one-half of the malt extract to this wort. Add water to bring brew pot volume to at least 3.5 gallons (13 L). Boil for 60 minutes, adding hops and Irish moss at times indicated. Add the kettle sugar and remaining malt extract in the final 15 minutes of the boil. Retain the dosage sugar to add in the secondary fermenter. Chill wort and transfer to fermenter. Add water to make 1 quart (1 L) shy of 5.0 gallons (19 L). Aerate and pitch yeast. Follow remaining instructions from all-grain recipe.

ADDING DOSAGE SUGAR

Additions of simple sugars to beers raise the original gravity (OG) of the beer, but not the final gravity (FG). This allows a brewer to make a beer that is stronger and drier than a comparable all-malt beer. Caramelized or other colored sugars can also add flavor to the beer. Usually, a brewer will add the sugar to his or her kettle. However, it can also—as in this recipe—be added in the secondary fermenter. Adding the sugar after primary fermentation is complete can be less stressful on the yeast than adding all the sugar upfront.

When adding a clear sugar, simmering it in water for about 5 minutes should sanitize the solution without darkening it too much. (And really, all you need to do is hold the temperature above 170°F [77°C] for this period of time.) This is especially true if the sugar solution is not very thick. If you plan ahead for the sugar addition, you can make your wort slightly lower in volume than your intended batch size. Then, make the sugar solution such that racking the beer into it yields your intended batch size.

There is no reason to add sugar in the fermenter in lower-gravity beers. However, if you are making a strong beer that contains a substantial amount of sugar, it's worth considering withholding some of it until secondary fermentation.

MAL COBB TRIPEL
TRIPEL

The Belgian tripel was popularized by the Westmalle Trappist Brewery as a stronger and lighter-colored beer than their dubbel. The name tripel is an indication of strength, but tripels do not have literally triple the strength of a Trappist single.

This beer is strong and dry, being brewed with about 20 percent sugar in the kettle. A very high level of carbonation enhances the sensation of dryness. Very similar to a Belgian golden strong ale, the yeast strain used for fermentation adds character to the beer. At high pitching rates and low fermentation temperatures, this yeast ferments very cleanly. At lower pitching rates and higher temperatures, it has a fruity aroma with some black pepper–like spice notes. The pitching rate and fermentation profile described here is meant to deliver a moderate amount of fruit and spice.

5.0 GALLONS (19 L) AT 9.0% ABV
OG = 1.083, FG = 1.013
35 IBU, 3.4 SRM

+ Wyeast 3787 (Trappist High Gravity) or White Labs WLP530 (Abbey Ale) yeast
+ A 3.5-qt. (3.3-L) yeast starter is recommended
+ 11 lb. 4 oz. (5.1 kg) Belgian Pils malt
+ 2 lb. 8 oz. (1.1 kg) cane sugar
+ 2.0 oz. (57 g) Tettnang hops at 4.5% alpha acids, boiled for 60 minutes (34 IBU)
+ 0.25 oz. (7.1 g) Saaz hops at 3.5% alpha acids, boiled for 5 minutes (1.3 IBU)
+ 0.50 tsp. yeast nutrient, boiled for 15 minutes
+ 1.0 tsp. Irish moss, boiled for 15 minutes
+ 8.0 oz. (230 g) corn sugar, to prime bottles for 3.5 volumes of CO_2

Make your yeast starter two to three days ahead of time. Heat 14 quarts (13 L) of brewing liquor to 161°F (72°C) and mash in grains. Mash at 150°F (66°C) for 60 minutes, stirring every 15 minutes if you can do so without losing too much heat from your mash tun. Heat or add boiling water to mash out to 168°F (76°C). Recirculate wort until clear, and then run off.

Sparge to collect about 7.3 gallons (28 L) of wort. Boil wort to reduce to just over 5.0 gallons (19 L), adding hops, Irish moss and yeast nutrients at times indicated. Chill wort, then rack to fermenter. Aerate wort thoroughly and pitch sediment from yeast starter. Begin fermenting at 65°F (18°C). After the most vigorous phase of fermentation is over, let the fermentation temperature climb to 72°F (22°C). When fermentation is over, bottle and carbonate to 3.5 volumes of CO_2. Use heavy bottles for this and store them where it will not be a problem if they burst. (Line a couple case boxes with garbage bags, just in case)

MALT EXTRACT OPTION

Add 6.0 pounds (2.7 kg) of liquid Pilsner malt extract to the recipe. Reduce the amount of Pilsner malt to 3.0 pounds (1.4 g). "Steep" the crushed Pilsner malt in 4.1 quarts (3.9 L) of water at 150°F (67°C) for 60 minutes. ("Steep" is in quotes because technically this is a partial mash.) Place the grain bag in a colander over your brew pot and rinse the grains with 2.0 quarts (1.9 L) of 170°F (77°C) water. Add roughly one-half of the malt extract to this wort. Add water to bring brew pot volume to at least 3.5 gallons (13 L). Boil for 60 minutes, adding hops and Irish moss at times indicated. Add the sugar and remaining malt extract in the final 15 minutes of the boil.

DETERMINING YOUR EVAPORATION RATE

Some brewers collect the same amount of wort for every beer. They collect an amount that they know they can reduce to their batch size in their allotted boil time. While this is convenient, it is not always the best practice. For beers with very small grain bills, collecting a full pre-boil wort volume may only be possible by oversparging the grain bed.

Conversely, for progressively larger beers, the brewer is leaving progressively more sugars behind in the grains. If you measure your boil-off rate, you can know how long it will take you to reduce any volume of wort.

If you normally collect a set amount of wort and boil for a set amount of time, you already know your boil-off rate. Just subtract your post-boil wort volume from your pre-boil wort volume, and divide by the time it took. It will likely be most useful to express the result in terms of gallons or liters per hour. Typical figures for homebrewers are around 1.0–1.5 gallons per hour (3.8–5.7 L/hour), with most brewers hovering around the lower end of that range.

If you don't know your evaporation rate, make a dipstick for your kettle. Pour water in half-gallon (or 2-L) increments into your kettle and make a mark on your dipstick for each increment. Then, every time you boil, measure the volume every 15 or 30 minutes. After a few brewing sessions, you will know your average evaporation rate. You can use this to estimate your total boil time whenever you collect a volume of wort you have never dealt with before.

A calibrated dip stick measures the volume of wort remaining as the boil proceeds.

GRIZZLY
AMERICAN BARLEYWINE

This is a huge American barleywine. To brew it, you will need a 15-gallon (57-L) mash tun, a 15-gallon (57-L) kettle, and at least 5 hours to boil the wort. (You can maybe get away with a 10-gallon (38-L) mash tun, but it will be filled to the brim. And, of course, you can cheat on the boil time by adding malt extract to the kettle.) The yeast will do its job well if you make the prescribed yeast starter. Don't even think about not doing so. This beer may age well, but then again it may not. It will taste fantastic as long as the hop aroma remains (about a year).

5.0 GALLONS (19 L) AT 10% ABV
OG = 1.107, FG = 1.027
91 IBU, 11 SRM

+ Wyeast 1056 (American Ale) or White Labs WLP001 (California Ale) yeast
+ A 5.8-qt. (5.5-L) yeast starter is recommended
+ 19.5 lb. (8.9 kg) 2-row pale ale malt (3°L)
+ 8.0 oz. (230 g) caramel malt (30°L)
+ 4.0 oz. (110 g) caramel malt (40°L)
+ 0.50 oz. (14 g) Summit hops at 17% alpha acids, boiled for 60 minutes (32 IBU)
+ 0.50 oz. (14 g) Warrior hops at 16% alpha acids, boiled for 60 minutes (30 IBU)
+ 0.25 oz. (7.1 g) Simcoe hops at 13% alpha acids, boiled for 30 minutes (9.2 IBU)
+ 0.50 oz. (14 g) Chinook hops at 13% alpha acids, boiled for 15 minutes (12 IBU)
+ 1.0 oz. (28 g) Centennial hops at 10% alpha acids, boiled for 5 minutes (7.5 IBU)
+ 1.0 oz. (28 g) Ahtanum hops at 6% alpha acids, boiled for 0 minutes (0 IBU)
+ 2.0 oz. (57 g) Cascade hops (dry hops)
+ 1.0 tsp. Irish moss, boiled for 15 minutes
+ 0.25 tsp. yeast nutrients, boiled for 10 minutes
+ 4.6 oz. (130 g) corn sugar, to prime bottles for 2.4 volumes of CO_2

Make your yeast starter two to three days ahead of time. Heat 25 quarts (24 L) of brewing liquor to 161°F (72°C) and mash in grains. Mash at 150°F (66°C) for 60 minutes, stirring every 15 minutes if you can do so without losing too much heat from your mash tun. Heat mash to 168°F (76°C) for a mash out. Recirculate wort until clear, and then run off. A fully-sparged grain bed will yield 13 gallons (50 L) of wort, so decide how much wort you want to collect and be ready to supplement wort with malt extract. If you have a 15-gallon (57-L) kettle and good burner, this is just over a 5-hour boil. Boil wort to reduce volume to just over 5.0 gallons (19 L), adding hops and Irish moss at times indicated. Add yeast nutrients in the final 10 minutes of boil.

Chill wort, then let it sit (covered) for at least an hour to let the hop debris settle. Rack to fermenter. Aerate wort thoroughly and pitch sediment from yeast starter. Ferment at 68°F (20°C). If fermentation does not start within 8 hours, give the wort a second shot of aeration. (Watch for excessive foaming when you do.) If the fermentation falters near the end, stir the beer with a sanitized stick to rouse the yeast. (Do this slowly so as not to cause the beer to foam excessively.) Allow the temperature to rise to 72°F (22°C)—or as high as 75°F (24°F) —if you've got just a few more gravity points to go and the yeast is still active.

Let the beer condition in secondary for about two months. Then, dry hop (still in secondary) for 10 days. Finally, keg or bottle and carbonate to 2.4 volumes of CO_2. If bottle conditioning, you might want to add ¼ teaspoon of Fermentis U.S.-05 dried yeast to the beer in your bottling bucket.

MALT EXTRACT OPTION

Add 9.5 pounds (4.3 kg) of light dried malt extract to the recipe. Reduce the amount of 2-row pale ale malt to 3 pounds 4 ounces (1.5 kg). This is a large partial mash. For best results, follow the general procedures for a countertop partial mash as explained on page 36. Here are the specifics for this beer. Mash the crushed malts at 150°F (66°C) for 60 minutes. Collect about 2.6 gallons (10 L) of wort. Stir in roughly one-third of the malt extract and add water to make at least 4.0 gallons (15 L). Boil for 60 minutes, adding hops, Irish moss and yeast nutrients at times indicated. As the boil progresses, dissolve small amounts of malt extract in wort and add to the boil.

Add malt extract at the pace of about 1 pound (~0.5 kg) every 10 minutes. Do not let boil volume dip below 3.5 gallons (13 L). Top up with boiling water, if needed. After boil, chill and let brew pot sit—covered—for about 2 hours to let the hop debris settle. Then, rack the beer to your fermenter, top up to 5.0 gallons (19 L) with cool water, aerate the wort and pitch the yeast. Pitch only the sediment from the yeast starter.

MAKING A SECOND BEER (CUB PALE ALE)

Whenever you're brewing a huge beer, you have the option of brewing two beers from the same mash. Here's one way to brew this Grizzly barleywine along with a Cub Pale Ale. You will need two kettles and burners, two fermenters and all the other things you need for two separate batches of beer. Your batch of pale ale will be much smaller than the batch of barleywine.

Mash as usual, and then begin to run off the wort. Run off the first half-gallon (~2 L) of first wort to the kettle for the pale ale. Then run off the remaining first wort—there should be about 3.3 gallons (12 L) total—to the kettle for the barleywine. Continue to collect wort in the barleywine until you are a gallon (3.8 L) short of your desired pre-boil volume. Then, divert the flow to the pale ale kettle. When you reach your desired pre-boil volume for the pale ale, divert the next gallon back to the kettle with the barleywine. Then proceed to boil the two worts. Pick any reasonable hop schedule for the pale ale.

You have 13 gallons (50 L) of wort to work with. If you use it all, your barleywine would be composed of about 10.5 gallons (40 L) of first wort and early sparged wort, plus the final 1.0 gallon (3.8 L) of sparged wort. The pale ale would contain one half-gallon (1.9 L) of first wort and 1.0 gallon (3.8 L) of sparged wort from late in the runoff. You can, of course, make adjustments to collect less wort overall, or to divert a higher percentage of the wort to the pale ale. If you divert any wort towards making a pale ale, the OG of your barleywine will, of course, be lower. You can either make up the difference with malt extract, or accept a beer that is not quite as strong. You may want to scale the hops back proportionally if you undershoot the OG by more than 10 percent.

GJALLARHORN ALE
REITERATED MASH BEER

This is a big ale made using an interesting method of wort production. The main wort for this beer is made by using wort as the brewing liquor. In short, you collect one batch of wort to use as brewing liquor, and use that to mash and sparge a second grist. I got this idea after learning that the Hürlimann Brewery, the original brewery to brew the strong lager Samichlaus, used the late runnings of one beer during wort production for Samichlaus. (I later learned that various breweries have tried something similar in the past.) You can make a very strong and very pale beer with this method.

5.0 GALLONS (19 L) AT UP TO 10% ABV
OG = UP TO 1.101, FG = 1.022 (OR LOWER)
56 IBU, 4.3 SRM (OR LESS)

+ Wyeast 1056 (American Ale), White Labs WLP001 (California Ale) or Fermentis Safale U.S.-05 yeast

+ A 5.2-qt. (4.9-L) yeast starter is recommended

FIRST MASH

+ 6.0 lb. (2.7 kg) U.S. 6-row pale malt

+ 1.0 lb. (450 g) U.S. 2-row pale malt

+ 3.0 lb. (1.4 kg) flaked maize

SECOND MASH

+ 6.0 lb. (2.7 kg) U.S. 2-row pale malt

+ 2.0 lb. (910 g) Vienna malt

+ 2.0 lb. (910 g) flaked maize

BOIL

+ 1.0 oz. (28 g) Magnum hops at 15% alpha acids, boiled for 60 minutes (56 IBU)

+ 1.0 tsp. Irish moss, boiled for 15 minutes

+ 5.0 oz. (140 g) corn sugar, to prime bottles for 2.5 volumes of CO_2

Make yeast starter two to three days ahead of time. The basic idea is to make a batch of wort and use this as your brewing liquor for your second mash. Make your first wort as quickly as possible. Don't bother to recirculate before running it off. Monitor the specific gravity of the wort from the second mash with a refractometer. It will take longer than an hour to reach a reasonable wort density. Run off the wort until the increase in wort density slows greatly.

Then, recirculate and collect your wort (chasing the last bit of wort used as sparge water with water). Boil wort and proceed as you normally would.

Make your yeast starter two to three days ahead of your brew day. You can use two 11.5-gram sachets of dried yeast instead of making a starter.

FIRST MASH

Mash flaked maize and crushed malts at 150°F (66°C) in 14 quarts (13 L) of strike water. After 20 minutes, test for starch conversion. If converted, run off wort to kettle, sparging with water hot enough to keep grain bed at 150–170°F (66–77°C). Collect around 6.5 gallons (25 L). Heat this wort to 161°F (72°C).

SECOND MASH

Quickly scoop and rinse mash tun and then mash flaked maize and crushed malts for second mash in 14 quarts (13 L) of wort from first mash. Mash temperature should be 150°F (66°C). Transfer remaining wort—a little over 3.0 gallons (11 L)—from kettle to a second brew pot. Heat this wort to 170°F (77°C). Stir mash frequently and monitor the specific gravity of wort from the grain bed with a refractometer every 5 minutes or so. Wort density will increase over time—quickly at first, then more slowly.

Decide when the rate of increase in wort density has slowed to the point that you wish to proceed. Recirculate and run off wort. Sparge with hot wort from first mash to yield roughly 5.0 gallons (19 L) of thick wort. Sparge with an additional 1.5 gallons (5.7 L) of water at 170°F (77°C) to make 6.5 gallons (25 L) of wort total.

BOIL AND BEYOND

Boil for 90 minutes, to reduce volume to just over 5.0 gallons (19 L). Add hops for final 60 minutes of boil. Add Irish moss for final 15 minutes of boil. Cool wort, aerate and pitch yeast. Ferment at 68°F (20°C). Finally, keg or bottle the beer.

REITERATED MASHING

The basic idea of reiterated mashing is that you make two worts—the first for your brewing liquor and the second as the wort you will ferment into beer. It took me a couple of tries to work some of the kinks out, but now the procedures are more workable. Expect this to be a long brew day; don't waste time on the first mash. Let it go for about 20 minutes, then start running off the wort. Don't bother recirculating, as it won't hurt if your brewing liquor is cloudy. The big key to getting this to work is patience during the second mash. It takes time for the starches to dissolve when there is already a lot of sugar in the mash liquid. Monitor the specific gravity every 5 to 10 minutes with a refractometer (or hydrometer) and keep mashing if the specific gravity is still rising quickly.

This really works best if you have a heatable mash and can stir the mash after each specific gravity reading. If you have an extra kettle, you can mash in it and transfer the mash to your lauter tun when it comes time to collect the wort.

The only reason to try this—beyond wanting to do something adventurous—is to brew a very strong beer that is very light in color. There are other, much easier, methods to brew any dark, strong beer. If you try this, be prepared to make adjustments as you go. For example, if you don't collect the full volume of wort from the first mash, you will need to adapt what you do for the second mash. (In this case, the easiest thing to do would be to add water to make the volume of the brewing liquor the expected volume.)

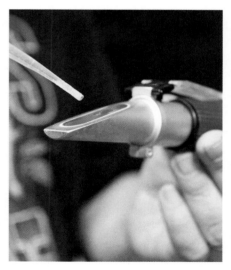

A refractometer comes in very handy when making this beer.

EURYPTERID BARLEYWINE
IMPERIAL BARLEYWINE

This is a huge barleywine that you can make even bigger by feeding the fermentation. You will need close to 15 gallons (57 L) of mash tun space and a 20-gallon (78-L) kettle to brew a 5.0-gallon (19-L) batch—but of course you can scale this down and brew a smaller volume of beer.

If you fully sparge the grain bed, you may need to boil for 7 hours or longer to reduce it, but of course you know you can cheat and use malt extract to hit the projected OG or just accept whatever OG you do hit. This beer is as much of a journey as a destination. If you hope to reach the end, you will need to take the yeast starter size recommendation seriously.

5.0 GALLONS (19 L) AT 12% ABV
OG = 1.122, FG = 1.028
92 IBU, 8.8 SRM

+ Wyeast 1056 (American Ale), White Labs WLP001 (California Ale) or Fermentis Safale U.S.-05 yeast
+ A 7.7-qt. (7.3-L) yeast starter is recommended
+ 23.0 lb. (10.4 kg) U.S. 2-row pale malt
+ 5.0 oz. (230 g) caramel malt (40°L)
+ 1.5 oz. (43 g) Columbus hops at 15% alpha acids, boiled for 60 minutes (84 IBU)
+ 1.0 oz. (28 g) Centennial hops at 10% alpha acids, boiled for 5 minutes (7.5 IBU)
+ 1.0 oz. (28 g) Cascade hops at 5% alpha acids, boiled for 0 minutes (0 IBU)
+ 2.5 oz. (71 g) Cascade hops (dry hops)
+ 1.0 tsp. Irish moss, boiled for 15 minutes
+ 0.50 tsp. yeast nutrients, boiled for 10 minutes
+ 5.0 oz. (140 g) corn sugar, to prime bottles for 2.5 volumes of CO_2

Make your yeast starter two to three days ahead of time. Alternately, you can pitch two 11.5-gram sachets of the dried yeast. If you do, it would be a good idea to rehydrate the yeast before pitching. Heat 30 quarts (28 L) of brewing liquor to 160°F (71°C) and mash in grains. Mash at 149°F (65°C) for 60 minutes, stirring every 15 minutes if you can. Heat to mash out to 168°F (76°C). Recirculate wort until clear, and then run off.

Sparge to collect about 15 gallons (58 L) of wort—or, whatever volume you are able and willing to boil. Boil the wort to reduce to just over 5.0 gallons (19 L), adding hops, Irish moss and yeast nutrients at times indicated. Chill wort, then let sit (covered) for about 2 hours to let hop debris settle. Rack clear wort to fermenter, aerate thoroughly and pitch sediment from yeast starter. Ferment at 67°F (19°C). You may need to rouse the yeast and raise the fermentation temperature—up to 72°F (22°C)—near the end of fermentation. Dry hop for seven days. After fermentation stops, decide whether to condition the beer for a few months, then bottle or keg or continue feeding the fermentation.

If you choose to feed to fermentation, follow these instructions. Mix a 2.0-quart (1.9-L) solution with one part malt extract and two parts cane sugar or corn sugar. Make the specific gravity of this solution SG 1.140. Add a pinch of yeast nutrients and heat solution to 170°F (77°C). Hold at this temperature for 5 minutes to sanitize the solution. Transfer to a sanitized container and cool. Add 8–12 fluid ounces (240–350 ml) to the secondary fermenter and check to see if fermentation is reinvigorated.

When renewed fermentation stops, repeat the addition of the feeding solution. Keep doing this until adding sugar no longer rouses the yeast. At some point, you may need to remove a small volume of beer from the fermenter to make room for the sugar mixture. Once the fermentation cannot be roused by adding more sugar, condition the beer for a few months and keg. (You likely won't have any luck bottle-conditioning it.) Your final ABV will depend on how much additional sugar the yeast produces.

MALT EXTRACT OPTION

Add 12 pounds (5.4 kg) of light dried malt extract to the recipe. Reduce the amount of 2-row pale ale malt to 2 pounds 8 ounces (1.1 kg). "Steep" the crushed grains in 4.1 quarts (3.9 L) of water at 149°F (65°C) for 60 minutes. ("Steep" is in quotes because technically this is a partial mash.) Place the grain bag in a colander over your brew pot and rinse the grains with 2.0 quarts (1.9 L) of 170°F (77°C) water. Add roughly one-quarter of the malt extract to this wort. Add water to bring brew pot volume to at least 5.0 gallons (19 L). Boil for 60 minutes, keeping boil topped up to 5.0 gallons (19 L) with boiling water throughout the boil. Add hops, Irish moss and yeast nutrients at times indicated. Add the remaining malt extract in small doses throughout the boil.

FEEDING A FERMENTATION

High-gravity fermentations can be stressful to yeast. Starting a beer at a very, very high original gravity (OG) can cause the yeast to drop out of solution. One solution for brewing stronger beer is to ferment a very strong beer, then "feed" the fermentation with sugar. The idea is that the yeast never face a solution with a daunting specific gravity. They are, however, expected to continue to work in a high-alcohol environment.

The base beer for *Eurypterid* Barleywine is a 12 percent ABV alcohol barleywine (OG 1.122). This is right at the edge of what most ale strains can ferment. The beer is then fed with small doses of an SG 1.140 sugar solution as long as the yeast will ferment it.

5

DARK AND AMBER LAGERS: RICH, MALTY AND SATISFYING

This section gives recipes for 10 lagers, amber or darker. They range from an OG 1.047 (4.7 percent ABV) American Bock to an OG 1.091 (8.8 percent) doppelbock that you can freeze and turn into a 12 percent ABV eisbock—with a Vienna lager, Octoberfest, dark bockbier and others in between. The color of these beers ranges from 11 SRM to over 40 SRM.

If you are treating your water, you should aim to have at least 100 ppm calcium (Ca^{+2}) ions, and between 90 ppm and 440 ppm bicarbonate (HCO_3^-), with the lower end being for beers around 11 SRM and the upper end for beers around 40 SRM. (When the boil starts, you may want to add 50 ppm more calcium.) You do not have to adjust your water chemistry to match your beer's SRM exactly. Being in the ballpark is all you need.

If you are making your water by adding minerals to 5.0 gallons (19 L) of distilled or RO water, start by adding 3 to 14 g of sodium bicarbonate ($NaHCO_3$, baking soda), with the low end of the range corresponding to beers around 11 SRM and the high end corresponding to beers around 40 SRM. (Note: Some brewers claim that your brewing water should not contain more than 50 ppm sodium [Na^{2+}]. Others say levels up to 100 ppm Na^{2+} are fine. Still others say levels up to 250 ppm Na^{2+} are fine. Over these limits and the beer will have a metallic taste, it is claimed.)

Following the instructions above, your water would contain 40–200 ppm sodium. If you brew a beer and it has a metallic taste, try reducing your sodium levels next time. Then choose a calcium addition depending on how much you want to accentuate the hops. For a balanced beer, add 4 g of calcium chloride ($CaCl_2*2H_2O$) and 4 g of calcium sulfate ($CaSO_4*2H_2O$, gypsum). For a beer in which the hops are to be accentuated, add 8 g of calcium sulfate ($CaSO_4*2H_2O$, gypsum). You will need to prepare more than 5.0 gallons (19 L) of brewing liquor for the all-grain versions of these beers.

For the extract versions, you only need to prepare brewing liquor (water with the correct mineral additions) of the grains you steep or mash. Use distilled water, RO water or naturally soft water for diluting the malt extract.

If you have a water report that describes what is in your water, you can use brewing software to plan your mineral additions. Remember to treat your water to remove any chlorine compounds, if present (as they are in all municipal water sources).

DIMEBOX BOCK
AMERICAN BOCK

American bock beers used to be a popular seasonal offering, but they mostly disappeared by the early 1970s. Conventional wisdom held that they came from "the bottom of the barrel" when the brewers "cleaned their tanks once a year." (As brewers, we of course know that beer at the bottom of the barrel is the same as that at the top and tanks get cleaned every single time they are used.) Recently, the style has made a bit of a resurgence thanks to Shiner Bock—brewed just up the road from me in Shiner, Texas.

American bocks are basically typical American lager beers with a bit of dark grains added. In some versions, only a bit of caramel coloring was used. In the best versions, the malt character is a little richer and the beer is slightly sweeter.

5.0 GALLONS (19 L) AT 4.7% ABV
OG = 1.047, FG = 1.011
17 IBU, 15 SRM

+ Wyeast 2035 (American Lager) or White Labs WLP940 (Mexican Lager) yeast
+ A 4.9-qt. (4.6-L) yeast starter is recommended
+ 3.0 lb. (1.4 kg) U.S. 2-row pale malt
+ 3.0 lb. (1.4 kg) Munich malt (8°L)
+ 2 lb. 11 oz. (1.2 kg) flaked maize
+ 11 oz. (310 g) crystal malt (60°L)
+ 2.0 oz. (57 g) black malt (500°L)
+ 0.50 oz. (14 g) Brewers Gold hops at 9% alpha acids, boiled for 60 minutes (17 IBU)
+ 1.0 tsp. Irish moss, boiled for 15 minutes
+ 4.5 oz. (130 g) corn sugar, to prime bottles for 2.5 volumes of CO_2

Make your yeast starter two to three days ahead of time. Heat 12 quarts (11 L) of brewing liquor to 161°F (72°C) and mash in grains. Mash at 150°F (66°C) for 60 minutes, stirring every 15 minutes, if you can do so without losing too much heat from your mash tun. Heat or add boiling water to mash out to 168°F (76°C). Recirculate wort until clear, and then run off. Sparge to collect about 6.2 gallons (23 L) of wort.

Boil wort for 60 minutes, adding hops and Irish moss at times indicated. Chill wort, then rack to fermenter. Aerate wort thoroughly and pitch sediment from yeast starter. Ferment at 56°F (13°C). When fermentation slows greatly, let fermentation temperature rise to 60°F (16°C) and hold for three days for a diacetyl rest. After the diacetyl rest, let beer lager at 40°F (4.4°C) for six weeks. Then, keg or add priming sugar and bottle and carbonate to 2.5 volumes of CO_2.

(continued)

MALT EXTRACT OPTION

Add 2 pounds 8 ounces (1.1 kg) of liquid Munich malt extract to the ingredient list. Replace the flaked maize with 1 pound 14 ounces (850 g) of corn sugar. Reduce the amount of 2-row pale malt to 1 pound 1 ounce (500 g). Reduce the amount of Munich malt to 1 pound 1 ounce (500 g). "Steep" the crushed grains in 4.1 quarts (3.9 L) of water at 150°F (66°C) for 60 minutes. ("Steep" is in quotes because technically this is a partial mash.) Place the grain bag in a colander over your brew pot and rinse the grains with 2.0 quarts (1.9 L) of 170°F (77°C) water. Add roughly one-third of the malt extract to this wort. Add water to bring brew pot volume to 3.0 gallons (11 L). Boil for 60 minutes, adding hops and Irish moss at times indicated. Add the sugar and remaining malt extract in the final 15 minutes of the boil.

DIACETYL REST

As brewers yeast ferments wort, it gives off a variety of chemical compounds, Ethanol and carbon dioxide (CO_2) are the major products of alcoholic fermentation, but there are plenty of minor by-products. One of these compounds, diacetyl, lends a buttery or butterscotch-like note to beer. It also gives the beer a tongue-coating slickness that most people find objectionable. Fortunately, although the yeast excrete (the precursor to) this molecule in early fermentation, they take diacetyl back up in the late stages of fermentation.

In ales, this generally happens without the brewer having to do anything. In lagers, however, the yeast sometimes need some help to clean up the beer. One way brewers encourage the yeast to reduce the amount of diacetyl is with a diacetyl rest. As fermentation nears the end, the temperature is allowed to rise from typical lager fermentation temperatures to about 60°F (16°C). The beer is held there for a couple of days and the yeast become more active. Within a couple of days, the diacetyl is usually gone.

Excess diacetyl is one of the major concerns in lager brewing. In large lager breweries, diacetyl levels are carefully tracked and the beer remains in the diacetyl rest until tests show the molecule has dropped below the threshold at which it can be detected. On a homebrew scale, a diacetyl rest of three days almost always clears up any residual diacetyl.

THIS BLACK LAGER'S NAME IS ROBERT PAULSON
SCHWARZBIER

Schwarzbier is a German lager with a hint of roasted malt flavor. The word "schwarzbier" means black beer, but the beer is never black like a stout or porter. Nor does it show that degree of roast character. The beer is fairly dry and hopped just enough for balance. Some examples have a bit of a sweet edge to them, but overall it is a very balanced, drinkable lager. Think of it as a balanced (not-too-hoppy) Pilsner with just enough dark malt to be noticeable.

5.0 GALLONS (19 L) AT 4.9% ABV
OG = 1.049, FG = 1.011
26 IBU, 20 SRM

+ Wyeast 2124 (Bohemian Lager), White Labs WLP830 (German Lager Yeast) or Fermentis Saflager W-34/70 yeast
+ A 5.3-qt. (5.0-L) yeast starter is recommended
+ 10 lb. (4.5 kg) German Munich malt (8°L)
+ 5.0 oz. (140 g) Carafa Special II malt (410°L)
+ 0.80 oz. (23 g) Perle hops at 8% alpha acids, boiled for 60 minutes (24 IBU)
+ 0.75 oz. (21 g) Hallertauer Mittelfrüher hops at 4.5% alpha acids, boiled for 5 minutes (2.5 IBU)
+ 0.50 oz. (14 g) Hallertauer Mittelfrüher hops at 0% alpha acids, boiled for 0 minutes (0 IBU)
+ 4.5 oz. (130 g) corn sugar, to prime bottles for 2.5 volumes of CO_2

If you are using one of the liquid yeasts, make your yeast starter two to three days ahead of time. Heat 13 quarts (12 L) of brewing liquor to 163°F (73°C) and mash in grains. Mash at 152°F (67°C) for 60 minutes, stirring every 15 minutes, if you can do so without losing too much heat from your mash tun. Heat or add boiling water to mash out to 168°F (76°C). Recirculate wort until clear, and then run off.

Sparge to collect about 6.7 gallons (25 L) of wort. Boil wort for 90 minutes, to reduce wort volume to just over 5.0 gallons (19 L). Add hops at times indicated. Chill wort, then rack to fermenter. Aerate wort thoroughly and pitch sediment from yeast starter. Ferment at 54°F (12°C). Perform a diacetyl rest at 60°F (16°C) for three days, then lager beer at 40°F (4.4°C) for six weeks. Then, keg or add priming sugar and bottle and carbonate to 2.5 volumes of CO_2.

MALT EXTRACT OPTION

Add 4.75 pounds (2.2 kg) of liquid Munich malt extract to the recipe. Reduce the amount of Munich malt to 2 pounds 11 ounces (1.2 kg). "Steep" the crushed grains in 4.1 quarts (3.9 L) of water at 152°F (67°C) for 60 minutes. ("Steep" is in quotes because technically this is a partial mash.) Place the grain bag in a colander over your brew pot and rinse the grains with 2.0 quarts (1.9 L) of 170°F (77°C) water.

Add roughly one-third of the malt extract to this wort. Add water to bring brew pot volume to 3.0 gallons (11 L). Boil for 60 minutes, adding hops at times indicated. Add the remaining malt extract in the final 15 minutes of the boil.

"LAGER STINK"

The first time a homebrewer brews a lager, he or she might think something has gone horribly wrong once fermentation starts. Some lager strains produce a lot of sulfur during fermentation, and the smell coming from the airlock—which some homebrewers informally call lager stink—can be quite off-putting. However, this is not evidence that the beer is contaminated. And, the resulting beer will not smell of rotten eggs. A few lager yeast strains leave a little residual sulfur in the finished beer, but nothing like the smell coming from the fermenter early in the fermentation.

RECIPE OPTIONS AND NOTES

Commercially, some schwarzbiers are brewed as a pale lager, then colored with malt color extracts—such as Weyermann's SINAMAR or Briess's Maltoferm—after fermentation. You can brew the beer that way by omitting the Carafa malt, then adding as much color as you desire with a coloring agent. At the level required to reach a reasonable color for a schwarzbier, these malt color extracts will lend an appropriate level of roasted malt character to the beer. (At lower levels, they are nearly neutral with respect to flavor.) These malt color extracts can also be added in the kettle.

A self-cooling conical fermenter is great for brewing lagers.

MOVIE NIGHT LAGER
AMBER LAGER

There are a lot of amber lagers in the world, and they vary in how they are made. Some are merely brewed as a pale lager with adjuncts, and then made a few shades darker with caramel coloring. Others, however, are all-malt beers with a pleasant malt profile. Amber lagers are generally not highly hopped and—although most are well attenuated—may show a hint of sweetness. This beer is a well-balanced amber lager with a moderate amount of malt and hop character. It would be welcome at both a homebrew club meeting and a picnic with friends who aren't into craft beers.

5.0 GALLONS (19 L) AT 4.9% ABV
OG = 1.050, FG = 1.011
26 IBU, 13 SRM

+ Wyeast 2035 (American Lager), Wyeast 2272 (North American Lager) or WLP840 (American Lager) yeast
+ A 5.6-qt. (5.3-L) yeast starter is recommended
+ 6.0 lb. (2.7 kg) U.S. 2-row pale malt
+ 3.0 lb. (1.4 kg) Munich malt (8°L)
+ 8.0 oz. (230 g) caramel malt (40°L)
+ 5.0 oz. (140 g) caramel malt (60°L)
+ 2.0 oz. (57 g) black malt (500°L)
+ 1.25 oz. (35 g) Willamette hops at 5% alpha acids, boiled for 60 minutes (23 IBU)
+ 0.50 oz. (14 g) Liberty hops at 4% alpha acids, boiled for 10 minutes (2.7 IBU)
+ 1.0 tsp. Irish moss, boiled for 15 minutes
+ 4.5 oz. (130 g) corn sugar, to prime bottles for 2.5 volumes of CO_2

Make your yeast starter two to three days ahead of time. Heat 15 quarts (14 L) of brewing liquor to 163°F (73°C) and mash in grains. Mash at 152°F (67°C) for 60 minutes, stirring every 15 minutes, if you can do so without losing too much heat from your mash tun. Heat or add boiling water to mash out to 168°F (76°C). Recirculate wort until clear, and then run off. Sparge to collect about 6.5 gallons (24 L) of wort. Boil wort for 90 minutes, to reduce volume to just over 5.0 gallons (19 L).

Add hops and Irish moss at times indicated. Chill wort, then rack to fermenter. Aerate wort thoroughly and pitch sediment from yeast starter. Ferment at 53°F (12°C). Perform a diacetyl rest at 60°F (16°C) for three days, then lager beer at 40°F (4.4°C) for six weeks. Then, keg or add priming sugar and bottle and carbonate to 2.5 volumes of CO_2.

On the "hot side," brewing lagers differ little from brewing ales.

An external thermostat controls the temperature inside a refrigerator used as a fermentation chamber.

MALT EXTRACT OPTION

Add 4.75 pounds (2.2 kg) of liquid Munich malt extract to the recipe. Omit the Munich malt. Reduce the amount of 2-row pale malt to 2 pounds 1 ounce (930 g). "Steep" the crushed grains in 4.1 quarts (3.9 L) of water at 152°F (67°C) for 60 minutes. ("Steep" is in quotes because technically this is a partial mash.) Place the grain bag in a colander over your brew pot and rinse the grains with 2.0 quarts (1.9 L) of 170°F (77°C) water. Add roughly one-third of the malt extract to this wort. Add water to bring brew pot volume to 3.0 gallons (11 L). Boil for 60 minutes, adding hops and Irish moss at times indicated. Add the remaining malt extract in the final 15 minutes of the boil.

FERMENTATION CHAMBER

Many homebrewers live where they can brew ales using ambient temperature control—or simple evaporative cooling—for at least part of the year. However, most require active temperature control to brew lagers. The most common lager fermentation setup for homebrewers is a refrigerator or chest freezer with an external thermostat. The thermostat plugs into the wall and the fridge or freezer plugs into an outlet on the thermostat. The brewer sets a temperature on the external thermostat. This is usually a few degrees below the intended fermentation temperature. When the temperature exceeds to set point, the thermostat relays power to the fridge. After cooling several degrees, it cuts power to the fridge and the cycle repeats. With this method, the air temperature inside the fermentation chamber varies by perhaps 4°F (2°C) as it cycles, but the fermenting beer stays at a much steadier temperature.

A pre-chiller—a second wort chiller, placed in line before the main chiller—may be necessary when chilling larger wort.

WIENER BLUT LAGER
VIENNA LAGER

Vienna lager is a moderate-strength amber lager with a rich, malty flavor. Interpretations of this style vary, from dry and fairly bitter to somewhat sweet. This version is relatively dry and fairly hoppy. It is well-balanced and the Vienna and Munich malt give the beer a bready/toasty malt character.

5.0 GALLONS (19 L) AT 5.0% ABV
OG = 1.052, FG = 1.013
29 IBU, 11 SRM

+ Wyeast 2247 (European Lager) or White Labs WLP920 (Old Bavarian Lager) yeast
+ A 6.0-qt. (5.7-L) yeast starter is recommended
+ 9 lb. 8 oz. (4.3 kg) German Vienna malt
+ 1.0 lb. (450 g) Munich malt
+ 1.5 oz. (43 g) Carafa Special II malt (430°L)
+ 1.25 oz. (35 g) Styrian Goldings hops at 6% alpha acids, boiled for 60 minutes (28 IBU)
+ 0.33 oz. (9.4 g) Tettnanger hops at 4.5% alpha acids, boiled for 5 minutes (1.1 IBU)
+ 0.33 oz. (9.4 g) Styrian Goldings hops at 6% alpha acids, boiled for 0 minutes (0 IBU)
+ 4.5 oz. (130 g) corn sugar, to prime bottles for 2.5 volumes of CO_2

Make your yeast starter two to three days ahead of time. Heat 13 quarts (12 L) of brewing liquor to 163°F (73°C) and mash in grains. Mash at 152°F (67°C) for 60 minutes, stirring every 15 minutes if you can do so. Heat or add boiling water to mash out to 168°F (76°C). Recirculate wort until clear, and then run off.

Sparge to collect about 6.9 gallons (26 L) of wort. Boil wort to reduce wort volume to just over 5.0 gallons (19 L), adding hops at times indicated. Chill wort, then rack to fermenter. Aerate wort thoroughly and pitch sediment from yeast starter. Ferment at 55°F (13°C). Perform a diacetyl rest at 60°F (16°C) for three days at end of primary fermentation. Then, lager beer at 40°F (4.4°C) for six weeks. Keg or add priming sugar and bottle and carbonate to 2.5 volumes of CO_2.

MALT EXTRACT OPTION

Add 5 pounds 2 ounces (2.3 kg) of liquid Vienna malt extract to the recipe. (Or, failing that, 2.0 pounds [910 g] of liquid Pilsner malt extract and 3 pounds 2 ounces [1.4 kg] of liquid Munich malt extract.) Reduce the amount of Vienna malt to 1 pound 15 ounces (870 g). "Steep" the crushed grains in 4.1 quarts (3.9 L) of water at 152°F (67°C) for 60 minutes. ("Steep" is in quotes because technically this is a partial mash.)

Place the grain bag in a colander over your brew pot and rinse the grains with 2.0 quarts (1.9 L) of 170°F (77°C) water. Add roughly one-third of the malt extract to this wort. Add water to bring brew pot volume to 3.0 gallons (11 L). Boil for 60 minutes, adding hops at times indicated. Add the remaining malt extract in the final 15 minutes of the boil.

RECIPE OPTIONS AND NOTES

The grain bill for a Vienna lager can be all Vienna malt or all Munich malt. Or it can be a blend of Pilsner malt and Munich malt or a blend of the three. A touch of dark roasted malt—2.0–3.0 ounces (57–85 g) can give the beer some color, as it does in this recipe. Some Vienna lagers use small amounts of crystal malt (or CaraMunich malt), but you should not add enough to give the beer a strong caramel flavor. In a 5.0-gallon (19-L) batch, keep the amount of crystal malt at 6.0 ounces (170 g) or less.

AND MIRRORS RAUCHBIER
RAUCHBIER

The "rauch" in "rauchbier" is smoke in German. Smoked beer is brewed using malt that has been smoked. The classic German rauchbier is a Märzen-style beer made with beechwood-smoked malt. Rauchbiers range from mildly smoky to "drinking a campfire." This recipe produces a very smoky rauchbier, for brewers who really like the smoke flavor in beer.

5.0 GALLONS (19 L) AT 5.2% ABV
OG = 1.053, FG = 1.013
23 IBU, 13 SRM

+ Wyeast 2206 (Bavarian Lager) or White Labs WLP820 (Octoberfest Lager) yeast
+ A 6.3-qt. (6.0-L) yeast starter is recommended
+ 9 lb. 12 oz. (4.4 kg) rauchmalz malt (smoked malt)
+ 8.0 oz. (230 g) CaraMunich malt (60°L)
+ 2.0 oz. (57 g) Carafa Special III malt (500°L)
+ 0.75 oz. (21 g) Perle hops at 8.2% alpha acids, boiled for 60 minutes (23 IBU)
+ 4.5 oz. (130 g) corn sugar, to prime bottles for 2.5 volumes of CO_2

Make your yeast starter two to three days ahead of time. Heat 13 quarts (12 L) of brewing liquor to 163°F (73°C) and mash in grains. Mash at 152°F (67°C) for 60 minutes, stirring every 15 minutes if you can. Heat or add boiling water to mash out to 168°F (76°C). Recirculate wort until clear, and then run off.

Sparge to collect about 6.7 gallons (26 L) of wort. Boil wort for about 90 minutes, to reduce volume to just over 5.0 gallons (19 L), adding hops at times indicated. Chill wort, then rack to fermenter. Aerate wort thoroughly and pitch sediment from yeast starter. Ferment at 55°F (13°C). Perform a diacetyl rest at 60°F (16 °C) for three days, and lager for seven weeks. Then, keg or add priming sugar and bottle and carbonate to 2.5 volumes of CO_2.

SMOKING MALT

You can smoke your own malt at home for use in smoked beers. For this, you'll need some (unpainted) screen door material, a spray bottle with volume markings on the side (or calibrate one yourself) and the hardwood of your choice. Any wood that is commonly used to smoke foods should work—mesquite, hickory, apple, cherry, pecan, oak, etc.

Soak chunks or chips of the hardwood in water at least 2 hours, or overnight. Cut the screen door material to fit the shape of your grill or smoker. Build a small fire, using only a handful of briquets. Wrap the wet hardwood in aluminum foil, and then poke 3–5 holes in the pouch. When the charcoal burns down to coals, lay the aluminum pouch on top of them. Take any base malt—2-row pale malt, 2-row pale ale malt, Pilsner malt, Vienna malt, Munich malt, etc.—and spray it with water. Use 0.50 fluid ounces (15 ml) per pound of grain (33 mL/kg).

You can also smoke small amounts of specialty malts in a shallow dish.

This recipe yields a very smoky beer, comparable to the smokiest commercial examples. You can dial back on the smoke by swapping Munich malt (8°L) for a portion of the rauchmalz on a 1:1 basis. At a minimum, you should retain at least 1.0 pound (450 g) of rauchmalz for a hint of smoke.

The intensity of smoked malt varies, so if you brew this recipe the same way several times, it will likely turn out with a different level of smoke each time.

When smoke starts emerging from the bag, spread the wetted malt on the screen door material in a layer at most two grains deep. Let the grains smoke as long as the aluminum pouch is smoking or until they are dried. If the grains are still moist after smoking, put them on a cookie sheet in a 275°F (135°C) oven until they are dry. (Do not let them sit until they begin toasting.) As an alternative, you can dry the malt in a food dehydrator. Place the grains in a paper bag, and let them sit for about a week "to mellow" before using them.

NIGHT OF THE LIVING DUNKEL
MUNICH DUNKEL

Munich Dunkel is a moderate-strength lager with a rich, malty flavor. The beer gets its malty character from Munich malt, often accentuated with some dark Munich malt, melanoidin malt or aromatic malt. A small amount of darkly roasted grains give it a brown color and sometimes a hint of roast character. This should not be strong, as in a porter or stout, however.

5.0 GALLONS (19 L) AT 5.4% ABV
OG = 1.055, FG = 1.013
25 IBU, 19 SRM

+ Wyeast 2124 (Bohemian Lager), White Labs WLP830 (German Lager) or Fermentis Saflager W-34/70 yeast
+ A 6.9-qt. (6.5-L) yeast starter is recommended
+ 9.0 lb. (4.1 kg) Munich malt (10°L)
+ 1.0 lb. (450 g) Pilsner malt
+ 12 oz. (340 g) melanoidin malt (23°L)
+ 5.0 oz. (140 g) CaraMunich malt (60°L)
+ 4.0 oz. (110 g) Carafa Special I malt (320°L)
+ 1.5 oz. (43 g) Hallertauer Hersbrucker hops at 4.5% alpha acids, boiled for 60 minutes (251 IBU)
+ 4.5 oz. (130 g) corn sugar, to prime bottles for 2.5 volumes of CO_2

Make your yeast starter two to three days ahead of time. You can make the starter half the recommended size if you aerate it once a day and swirl the starter vessel to rouse the yeast. Heat 15 quarts (14 L) of brewing liquor to 163°F (73°C) and mash in grains. Mash at 152°F (67°C) for 60 minutes, stirring every 15 minutes if you can. Heat or add boiling water to mash out to 168°F (76°C). Recirculate wort until clear, and then run off.

Sparge to collect about 7.4 gallons (28 L) of wort. Boil wort to reduce volume to just over 5.0 gallons (19 L), adding hops at times indicated. Chill wort, then rack to fermenter. Aerate wort thoroughly and pitch sediment from yeast starter. Ferment at 54°F (12°C). Perform a diacetyl rest at 60°F (16°C) for three days. Lager for seven weeks at 40°F (4.4°C). Then, keg or add priming sugar and bottle and carbonate to 2.5 volumes of CO_2.

MALT EXTRACT OPTION

Most Munich malt extract is made from a 50:50 blend of Munich malt and a pale base malt (such as Pilsner). As such, it's not possible to formulate an exact match for the above all-grain recipe. This, however, is pretty close. Add 5.25 pounds (2.4 kg) of liquid Munich malt extract to the recipe. Omit the Pilsner malt. Reduce the amount of Munich malt to 1 pound 11 ounces (770 g). "Steep" the crushed grains in 4.1 quarts (3.9 L) of water at 152°F (67°C) for 60 minutes. ("Steep" is in quotes because technically this is a partial mash.)

Place the grain bag in a colander over your brew pot and rinse the grains with 2.0 quarts (1.9 L) of 170°F (77°C) water. Add roughly one-third of the malt extract to this wort. Add water to bring brew pot volume to 3.0 gallons (11 L). Boil for 60 minutes, adding hops at times indicated. Add the remaining malt extract in the final 15 minutes of the boil.

LAGERING

Lagering is a process in which beer is stored cold for a period of conditioning. During this time, the "green" lager beer produced by primary fermentation loses a variety of off flavors and aromas and becomes a clean lager beer. The word "lager" means "to store" in German.

At home, most homebrewers lager in a temperature-controlled fermentation chamber. After the diacetyl rest (if this is done), the beer is racked to a secondary fermenter or keg. Preferably, the fermenter has little headspace. If using a keg, the headspace should be purged with CO_2. The temperature of the beer can be lowered a few degrees each day until lagering temperature is reached. Any temperature below 40°F (4.4°C), but above the temperature at which the beer freezes, will work. A general rule of thumb is to lager (cold condition) the beer for a week for every 2°Plato (SG 1.008). (Divide the OG, in "gravity points," by 8 to estimate how long to lager the beer. For example, a beer with an OG of 1.064 would need to be lagered for [64/8=] 8 weeks.) Note that this is just an estimate. Use your palate as a guide to judging if the beer is ready. Fining or filtering the beer can shorten the required lagering time. If you lager in a keg, you can also carbonate the beer while lagering.

A pot with a spigot and false bottom makes a great mash/water tun.

LATER, HOSER FESTBIER
OCTOBERFEST

Octoberfest is a malty amber lager, often with an orangey hue, associated with the German beer celebration Octoberfest. This recipe makes a beer similar to the Octoberfests imported from German into the United States. The beer is malty, with the toasty flavor of Munich and melanoidin malt, and fairly strong. Overall, it's very balanced without being too sweet or too hoppy.

5.0 GALLONS (19 L) AT 5.9% ABV
OG = 1.060, FG = 1.014
21 IBU, 15 SRM

+ Wyeast 2124 (Bohemian Lager), White Labs WLP830 (German Lager) or Fermentis Saflager W-34/70 yeast
+ An 8.5-qt. (8.0-L) yeast starter is recommended
+ 10 lb. 4 oz (4.7 kg) Vienna malt
+ 1 lb. 4 oz. (570 g) Munich malt (10°L)
+ 4.0 oz. (110 g) melanoidin malt (23°L)
+ 6.0 oz. (170 g) CaraMunich malt (60°L)
+ 2.0 oz. (57g) Carafa Special III malt (525°L)
+ 1.25 oz. (35 g) Tettnanger hops at 4.5% alpha acids, boiled for 60 minutes (21 IBU)
+ 4.5 oz. (130 g) corn sugar, to prime bottles for 2.5 volumes of CO_2

If you are using one of the liquid yeasts, make your yeast starter two to three days ahead of time. (An 8.5-quart [8.0-L] yeast starter is optimal, but one-half this size would yield similar results—a slower start to fermentation would be the most obvious difference. The finished beer would not likely taste much different, however. This is especially true if you aerated the starter and roused the yeast once a day.) Heat 16 quarts (15 L) of brewing liquor to 163°F (73°C) and mash in crushed malts. Mash at 152°F (67°C) for 60 minutes, stirring every 15 minutes if you can. Heat or add boiling water to mash out to 168°F (76°C). Recirculate wort until clear, and then run off.

Sparge to collect about 8.0 gallons (30 L) of wort. Boil wort to reduce the volume to just over 5.0 gallons (19 L). (This should take two to three hours.) Add hops at times indicated. Chill wort, then rack to fermenter. Aerate wort thoroughly and pitch sediment from yeast starter. Ferment at 54°F (12°C). When fermentation slows greatly, allow the temperature to rise to 60°F (16°C) and stay at that temperature for at least three days for a diacetyl rest. Lager around 40°F (4.4°C) for at least eight weeks. Keg or add priming sugar and bottle. Carbonate to 2.5 volumes of CO_2.

MALT EXTRACT OPTION

Add 6 pounds 2 ounces (1.3 kg) liquid Vienna malt extract—or, failing that, liquid Munich malt extract—to the recipe. Lower the amount of Vienna malt to 1.0 pound (450 g). In your brew pot, steep the 3.0 pounds (1.4 kg) total of crushed grains in 4.1 quarts (3.9 L) of water at 152°F (67°C) for 60 minutes. (This is really a mash, so follow the temperature and volume guidelines closely.) After steeping, place the grain bag in a large colander over your brew pot. Rinse the grains with 2.0 quarts (1.9 L) of 170°F (77°C) water. Add roughly a fourth of the malt extract to the wort collected and adjust the wort volume with water to make 3.0 gallons (11 L) of wort. Boil for 60 minutes, adding hops at times indicated. Add remaining malt extract in the final 10 minutes of the boil.

TIMING YOUR OCTOBERFEST

Octoberfest beers can be enjoyed year-round. However, they are usually thought of as a seasonal beer. If you want an Octoberfest beer ready for Octoberfest—which was traditionally held in the 16 days prior to the first Sunday in October—you'll need to get it started by early July. If you can start it earlier, all the better, because sometimes it takes longer to lager a beer than planned.

Homebrew lagering in a refrigerator.

RECIPE OPTIONS AND NOTES

Bockbiers can be dark (dunkles bock) or pale (helles bock). To brew a helles bock, decrease the amount of Munich malt and replace it with an equal amount of Pilsner malt. And of course, omit the dark malt. Shoot for a beer of 11 SRM or lighter, but at the same strength as a dunkles bock. Helles bocks are generally a bit drier and hoppier, so decrease the mash temperature by a few degrees and add about 15 percent more bittering hops.

The long boil required to condense the wort will contribute to the melanoidin-rich malt character of the dunkles bock. You can enhance this even further, by making your wort via a decoction mash. (See the recipe on page 180 for information on how to do this.)

BOTTOM OF THE BARREL BOCK
BOCKBIER (OR DUNKLES BOCK)

Bock is a strong German lager. Bockbiers are richly malty, often with just a hint of sweetness. This recipe is for a dunkles bock, or dark bock.

5.0 GALLONS (19 L) AT 6.4% ABV
OG = 1.064, FG = 1.015
23 IBU, 16 SRM

+ Wyeast 2206 (Bavarian Lager) or White Labs WLP820 (Octoberfest Lager) yeast
+ A 9.6-qt. (9.1-L) yeast starter is recommended
+ 5 lb. 4 oz. (2.4 kg) Vienna malt
+ 8.0 lb. (3.6 kg) Munich malt (10°L)
+ 2.0 oz. (57 g) Carafa Special II malt (430°L)
+ 1.25 oz. (35 g) Hallertauer Hersbrucker hops at 4.5% alpha acids, boiled for 60 minutes (21 IBU)
+ 0.25 oz. (7.1 g) Hallertauer Hersbrucker hops at 4.5% alpha acids, boiled for 10 minutes (1.5 IBU)
+ 4.5 oz. (130 g) corn sugar, to prime bottles for 2.5 volumes of CO_2

Make your yeast starter two to three days ahead of time. You can make the yeast starter half this size if you aerate it once a day, and then swirl the starter vessel to rouse the yeast. Heat 17 quarts (16 L) of brewing liquor to 163°F (73°C) and mash in grains. Mash at 152°F (67°C) for 60 minutes, stirring every 15 minutes if you can. Heat or add boiling water to mash out to 168°F (76°C). Recirculate wort until clear, and then run off.

Sparge to collect up to 8.6 gallons (33 L) of wort. Boil wort to reduce volume to just over 5.0 gallons (19 L), adding hops at times indicated. Chill wort, then rack to fermenter. Aerate wort thoroughly and pitch sediment from yeast starter. Ferment at 54°F (12°C). Perform a diacetyl rest at 60°F (16°C) for three days. Lager for eight weeks at 40°F (4.4°C). Then, keg or add priming sugar and bottle and carbonate to 2.5 volumes of CO_2.

(continued)

MALTMEISTER DOPPLEBOCK
DOPPELBOCK

Doppelbock is a strong dark German lager. The "doppel" in "doppelbock" means double, although the beer is not literally double the strength of a normal bock. Although there are a few very high-gravity versions commercially available, most commercial examples weigh in at around 7 percent ABV, the legal minimum required to label them as doppelbock. Doppelbocks are very malty, but well attenuated given their size. As such, they do not taste overly sweet.

5.0 GALLONS (19 L) AT 7.5% ABV
OG = 1.076, FG = 1.018
21 IBU, 20 SRM

+ Wyeast 2206 (Bavarian Lager) or White Labs WLP820 (Octoberfest Lager) yeast
+ A 14-qt. (13-L) yeast starter is recommended
+ 5.0 lb. (2.3 kg) Pilsener malt
+ 8.0 lb. (3.6 kg) Munich malt (10°L)
+ 1 lb. 8 oz. (680 g) dark Munich malt (20°L)
+ 12 oz. (340 g) aromatic malt (23°L)
+ 3.0 oz. (85 g) Carafa Special II malt (430°L)
+ 1.25 oz. (35 g) Hallertau Hersbrücker hops at 4.5% alpha acids, boiled for 60 minutes (21 IBU)
+ 4.5 oz. (130 g) corn sugar, to prime bottles for 2.5 volumes of CO_2

Make your yeast starter two to three days ahead of time. Obviously, the recommended starter size for this strong lager is huge. You may want to consider brewing 5.0 gallons (19 L) of a low-gravity lager—OG 1.040–1.044—in place of your yeast starter. Alternately, you can make the starter half this size if you aerate it once a day, and then swirl the starter vessel to rouse the yeast. Heat 19 quarts (18 L) of brewing liquor to 161°F (72°C) and mash in grains.

Mash at 150°F (66°C) for 60 minutes, stirring every 15 minutes if you can. Heat mash to 168°F (76°C) for a mash out. Recirculate wort until clear, and then run off. Fully sparging the grain bed will allow you to collect up to 10 gallons (38 L) of wort. Boil wort to reduce volume to just over 5.0 gallons (19 L). Add the hops for final hour of the boil. Chill wort, then rack to fermenter.

Aerate wort thoroughly and pitch sediment from yeast starter. If fermentation has not started within 8 hours, aerate the wort a second time. Ferment at 53°F (12°C). Perform a diacetyl rest at 60°F (16°C) for three days. (Check by tasting to see if diacetyl is gone before lagering.) Lager for 10 weeks at 40°F (4.4°C). Then, keg or add priming sugar and bottle and carbonate to 2.5 volumes of CO_2.

This is a malt-focused beer. Use only the highest quality malts.

MALT EXTRACT OPTION

Add 7 pounds 10 ounces (3.5 kg) of light dried malt extract to the recipe. Omit the Pilsner malt. Reduce the amount of Munich malt to 1 pound 9 ounces (710 g). Follow the general directions for a countertop partial mash (see page 36), with these specifics. Mash at 150°F (66°C) for 60 minutes. Collect 2.6 gallons (9.8 L) of wort. Add one-quarter of the mash extract and water to make at least 4.0 gallons (15 L). Boil for 60 minutes, adding hops at beginning of boil. Stir in the malt extract in small doses during the final 30 minutes of the boil.

BOTTLE CONDITIONING A BIG LAGER

Bottle conditioning an average-strength ale is no problem—just add the priming sugar and let the bottles sit somewhere warm for about a week. Bottle conditioning a strong lager or very strong ale, however, can be problematic. By the end of a high-gravity fermentation, followed by a period of cold conditioning (lagering), the yeast may not be healthy enough to quickly ferment the priming sugar. You can help them by adding a small amount of dried yeast (or healthy yeast harvested from another fermentation) at bottling. Any neutral yeast strain will work—you can even bottle condition a lager with an ale strain.

The yeast only ferment the priming sugar, so this secondary fermentation doesn't appreciably change the character of the beer (unless you use an ale yeast strain that produces lots of esters or phenols). To prime 5.0 gallons (19 L) of beer, add the required amount of priming sugar and ¼ teaspoon of yeast. You only need enough yeast cells to ferment the priming sugar, so this amount of yeast is plenty.

POLAR VORTEX EISBOCK
EISBOCK

An eisbock is a doppelbock that has been frozen and had ice crystals removed from it. This concentrates the beer, increasing the alcoholic strength and all the flavors. You can turn any doppelbock into an eisbock, but this recipe gives a high-gravity doppelbock to start with. With a higher-gravity base beer, you need to remove less water (as ice) to concentrate the beer. However, the higher the alcohol content, the lower the freezing point of the beer. If you live in the northern U.S., your best bet is to brew the beer in the late spring, lager it and wait for an intensely cold snap over the winter. Place the keg outside and wait until you hear rattling around when you jostle it.

5.0 GALLONS (19 L) AT 8.8% ABV
(AFTER FREEZING AND REMOVING ICE, LESS THAN 5.0 GALLONS [19 L]
AND MORE THAN 8.8% ABV)
OG = 1.091, FG = 1.023
21 IBU, 16 SRM

+ Wyeast 2206 (Bavarian Lager) or White Labs WLP820 (Octoberfest Lager) yeast

+ A 8.2-qt. (7.8-L) yeast starter is recommended—two vials or packs of yeast are required

+ 8.0 lb. (3.6 kg) Pilsener malt

+ 9.0 lb. (4.1 kg) German Munich malt (8°L)

+ 12 oz. (340 g) dark Munich malt (20°L)

+ 4.0 oz. (110 g) melanoidin malt (23°L)

+ 2.0 oz. (57 g) Carafa Special II malt (430°L)

+ 1.25 oz. (35 g) Hallertau Hersbrücker hops at 4.5% alpha acids, boiled for 60 minutes (21 IBU)

Make your yeast starter two to three days ahead of time, pitching two vials or smack packs of yeast. Consider aerating the starter once a day and swirling the starter vessel to rouse the yeast. Watch for excessive foaming. Heat 23 quarts (22 L) of brewing liquor to 160°F (71°C) and mash in grains. Mash at 149°F (65°C) for 60 minutes, stirring every 15 minutes if you can. Heat mash to mash out to 168°F (76°C). Recirculate wort until clear, and then run off. A fully sparged grain bed will yield up to 12 gallons (45 L) of wort.

Boil wort to reduce volume to just over 5.0 gallons (19 L), adding hops at the beginning of the boil. Chill wort, then rack to fermenter. Aerate wort thoroughly and pitch sediment from yeast starter. Ferment at 52°F (11°C). Perform a diacetyl rest at 60°F (16°C) for three days. (Check by tasting to see if diacetyl is gone before lagering.) Lager for 11 weeks at 40°F (4.4°C). Then, keg (if not already kegged) and freeze. Wait until a significant amount of ice is formed and then remove it from the beer. (You can do this with a sanitized strainer.) Carbonate keg to 2.5 volumes of CO_2.

MALT EXTRACT OPTION

Add 10 pounds 4 ounces (4.7 kg) of liquid Munich malt extract to the recipe. Reduce the amount of Pilsner malt to 14 ounces (390 g). Reduce the amount of Munich malt to 1.0 pound (450 g). "Steep" the crushed grains in 4.1 quarts (3.9 L) of water at 149°F (65°C) for 60 minutes. ("Steep" is in quotes because technically this is a partial mash.) Place the grain bag in a colander over your brew pot and rinse the grains with 2.0 quarts (1.9 L) of 168°F (76°C) water. Add roughly one-quarter of the malt extract to this wort. Add water to bring brew pot volume to at least 4.0 gallons (15 L). Boil for 60 minutes, adding hops at the beginning of the boil. Add the remaining malt extract in small doses throughout the boil.

CALCULATING THE ALCOHOL CONTENT OF AN EISBOCK

If you make an eisbock, you'll assuredly want to know how strong it is after you have removed the ice. There is a simple way to estimate this. You will know the initial volume of your doppelbock and can calculate its alcoholic content from the OG and FG of the beer. After you remove the ice, you will need to measure the volume of beer that remains. Then, use the CV = CV equation. "C" and "V" stand for concentration and volume. If you had 5.0 gallons of 8.8 percent ABV dopplebock and ended up with 4.5 gallons of eisbock, its alcoholic content can be estimated by solving this equation—8.8(5.0) = X(4.5). Solving for X yields, 9.777, so your alcohol content would be—when rounded to the correct number of significant digits—9.8 percent ABV. In practice, it is not too difficult to get eisbocks up to around 12 percent ABV.

6

PALE LAGERS: CRISP AND CLEAN

The section gives the recipes for seven pale lagers. They range from an OG 1.046 (4.5 percent ABV) Munich Helles to an OG 1.069 (6.9 percent ABV) Maibock—with a Dortmunder Export, Pilsners and others in between. The color of these beers ranges from 3.0 SRM to 10 SRM.

If you are treating your water, you should aim to have at least 100 ppm calcium (Ca^{+2}) ions, and between 0 ppm and 60 ppm bicarbonate (HCO_3^-), with the lower end for beers around 3 SRM and the upper end for beers around 10 SRM. (When the boil starts, you may want add 50 ppm more calcium.) As with the darker ales, you do not have to adjust your water chemistry to match your beer's SRM exactly. Being in the ballpark is all you need.

If you are making your water by adding minerals to 5.0 gallons (19 L) of distilled or RO water, start by adding 0 to 2 g of sodium bicarbonate ($NaHCO_3$, baking soda), with no addition corresponding to beers around 3 SRM and the high end corresponding to beers around 10 SRM. Then choose a calcium addition depending on how much you want to accentuate the hops. For a balanced beer, add 4 g of calcium chloride ($CaCl_2*2H_2O$) and 4 g of calcium sulfate ($CaSO_4*2H_2O$, gypsum). For a beer in which the hops are to be accentuated, add 8 g of calcium sulfate ($CaSO_4*2H_2O$, gypsum). You will need to prepare more than 5.0 gallons (19 L) of brewing liquor for the all-grain versions of these beers.

For the extract versions, you only need to prepare brewing liquor (water with the correct mineral additions) of the grains you steep or mash. Use distilled water, RO water or naturally soft water for diluting the malt extract.

If you have a water report that describes what is in your water, you can use brewing software to plan your mineral additions. Remember to treat your water to remove any chlorine compounds, if present (as they are in all municipal water sources).

AUTOBAHN TO HELLES
MUNICH HELLES

Munich Helles is a light, malty lager focused on the flavor and aroma of Pilsner malt. The beer is well attenuated and is not overly sweet. Hop bitterness and aroma are subdued. This recipe uses a single decoction mash, which will enhance the grainy-malty character of the beer.

5.0 GALLONS (19 L) AT 4.5% ABV
OG = 1.046, FG = 1.011
20 IBU, 2.9 SRM

+ Wyeast 2124 (Bohemian Lager), White Labs WLP830 (German Lager) or Fermentis Saflager W-34/70 yeast
+ A 4.7-qt. (4.4-L) yeast starter is recommended
+ 8 lb. 10 oz. (3.9 kg) undermodified Pilsner malt
+ 1.0 oz. (28 g) Saaz hops at 5% alpha acids, boiled for 60 minutes (19 IBU)
+ 0.25 oz. (7.1 g) Saaz hops at 5% alpha acids, boiled for 5 minutes (0.9 IBU)
+ 4.5 oz. (130 g) corn sugar, to prime bottles for 2.5 volumes of CO_2

If you are using one of the liquid yeasts, make your yeast starter two to three days ahead of time. Heat 11 quarts (10 L) of brewing liquor to 133°F (56°C) and mash in grains at 122°F (50°C). After 20 minutes, stir the mash and scoop out roughly 40 percent of it. Try not to get only the thickest portion of the mash. Heat the removed mash (the decoction) to a boil and boil for 20 minutes. You must stir this boiling decoction almost constantly.

Return the decoction to the main mash. This should raise the temperature of the combined mash to around 150°F (66°F). Let the mash rest for another 45 minutes, then heat or add boiling water to mash out to 168°F (76°C). Recirculate wort until clear, and then run off. Sparge to collect about 5.6 gallons (21 L) of wort. Add water to make 6.5 gallons (24 L). Boil wort for 90 minutes, to reduce volume to just over 5.0 gallons (19 L), adding hops at times indicated. Chill wort, then rack to fermenter.

Aerate wort thoroughly and pitch sediment from yeast starter. Ferment at 54°F (12°C). Perform a diacetyl rest for three days at 60°F (16°C). Lager for six weeks. Then, keg or add priming sugar and bottle and carbonate to 2.5 volumes of CO_2.

MALT EXTRACT OPTION

Add 4.0 pounds (1.8 kg) of liquid Pilsner malt extract to the recipe. Reduce the amount of Pilsner malt to 3.0 pounds (1.4 kg). Use fully modified Pilsner malt for extract version. "Steep" the crushed grains in 4.1 quarts (3.9 L) of water at 152°F (67°C) for 60 minutes. ("Steep" is in quotes because technically this is a partial mash.) Place the grain bag in a colander over your brew pot and rinse the grains with 2.0 quarts (1.9 L) of 170°F (77°C) water. Add roughly one-third of the malt extract to this wort. Add water to bring brew pot volume to 3.0 gallons (11 L). Boil for 60 minutes, adding hops and Irish moss at times indicated. Add the remaining malt extract in the final 15 minutes of the boil.

The decoction should be stirred constantly.

SINGLE DECOCTION MASH

A decoction mash is a mash in which part of the mixture of grains and water is removed, boiled and then returned to the mash. As you might guess, a single decoction is a decoction mash in which this is done once. The single decoction mash shown in this recipe is mashed in to 122°F (50°C). At this temperature, any excess gums in the mash are degraded, which will aid in lautering. A thin decoction of about 40 percent is pulled, boiled and returned to the main mash.

In commercial brewing, brewers usually pull a thick decoction around 33 percent. However, at home, the thinner decoction is easier to boil without scorching. Once the decoction is returned to the main mash, the temperature of the combined mash falls near the low end of the saccharification range. (The whole range is often given as 148–162°F [64–72°C].) After this, the brewer performs a mash out as usual and continues brewing.

These days, most malts are manufactured to be single infusion mashed. When decoction mashing, you are better off selecting an undermodified Pilsner malt. Undermodified malts will be identified as such and are meant to encounter a rest in the 113–122°F (45–50°C) range. At this temperature the level of gums can be reduced without negatively impacting foam. In a "normal," fully modified malt, a rest in this range can degrade the proteins required for a nice foam stand.

Some brewers may wonder if boiling a decoction will extract excess tannins from their malt. After all, they are advised not to exceed 170°F (77°C) while sparging to limit tannin extraction. However, tannin extraction is increased at higher pH levels. In a decoction, the pH should be in the 5.2–5.4 range, while it may be as high as 5.8 near the end of lautering. The lower pH of the decoction being boiled does not favor tannin extraction to the degree that the higher pH in lautering does. Some tannins are extracted when a decoction is boiled, but in practice the amount is below that which leads to an objectionable level of astringency.

BIERGARTEN PILS

GERMAN PILS

A good German Pilsner exhibits the best qualities of Pilsner malt. It's a pale-to-golden, fairly dry lager with an assertive hop bitterness. The dry nature of the beer, ample bitterness and crisply clean lager character make the beer very refreshing.

5.0 GALLONS (19 L) AT 5.0% ABV
OG = 1.050, FG = 1.011
39 IBU, 3.0 SRM

+ Wyeast 2007 (Pilsen Lager) or White Labs WLP840 (American Pilsner Lager) yeast
+ A 5.6-qt. (5.3-L) yeast starter is recommended
+ 9 lb. 6 oz. (4.3 kg) German Pilsner malt
+ 2.25 oz. (64 g) Tettnanger hops at 4.5% alpha acids, boiled for 60 minutes (38 IBU)
+ 0.25 oz. (7.1 g) Hallertau Mittelfrüher hops at 4.5% alpha acids, boiled for 5 minutes (0.84 IBU)
+ 0.33 oz. (9.4 g) Hallertau Mittelfrüher hops at 4.5% alpha acids, boiled for 0 minutes (0 IBU)
+ 4.5 oz. (130 g) corn sugar, to prime bottles for 2.5 volumes of CO_2

Make your yeast starter two to three days ahead of time. Heat 12 quarts (11 L) of brewing liquor to 163°F (73°C) and mash in grains. Mash at 152°F (67°C) for 60 minutes, stirring every 15 minutes if you can. Heat or add boiling water to mash out to 168°F (76°C). Recirculate wort until clear, and then run off.

Sparge to collect about collect 6.1 gallons (23 L) of wort. Boil wort for 60 minutes, to reduce volume to just over 5.0 gallons (19 L), adding hops at times indicated. Chill wort, then rack to fermenter. Aerate wort thoroughly and pitch sediment from yeast starter. Ferment at 52°F (11°C). Perform a diacetyl rest for three days at 60°F (16°C). Lager for six weeks. Then, keg or add priming sugar and bottle and carbonate to 2.5 volumes of CO_2.

MALT EXTRACT OPTION

Add 4 pounds 10 ounces (2.1 kg) of liquid Pilsner malt extract to the recipe. Reduce the amount of Pilsner malt to 3.0 pounds (1.4 kg). "Steep" the crushed grains in 4.1 quarts (3.9 L) of water at 152°F (67°C) for 60 minutes. ("Steep" is in quotes because technically this is a partial mash.) Place the grain bag in a colander over your brew pot and rinse the grains with 2.0 quarts (1.9 L) of 170°F (77°C) water. Add roughly one-third of the malt extract to this wort. Add water to bring brew pot volume to 3.0 gallons (11 L). Boil for 60 minutes, adding hops at times indicated. Add the remaining malt extract in the final 15 minutes of the boil.

DEXTRINE MALT

Dextrine malts are a type of crystal malt that lend dextrins—carbohydrates that contain more sugar residues than simple sugars, but fewer than starches—to the beer. The malt helps with foam retention and makes the beer seem more full-bodied.

LAND OF OPPORTUNITY PILSNER
CLASSIC AMERICAN PILSNER

A classic American Pilsner is meant to reproduce what American Pilsners were like before Prohibition. Both slightly maltier—due to a smaller percentage of adjuncts—and considerably hoppier, they are a flavorful take on "American beer."

This recipe uses a classic American hop (Cluster) for bittering and the noble hop Saaz for aroma. If you brew one in late September, it can be ready by December 5—the day in 1933 when Prohibition was repealed.

5.0 GALLONS (19 L) AT 5.5% ABV
OG = 1.055, FG = 1.013
35 IBU, 3.6 SRM

+ Wyeast 2042 (Danish Lager) or White Labs WLP940 (Mexican Lager) yeast
+ A 6.9-qt. (6.5-L) yeast starter is recommended
+ 2 lb. 8 oz. (1.1 kg) U.S. 2-row pale malt
+ 5 lb. 8 oz. (2.5 kg) U.S. 6-row pale malt
+ 3.0 lb. (1.4 kg) brewer's corn grits
+ 1.25 oz. (35 g) Cluster hops at 7% alpha acids, boiled for 60 minutes (33 IBU)
+ 1.0 oz. (28 g) Saaz hops at 3.5% alpha acids, boiled for 5 minutes (2.6 IBU)
+ 0.75 tsp. Irish moss, boiled for 15 minutes
+ 4.5 oz. (130 g) corn sugar, to prime bottles for 2.5 volumes of CO_2

Make your yeast starter two to three days ahead of time. Heat 10 quarts (9.5 L) of brewing liquor to 151°F (66°C) and mash in malts, withholding about 0.50 pound (230 g) of crushed malt. Mash at 140°F (60°C). After the main mash has rested for about 10 minutes, mix corn grits and remaining malt in 5.0 quarts (4.7 L) of water and bring to a boil. Boil this cereal mash for 15 minutes, stirring often. Add the cereal mash to main mash, which should raise the combined mash temperature to 152°F (67°C). (Adjust temperature if needed.) Let mash rest for 45 minutes, then heat or add boiling water to mash out to 168°F (76°C). Recirculate wort until clear, and then run off.

Sparge to collect about 7.2 gallons (27 L) of wort. Boil wort for 90–120 minutes, to reduce volume to just over 5.0 gallons (19 L), adding hops and Irish moss at times indicated. Chill wort, then rack to fermenter. Aerate wort thoroughly and pitch sediment from yeast starter. Ferment at 54°F (12°C). Perform a diacetyl rest for three days at 60°F (16°C). Lager for seven weeks. Then, keg or add priming sugar and bottle and carbonate to 2.5 volumes of CO_2.

(continued)

MALT EXTRACT OPTION

Add 2 pounds 12 ounces (1.3 kg) of extra-light dried malt extract and 2 pounds 2 ounces (960 g) of corn sugar to the recipe. Reduce the amount of 6-row malt to 2.0 pounds (910 g). Reduce the amount of 2-row pale malt to 1.0 pound (450 g). "Steep" the crushed grains in 4.1 quarts (3.9 L) of water at 152°F (67°C) for 60 minutes. ("Steep" is in quotes because technically this is a partial mash.) Place the grain bag in a colander over your brew pot and rinse the grains with 2.0 quarts (1.9 L) of 170°F (77°C) water.

Add roughly one-third of the malt extract to this wort. Add water to bring brew pot volume to 3.0 gallons (11 L). Boil for 60 minutes, adding hops and Irish moss at times indicated. Add the remaining malt extract in the final 15 minutes of the boil.

CEREAL MASH

American Pilsners are made with 30–40 percent corn, rice or both as an adjunct. Flaked maize or flaked rice can be stirred into a single infusion mash. However, raw (degerminated) corn or raw rice must be cereal mashed because the starches in these cereals do not gelatinize at mash temperatures.

A cereal mash combines the corn or rice being mashed with 10–15 percent malted barley. This mixture is boiled to gelatinize the starches in the cereal, and then added to the main mash. The main mash begins at around 140°F (60°C)—in the range where the enzyme beta amylase works well—and adding the cereal mash boosts the temperature of the combined mash into the saccharification range.

If corn is used as the adjunct, the corn must be degerminated or it will be too oily. Degerminated corn processed for brewing is called brewer's corn grits. You will get a much "cornier" tasting beer by using a cereal mash than you will with flaked maize. Any white rice can be used as an adjunct.

AUSLÄNDER LAGER
DORTMUNDER EXPORT

In Germany, export beers are generally higher in strength than their domestic counterparts. A Dortmunder export is a golden lager that's stronger than a typical Pilsner (although the pale lager styles overlap somewhat). It's a balanced beer, showcasing both the malts and hops used to brew it. As such, it is less hoppy than the most bitter examples of Pils. These beers are often brewed in water that contains a high amount of sulfates.

5.0 GALLONS (19 L) AT 5.5% ABV
OG = 1.055, FG = 1.013
25 IBU, 4.4 SRM

+ Wyeast 2042 (Danish Lager) or White Labs WLP850 (Copenhagen Lager) yeast
+ A 6.9-qt. (6.5-L) yeast starter is recommended
+ 9 lb. 8 oz. (4.3 kg) Pilsner malt
+ 1.0 lb. (450 g) Munich malt (10°L)
+ 0.33 oz. (9.4 g) Perle hops at 3.5% alpha acids, FWH (10 IBU)
+ 0.40 oz. (11 g) Perle hops at 8% alpha acids, boiled for 60 minutes (12 IBU)
+ 0.25 oz. (7.1 g) Tettnanger hops at 4.5% alpha acids, boiled for 10 minutes (1.5 IBU)
+ 0.25 oz. (7.1 g) Spalt Spalter hops at 4.5% alpha acids, boiled for 5 minutes (0.84 IBU)
+ 0.20 oz. (7.1 g) Spalt Spalter hops at 4.5% alpha acids, boiled for 0 minutes (0 IBU)
+ 4.5 oz. (130 g) corn sugar, to prime bottles for 2.5 volumes of CO_2

Make your yeast starter two to three days ahead of time. If you are following the water chemistry suggestions from the section opener, add an extra 0.25 teaspoon of gypsum per 5.0 gallons (19 L) of brewing water. Add 1.0 teaspoon of gypsum to the boil, just after the first bit of hot break shows. Heat 14 quarts (13 L) of brewing liquor to 163°F (73°C) and mash in grains. Mash at 152°F (67°C) for 60 minutes, stirring every 15 minutes if you can. Heat or add boiling water to mash out to 168°F (76°C). Recirculate wort until clear, and then run off.

Sparge to collect about 6.8 gallons (26 L) of wort. Boil wort for 90 minutes, to reduce volume to just over 5.0 gallons (19 L), adding hops at times indicated. (FWH refers to first wort hopping. Add these hops while collecting your wort.) Chill wort, then rack to fermenter. Aerate wort thoroughly and pitch sediment from yeast starter. Ferment at 54°F (12°C). Perform a diacetyl rest for three days at 60°F (16°C). Lager for seven weeks. Then, keg or add priming sugar and bottle and carbonate to 2.5 volumes of CO_2.

(continued)

MALT EXTRACT OPTION

Add 5 pounds 6 ounces (2.4 kg) of liquid Pilsner malt extract to the recipe. Reduce the amount of Pilsner malt to 2.0 pounds (910 g). "Steep" the crushed grains in 4.1 quarts (3.9 L) of water at 152°F (67°C) for 60 minutes. ("Steep" is in quotes because technically this is a partial mash.) Place the grain bag in a colander over your brew pot and rinse the grains with 2.0 quarts (1.9 L) of 170°F (77°C) water.

Add roughly one-third of the malt extract to this wort. Add water to bring brew pot volume to 3.0 gallons (11 L). Boil for 60 minutes, adding hops at times indicated. Add the remaining malt extract in the final 15 minutes of the boil.

FIRST WORT HOPPING (FWH)

First wort hopping, often abbreviated to FWH, is the practice of adding hops to the first wort that flows into the kettle. First wort hops are added before the boil and steep in wort while it is being collected and heated towards a boil. Advocates of first wort hopping claim that it gives the beer a smoother hop character. Skeptics do not believe that this has been sufficiently demonstrated, but most will admit that it can't hurt anything. Some studies have shown that beers that were first wort hopped were perceived as less bitter than their IBUs would indicate. So, if you're looking to make a beer with an exceptionally smooth bitterness, try first wort hopping.

DIDDLEY PILS
BOHEMIAN PILSNER

Bohemian Pilsner, or Czech Pilsner, is a balanced Pilsner beer with a "soft," slightly sweet, malt character. A "Bo Pils" may be as heavily hopped as German Pils, but often doesn't seem as bitter due to the soft water used for the brewing liquor. The delicate aroma of noble hops—Saaz in the most famous example of the style, Pilsner Urquell—complements the enticing malt aroma. This recipe calls for a triple decoction mash to bring out the full malt character of the Pilsner malt. A small amount of acidulated malt is added to counter the fact that the brewing liquor contains less calcium than most brewing liquors.

5.0 GALLONS (19 L) AT 5.6% ABV
OG = 1.056, FG = 1.012
39 IBU, 3.3 SRM

+ Wyeast 2124 (Bohemian Lager), White Labs WLP830 (German Lager) or Fermentis Saflager W-34/70 yeast
+ A 7.2-qt. (6.8-L) yeast starter is recommended
+ 9 lb. 12 oz. (4.4 kg) undermodified Pilsner malt
+ 8.0 oz. (230 g) Cara-Pils malt (1.3°L)
+ 4.0 oz. (110 g) acidulated malt
+ 2.5 oz. (71 g) Saaz hops at 3.5% alpha acids, boiled for 60 minutes (33 IBU)
+ 1.0 oz. (28 g) Saaz hops at 3.5% alpha acids, boiled for 15 minutes (6.6 IBU)
+ 1.0 oz. (28 g) Saaz hops at 3.5% alpha acids, boiled for 0 minutes (0 IBU)
+ 4.5 oz. (130 g) corn sugar, to prime bottles for 2.5 volumes of CO_2

If you are using one of the Wyeast yeasts, make your yeast starter two to three days ahead of time. Bohemian Pilsners (Czech Pilsners) are generally brewed from soft water. If you are following the instructions for water treatment in the section intro, decrease the amount of calcium you add to your brewing liquor by half. Heat 13 quarts (12 L) of brewing liquor to 106°F (4°C) and mash in grains to 95°F (35°C). Hold for 20 minutes, then stir and pull a decoction of roughly 35 percent of the mash. Boil the first decoction for 20 minutes, and then return to main mash. The temperature should settle in to around 122°F (50°C). Hold for 10 minutes, then stir and pull another decoction (around 40 percent of the mash volume) and boil for 15 minutes.

Return second decoction to main mash and let combined mash rest at around 154°F (68°C) for 45 minutes. Stir mash, pull a third decoction (roughly 40 percent of the mash volume), boil for 10 minutes and return to main mash to mash out to 168°F (76°C). Recirculate wort until clear, and then run off. Sparge to collect about 6.5 gallons (25 L) of wort. Boil wort for 90 minutes, to reduce volume to just over 5.0 gallons (19 L). Add hops at times indicated. Chill wort, then rack to fermenter. Aerate wort thoroughly and pitch sediment from yeast starter. Ferment at 54°F (12°C). Perform a diacetyl rest for three days at 60°F (16°C). Lager for seven weeks. Then, keg or add priming sugar and bottle and carbonate to 2.5 volumes of CO_2.

You must stir the boiling decoctions almost constantly.

MALT EXTRACT OPTION

Add 5 pounds 6 ounces (2.4 kg) of liquid Pilsner malt extract and 2 pounds 8 ounces (1.1 kg) Pilsner malt to the recipe. Omit the undermodified Pilsner malt and acidulated malt. "Steep" the crushed grains in 4.1 quarts (3.9 L) of water at 152°F (67°C) for 60 minutes. ("Steep" is in quotes because technically this is a partial mash.) Place the grain bag in a colander over your brew pot and rinse the grains with 2.0 quarts (1.9 L) of 170°F (77°C) water. Add roughly one-third of the malt extract to this wort. Add water to bring brew pot volume to 3.0 gallons (11 L). Boil for 60 minutes, adding hops and Irish moss at times indicated. Add the remaining malt extract in the final 15 minutes of the boil.

TRIPLE DECOCTION MASH

A triple decoction mash employs three decoctions to move the mash through four rests—an acid rest (around 95°F [35°C]), a beta glucan rest (113–122°F [45–50°C]), the saccharification rest (148–162°F [64–72°C]), and the mash out (around 176°F [76°F]). The size of each decoction varies and a thicker decoction raises the temperature more than thinner ones. Hitting the target temperatures is difficult in a homebrewery. The easiest way to do a triple decoction mash at home is to mash in your kettle. If you undershoot a rest temperature, just heat the mash to the proper temperature. If you overshoot, stir in cool water to correct the problem. When you have mashed out, scoop the mash over to your lauter tun and proceed.

LAND O' CALORIES IAN
AMERICAN MALT LIQUOR

American malt liquor is a strong version, generally 6–9 percent ABV, of an American Pilsner. In fact, most American Pilsners are brewed as a strong beer, and then diluted to working strength at packaging. Often a 14–16°Plato (OG 1.056–1.064) malt liquor is diluted to an 11–13°Plato (OG 1.044–1.052) American Pilsner. This recipe produces 5.0 gallons (19 L) of a 6.5 percent ABV malt liquor. However, you can dilute it to 6.5 gallons (25 L) of a 5.0 percent ABV American Pilsner.

5.0 GALLONS (19 L) AT 6.5% ABV
OG = 1.064, FG = 1.014
22 IBU, 3.9 SRM

+ Wyeast 2035 (American Lager) or White Labs WLP840 (American Pilsner Lager) yeast; A 9.5-qt. (9.0-L) yeast starter is recommended
+ 2 lb. 12 oz. (1.3 kg) 2-row pale malt
+ 6.0 lb. (2.7 kg) 6-row pale malt
+ 4.0 lb. (1.8 kg) brewers corn grits
+ 0.66 oz. (19 g) Brewers Gold hops at 9% alpha acids, boiled for 60 minutes (22 IBU)
+ 0.25 oz. (7.1 g) U.S. Hallertau hops at 4.5% alpha acids, boiled for 0 minutes (0 IBU)
+ 1.0 tsp. Irish moss, boiled for 15 minutes
+ 4.5 oz. (130 g) corn sugar, to prime bottles for 2.5 volumes of CO_2

Make your yeast starter two to three days ahead of time. Heat 11 quarts (10 L) of brewing liquor to 151°F (66°C) and mash in grains, reserving 0.75 pound (340 g) of malt. Mash at 140°F (60°C). After main mash rests for 20 minutes, mix 5.6 quarts (5.3 L) of water with corn and remaining malt to make cereal mash. Heat cereal mash to a boil, stirring almost constantly. Boil cereal mash for 30 minutes, then add to main mash to reach a mash temperature of 150°F (66°C). (You may need to adjust the temperature downward with some cool water.) Hold combined mash at 150°F (66 °C) for 45 minutes. Heat or add boiling water to mash out to 168°F (76°C).

Recirculate wort until clear, and then run off. Sparge to collect about 8.3 gallons (31 L) of wort. Boil to reduce volume to just over 5.0 gallons (19 L), adding hops and Irish moss at times indicated. Chill wort, then rack to fermenter. Aerate wort thoroughly and pitch sediment from yeast starter. Ferment at 54°F (12°C). Perform a diacetyl rest for three days at 60°F (16°C). Lager for eight weeks. Then, keg or add priming sugar and bottle and carbonate to 2.5 volumes of CO_2.

MALT EXTRACT OPTION

Add 3 pounds 2 ounces (1.4 kg) of extra-light dried malt extract and 2 pounds 14 ounces (1.3 kg) of corn sugar to the recipe. Reduce the amount of 6-row pale malt to 2.0 pounds (910 g). Reduce the amount of 2-row pale malt to 1.0 pound (450 g). "Steep" the crushed grains in 4.1 quarts (3.9 L) of water at 152°F (67°C) for 60 minutes. ("Steep" is in quotes because technically this is a partial mash.)

Place the grain bag in a colander over your brew pot and rinse the grains with 2.0 quarts (1.9 L) of 170°F (77°C) water. Add roughly one-third of the malt extract to this wort. Add water to bring brew pot volume to 3.0 gallons (11 L). Boil for 60 minutes, adding hops and Irish moss at times indicated. Add the remaining malt extract in the final 15 minutes of the boil.

HIGH-GRAVITY BREWING

High-gravity brewing is the practice of brewing a strong beer, then diluting it to working strength after fermentation. This is also called blending for volume. Large commercial brewers use this method because it is cheaper to dilute the beer at packaging than to buy and maintain the added tanks that would be required to hold their beer at working strength. For homebrewers, it can be a way to get more beer from your fermenters.

Beer goes stale quickly when exposed to oxygen, so any oxygen present in the dilution water must be minimized. Most tap water will have around 8–9 ppm oxygen dissolved in it at groundwater temperature. Boiling this water for 15 minutes will knock the amount of oxygen down to around 1 ppm. If you cool it quickly and quietly, you can rack this water to a keg or bottling bucket and it will take awhile before the oxygen levels in it rise appreciably. Because there is a little oxygen left in the water, homebrew made this way will go stale faster than regular homebrew. However, it doesn't happen instantaneously. You have at least a couple months to enjoy the beer before it starts showing signs of age.

You can brew any type of beer this way. At home, a very workable method is to formulate all your recipes as 6.0-gallon (23-L) recipes, but brew them so they yield 5.0 gallons (19 L) of beer at 1.2X their intended strength. Then, dilute the beers when kegging or bottling to 6.0 gallons (23 L). This uses proportionally less dilution water than the recipe above, so the oxygen issue is lessened. If you keg your beer in Cornelius kegs, you could rack 0.83 gallons (3.2 L) of deaerated water to a keg, then fill it to 5.0 gallons (19 L) to make the working strength beer. You could then bottle the final 0.83 gallons (3.2 L) of beer as strong beer.

Some homebrewers worry that using this method will make their homebrew "watery." It won't. Higher-gravity beers finish at progressively higher final gravities. When the beer is diluted, the "virtual FG" becomes the FG that would have been achieved if you brewed the beer at working strength. American Pilsners brewed this way have little body because they are formulated to lack body; it is not a consequence of this technique.

RECIPE OPTIONS AND NOTES

Blend this 6.5 percent ABV malt liquor with deaerated water to make a 5.0 percent ABV American Pilsner. To do this, boil 1.8 gallons (6.8 L) vigorously, until the volume is reduced to 1.5 gallons (5.7 L). This will (mostly) deaerate the water. Quickly cool the water without splashing or otherwise aerating it. Transfer 1.2 gallons (4.4 L) of the deaerated water to a 5.0-gallon (19-L) Cornelius keg and rack malt liquor into it to make 5.0 gallons (19 L) of American Pilsner. You can combine the remaining malt liquor and water—in another keg or in a bottling bucket—to make 1.5 gallons (5.7 L) more American Pilsner, or package the remaining malt liquor by itself.

RAM OF SPRING HELLES BOCK
MAIBOCK (HELLES BOCK)

Maibock is golden bockbier. It is a strong, malty lager, which is usually more attenuated and hoppier than a dunkles bock (dark bock). The "Mai" in "Maibock" means May in German and these beers are often brewed as spring seasonals. The beer can also be called a Helles Bock.

The key to making a great Maibock is to run an efficient, ordered fermentation. You can help yourself out in this respect by pitching the recommended amount of yeast and kräusening the beer, as described in the procedures.

5.0 GALLONS (19 L) AT 6.9% ABV
OG = 1.069, FG = 1.016
27 IBU, 6.4 SRM

+ Wyeast 2206 (Bavarian Lager) or White Labs WLP820 (Octoberfest Lager) yeast
+ A 12-qt. (11-L) yeast starter is recommended
+ 7 lb. 8 oz. (3.4 kg) Pilsner malt
+ 5.0 lb. (2.3 kg) Vienna malt
+ 1.0 lb. (450 g) Munich malt (10°L)
+ 0.50 oz. (14 g) Magnum hops at 14.5% alpha acids, boiled for 60 minutes (27 IBU)
+ 0.50 oz. (14 g) Saaz hops at 3.5% alpha acids, boiled for 0 minutes (0 IBU)
+ 4.25 oz. (120 g) corn sugar, to prime bottles for 2.5 volumes of CO_2

Make your yeast starter two to three days ahead of time. Heat 17 quarts (16 L) of brewing liquor to 163°F (73°C) and mash in grains. Mash at 152°F (67°C) for 60 minutes, stirring every 15 minutes if you can. Heat or add boiling water to mash out to 168°F (76°C). Recirculate wort until clear, and then run off.

Sparge to collect about 8.8 gallons (33 L) of wort. Boil wort to reduce volume to just over 5.0 gallons (19 L), adding hops at times indicated. Chill wort, and then rack most of it to your fermenter. Divert 2.0 quarts (1.9 L) to a sanitized vessel and refrigerate. Aerate wort thoroughly and pitch sediment from yeast starter. Retain about 1.0 teaspoon of yeast slurry. Place it in a small, sanitized jar and refrigerate.

Ferment at 52°F (11°C). When main fermentation slows substantially, pitch the remaining yeast to the wort being held aside and let it begin fermenting. (Warm the wort up to lager temperature before pitching yeast.) This is your kräusen beer. Once the kräusen beer is fermenting vigorously, add it to your main batch of beer. Allow fermentation to complete at 52°F (11°C). Cool beer and lager for nine weeks. Then, keg or add priming sugar and bottle and carbonate to 2.5 volumes of CO_2.

Kräusening helps with attenuation in strong lagers.

MALT EXTRACT OPTION

Add 5 pounds 6 ounces (2.4 kg) of liquid Pilsner malt extract and 2.0 pounds (910 g) of liquid Munich malt extract to the recipe. Omit Pilsner malt and Munich malt. Reduce the amount of Vienna malt to 3.0 pounds (1.4 kg). "Steep" the crushed grains in 4.1 quarts (3.9 L) of water at 152°F (67°C) for 60 minutes. ("Steep" is in quotes because technically this is a partial mash.) Place the grain bag in a colander over your brew pot and rinse the grains with 2.0 quarts (1.9 L) of 170°F (77°C) water. Add roughly one-third of the malt extract to this wort. Add water to bring brew pot volume to 3.0 gallons (11 L). Boil for 60 minutes, adding hops and Irish moss at times indicated. Add the remaining malt extract in the final 15 minutes of the boil.

KRÄUSENING

Kräusening is the practice of adding a small amount of actively fermenting lager beer to the end of a lager beer fermentation. The active yeast clean up the diacetyl from the main fermentation and can help the beer reach its final gravity (FG) more quickly. The carbon dioxide being released can also be trapped and used to carbonate the beer—although that's tricky to do at home (unless you have something called a spunding valve). Usually, the volume of kräusen beer added is 10–17 percent of the volume of the main batch of beer, and the kräusen beer should be at its most active stage (i.e., high kräusen) when used. This takes a bit of planning to pull off at home, but can be very useful when brewing strong lagers.

7

BEER BREWED WITH SPECIALTY YEAST OR BACTERIA: TAKE A WALK ON THE WILD SIDE

The section gives the recipes for 10 beers brewed with microorganisms other than normal ale and lager yeast. These include German wheat beers, a special Belgian ale and sour beers. They range from an OG 1.031 (3.2 percent ABV) Berliner weisse to an OG 1.065 (7.1 percent ABV) Saison—with lambics, wheat beers and others in between. The color of these beers ranges from 2.6 SRM to 16 SRM, with most on the pale end of that range.

If you are treating your water, you should aim to have at least 100 ppm calcium (Ca^{+2}) ions, and between 0 ppm and 60 ppm bicarbonate (HCO_3^-), with the lower end for beers around 3 SRM and the upper end for beers around 10 SRM. (When the boil starts, you may want to add 50 ppm more calcium.) As with the other beers, you do not have to adjust your water chemistry to match your beer's SRM exactly. Being in the ballpark is all you need.

If you are making your water by adding minerals to 5.0 gallons (19 L) of distilled or RO water, start by adding 0 to 2 g of sodium bicarbonate ($NaHCO_3$, baking soda), with no addition corresponding to beers around 3 SRM and the high end corresponding to beer around 10 SRM. Then choose a calcium addition depending on how much you want to accentuate the hops. For a balanced beer, add 4 g of calcium chloride ($CaCl_2*2H_2O$) and 4 g of calcium sulfate ($CaSO_4*2H_2O$, gypsum). For a beer in which the hops are to be accentuated, add 8 g of calcium sulfate ($CaSO_4*2H_2O$, gypsum). You will need to prepare more than 5.0 gallons (19 L) of brewing liquor for the all-grain versions of these beers.

For the extract versions, you only need to prepare brewing liquor (water with the correct mineral additions) of the grains you steep or mash. Use distilled water, RO water or naturally soft water for diluting the malt extract.

If you have a water report that describes what is in your water, you can use brewing software to plan your mineral additions. Remember to treat your water to remove any chlorine compounds, if present (as they are in all municipal water sources).

HEART OF TARTNESS EXILE ALE
BERLINER WEISSE

Berliner weisse is a tart wheat beer. It is low in gravity, straw in color and highly carbonated. Napoleon referred to it as "the Champagne of the north." Unlike lambic—which sours over a long period—Berliner weisse is quickly soured during fermentation with a large pitch of *Lactobaccilus* (which is in the yeast blends recommended). The beer is traditionally served in goblets with raspberry or woodruff syrup, which sweetens the beer (to balance the tartness) and adds a red or green color.

5.0 GALLONS (19 L) AT 3.2% ABV
OG = 1.031, FG = 1.006 (OR LOWER)
6.4 IBU, 2.6 SRM

+ Fermentis Safale US-05 dried yeast (or any similar neutral ale yeast)
+ Wyeast 3191 (Berliner Weisse Blend) or White Labs WLP630 (Berliner Weisse Blend) yeast
+ A 2.1-qt. (2.0-L) yeast starter is recommended
+ 2 lb. 14 oz. (1.3 kg) Pilsner malt
+ 2 lb. 14 oz. (1.3 kg) wheat malt
+ 0.50 oz. (14 g) Hallertau hops at 4.5% alpha acids, boiled for 30 minutes (6.4 IBU)
+ 7.4 oz. (210 g) corn sugar, to prime bottles for 3.2 volumes of CO_2

Make your yeast starter two to three days ahead of time. Make 2.1 quarts (2.0 L) of your yeast starter with a starting gravity of OG 1.030 from wheat malt extract, aerate starter wort and pitch with roughly 2 g of dried yeast (about ⅓ of the package). Seal dried yeast package and refrigerate. The next day, pitch Berliner weisse blend to starter. Do not aerate the wort at this point. Let the starter incubate for one to two weeks at room temperature or (preferably) slightly above before brewing Berliner weisse.

On brew day, heat 7.1 quarts (6.8 L) of brewing liquor to 163°F (73°C) and mash in grains. Mash at 152°F (66°C) for 60 minutes, stirring every 15 minutes if you can do so. Heat or add boiling water to mash out to 168°F (76°C). Recirculate wort until clear, and then run off. Sparge to collect about 3.7 gallons (14 L) of wort. Add water to make a pre-boil volume you can boil down to 4.5 gallons (17 L) in 30 minutes. Add hops at beginning of boil. Chill wort, then rack to fermenter.

Aerate wort thoroughly and pitch entire volume of yeast starter, which will bring the batch volume up to 5.0 gallons (19 L). You may also want to pitch a couple more grams of dried yeast. Ferment at 70°F (21°C). After fermentation stops, let the beer condition for two weeks, preferably at 75—80°F (24–27°C). Keg or bottle and carbonate to 3.2 volumes of CO_2. Bottle it in heavy bottles.

(continued)

MALT EXTRACT OPTION

Add 1 pound 12 ounces (790 g) of dried wheat malt extract to the recipe. Reduce the amount of Pilsner malt and wheat malt to 1 pound 8 ounces (680 g) each. "Steep" the crushed grains in 4.1 quarts (3.9 L) of water at 152°F (67°C) for 60 minutes. ("Steep" is in quotes because technically this is a partial mash.) Place the grain bag in a colander over your brew pot and rinse the grains with 2.0 quarts (1.9 L) of 170°F (77°C) water. Add roughly one-half of the malt extract to this wort. Add water to bring brew pot volume to 3.0 gallons (11 L). Boil for 30 minutes, and then add hops at the beginning of the boil. Add the remaining malt extract in the final 15 minutes of the boil.

LACTIC ACID BACTERIA

Few bacteria can survive in beer. The alcohol content and low pH exclude the vast majority of potential contaminants in beer. One type that can is a bacterium that ferment sugar (primarily) into lactic acid. Lactic acid bacteria are generally not wanted in beer as they turn it sour. Also, some types of lactic acid bacteria produce other compounds—including diacetyl—along with the lactic acid that gives an unpleasant flavor.

However, most intentionally sour beers are inoculated with strains of *Lactobacillus*—and often other microorganisms, including *Pediococcus*—that produce a "clean" sour character. *Lactobacillus* can live in either aerobic or anaerobic conditions, but thrives in environments that contain a tiny concentration of oxygen.

Various *Lactobacillus* species are also involved in the production of fermented foods, including yogurt, sauerkraut, kimchi, cheese and sourdough bread.

RUBY RED FRAMBOISE
RASPBERRY LAMBIC

A raspberry lambic (or framboise) is a sour Belgian wheat beer flavored with raspberries. This recipe is a homebrewed interpretation that produces an intensely flavored fruit lambic with a deep red color. It is dry, sour and shows a hint of astringency (from the berries and high sparging temperature).

5.0 GALLONS (19 L) AT 4.8% ABV
OG = 1.048, FG = 1.011 (OR LOWER)
13 IBU, 3.8 SRM

+ Wyeast 3278 (Belgian Lambic Blend) or White Labs WLP655 (Belgian Sour Mix 1) yeast
+ Do not make a yeast starter
+ 6.0 lb. (2.7 kg) Belgian 2-row pale malt
+ 2 lb. 4 oz. (1.0 kg) white wheat malt
+ 1.0 lb. (450 g) flaked wheat
+ 5.0 lb. (2.3 kg) raspberries
+ 1.0 oz. (28 g) Saaz hops at 3.5% alpha acids, boiled for 60 minutes (13 IBU)
+ 1.0 tsp. Irish moss, boiled for 15 minutes
+ 6.7 oz. (190 g) corn sugar, to prime bottles for 2.9 volumes of CO_2

Brew this beer when raspberries are in season (but you won't need to buy them until the next year). Heat 12 quarts (11 L) of brewing liquor to 163°F (73°C) and mash in grains. Mash at 152°F (67°C) for 60 minutes, stirring every 15 minutes if you can. Heat or add boiling water to mash out to 168°F (76°C). Recirculate wort until clear, and then run off.

Sparge to collect about 6.0 gallons (23 L) of wort. Sparge with water hot enough to raise the grain bed temperature to 176°F (80°C), if you'd like a hint of astringency in the beer. Boil wort for 60 minutes, to reduce wort volume to just over 5.0 gallons (19 L). Add hops at times indicated. Chill wort, then rack to a bucket fermenter.

Aerate wort thoroughly and pitch blend of microorganisms. Ferment initially at 70°F (21°C). After a couple of weeks, let the temperature drift a little higher—up to 78°F (26°C). If you'd like, you could rack the beer to a carboy after three months. Let the beer sour for one year.

When raspberries are at their peak, place them in a nylon steeping bag and put them in a sanitized bucket fermenter. Crush berries lightly with a potato masher (or similar device). Rack lambic into berries. Let beer infuse fruit for at least three months. Keg or bottle and carbonate to 2.9 volumes of CO_2. (You can bottle this in heavier bottles and carbonate more highly, if you'd like.)

(continued)

RECIPE OPTIONS AND NOTES

This recipe uses more raspberries than is typically found in commercial examples. For a more authentic degree of fruit character, try adding 1.0–3.0 pounds (0.45–1.4 kg) of raspberries per 5.0-gallon (19-L) batch. At the bottom end of this range, the fruit will be faint.

You can also add cherries to this beer, to make a cherry lambic (or kriek). For a level typical of commercial examples, use 2 pounds 8 ounces (1.1 kg) of cherries per 5.0-gallon (19-L) batch. For a more intense cherry flavor, add up to 10 pounds (4.5 kg). Mash the cherries to split them open before you rack the lambic onto them. You do not need to pit the cherries.

Lambic-style beers take much longer to brew than normal ales or lagers.

MALT EXTRACT OPTION

Add 3 pounds 10 ounces (1.6 kg) of light dried malt extract to the recipe. Reduce amount of Belgian pale malt to 3.0 pounds (1.4 kg). Omit wheat malt and flaked wheat. "Steep" the crushed grains in 4.1 quarts (3.9 L) of water at 152°F (67°C) for 60 minutes. ("Steep" is in quotes because technically this is a partial mash.) Place the grain bag in a colander over your brew pot and rinse the grains with 2.0 quarts (1.9 L) of 170°F (77°C) water. Add roughly one-third of the malt extract to this wort. Add water to bring brew pot volume to 3.0 gallons (11 L). Boil for 60 minutes, adding hops at times indicated. Add the remaining malt extract in the final 15 minutes of the boil.

GILLIGAN'S GUEUZE
GUEUZE

Gueuze is a blended lambic. It is made from three lambics brewed in three consecutive years. Gueuze is typically dry and very sour. It may have a "funky" aroma that includes elements labeled as barnyard or horse blanket. (Some even have a faint baby diaper aroma.) Or it might be cleanly sour.

Gueuzes are well carbonated, but the level of carbonation may decrease with age. Brewing a gueuze is a challenge, mostly because of the time involved, but for sour beer–loving homebrewers, the result will be worth it.

5.0 GALLONS (19 L) AT 5.2% ABV
OG = 1.048–1.052, FG = 1.011 (OR LOWER)
LESS THAN 10 IBU, 4–6 SRM

+ 5.0 gallons (19 L) lambic, aged three years
+ 5.0 gallons (19 L) lambic, aged two years
+ 5.0 gallons (19 L) lambic, aged one year
+ Cane sugar for priming bottles (amount depends on volume of blended beer)

The overall idea is to blend three lambics, aged for different amounts of time, into a gueuze. The three-year-old lambic is likely to be the most dry. The one-year-old lambic is likely to have the most residual carbohydrates, resulting in a higher FG and relatively sweeter taste. The level of "funk" in the three beers may vary substantially. Sample roughly a pint from each batch in a manner that disturbs the beer the least (and especially, lets in the least amount of oxygen).

Make small test blends to determine the ratio of your final blend. Many commercial producers base their blend on the three-year-old lambic, blending in lesser volumes of two-year-old lambic and just enough of the one-year-old lambic to mellow the blend slightly. Once you've decided the ratio of your blend, make the blend and bottle, adding cane sugar for priming.

Using 2.0–2.6 ounces (55–74 g) of corn sugar per gallon will yield around 4–5 volumes of CO_2. Bottle in heavy bottles—such as Champagne bottles—that can take this level of carbonation. Otherwise, use 1.4 ounces (38 g) of sugar per gallon to yield about 3 volumes of CO_2. Bottle in heavy bottles, such as those used for German wheat beers. Unless you have a vessel capable of containing the full volume of the blend, you may have to blend in batches.

(continued)

You can also age lambic-sytle beers in a barrel.

Rack the beer with the least volume contributing to the blend into the bottling bucket first. Rack the most abundant beer last and stir gently, using both side-to-side and up-and-down motions. Stir enough to gently mix the solution, but not so much as to cause splashing or a whirlpool in the bottling bucket. Age the blended beer in bottles for at least a couple of weeks at room temperature or higher—up to 80°F (27°C). Then, let them age at cool temperatures for at least a few months more. Use the remaining lambic to make fruit beers or continue to age for future gueuzes.

PLANNING FOR A GUEUZE

Making a full-on gueuze is a large undertaking. You will not be drinking it for at least 3.5 years after brewing the first component batch. If you enjoy gueuze, you can plan to have a steady "pipeline" of lambic for eventual blending, plus some young lambic each year to drink or make into fruit lambic. Bucket fermenters are cheap. If you have an out-of-the-way place to store multiple buckets of lambic, you can start a small "lambic farm" in a back room.

The key to having a steady supply of lambic is to brew a lambic at least once a year and brew enough that some can be used after souring for one year and the rest can be saved for later. For example, let's say you brewed 10 gallons (38 L) every year, split into two bucket fermenters. After each year, you would use one of the buckets from the previous year's "vintage" for a fruit lambic, and keep the rest for extended aging. After three years, you would have used three buckets of lambics, but have three left over—a one-year-old, two-year-old and a three-year-old.

And if you brewed two buckets worth that year, you could start saving up for another gueuze three years down the line. If you wanted to blend a gueuze every single year, you would need to make at least three buckets of lambic each year—four if your wanted to make a fruit lambic each year.

If you keep a number of aged lambics around, remember to check the airlocks once a month and keep them topped up.

UTILITY LAMBIC
LAMBIC

Lambic is a sour beer fermented with brewer's yeast and soured by lactic acid bacteria. The wild yeast Brettanomyces adds "funk" to the beer. A young (one-year-old) lambic can be enjoyed on its own or used to make a fruit lambic. It can also be used as part of a blended lambic.

5.0 GALLONS (19 L) AT 5.2% ABV
OG = 1.052, FG = 1.011 (OR LOWER)
8.9 IBU, 4.7 SRM

+ Wyeast 3278 (Belgian Lambic Blend) or White Labs WLP655 (Belgian Sour Mix 1) yeast and bacteria blend
+ Do not make a yeast starter
+ 6 lb. 2 oz. (2.8 kg) Belgian 2-row pale malt
+ 2 lb. 8 oz. (1.1 kg) wheat malt (white)
+ 1.0 lb. (450 g) flaked wheat
+ 0.75 oz. (21 g) Strisselspalt hops at 3.2% alpha acids, boiled for 60 minutes (8.9 IBU)
+ 12.8 oz. (362 g) corn sugar, to prime bottles for 5.0 volumes of CO_2

Heat 13 quarts (12 L) of brewing liquor to 163°F (73°C) and mash in grains. Mash at 152°F (67 °C) for 60 minutes, stirring every 15 minutes if you can. Do not mash out. Recirculate wort until clear, and then run off. Sparge to collect about 6.3 gallons (24 L) of wort, using sparge water heated to 194°F (90°C). Boil wort for 60–90 minutes, to reduce wort volume to just over 5.0 gallons (19 L). Add hops for final 60 minutes of the boil. Chill wort, then rack to a bucket fermenter.

Aerate wort thoroughly and pitch yeast and bacteria blend. Ferment initially at 68°F (20°C). After a couple of weeks, allow temperature to climb—as high as 78°F (26°C)—as the beer sours. Let the beer sour for a year. After a few months, you can rack the beer off the yeast and into a glass carboy if you choose. Check on the airlock once a month so it doesn't dry out. Bottle and carbonate to up to 5.0 volumes of CO_2. Use Champagne bottles for highly carbonated lambics. Another option is to carbonate to 3.0 volumes of CO_2 in heavy beer bottles.

(continued)

RECIPE OPTIONS AND NOTES

Real lambics are heavily hopped with aged hops. If you have any hops that are older than a year, and don't smell cheesy, estimate that they have lost half their alpha acids each year, and add hops to reach just under 10 IBU.

Instead of bottling this lambic, you can add fruit and make a fruit lambic. Use 3.0 pounds (1.4 kg) of raspberries for a framboise or 2.5 pounds (1.1 kg) of tart cherries (with pits) for a kriek.

Instead of bottling this lambic, you could leave it in the fermenter and let it age for later use in a gueuze (see page 203).

Barrel aging can add another dimension to aging sour beers.

MALT EXTRACT OPTION

Add 4.0 pounds (1.8 kg) of dried wheat malt extract to the recipe. Reduce the amount of pale malt to 2.0 pounds (910 g). Reduce the amount of wheat malt to 1.0 pound (450 g). Omit the flaked wheat. "Steep" the crushed grains in 4.1 quarts (3.9 L) of water at 152°F (67°C) for 60 minutes. ("Steep" is in quotes because technically this is a partial mash.) Place the grain bag in a colander over your brew pot and rinse the grains with 2.0 quarts (1.9 L) of 170°F (77°C) water. Add roughly one-third of the malt extract to this wort. Add water to bring brew pot volume to 3.0 gallons (11 L). Boil for 60 minutes, adding hops at times indicated. Add the remaining malt extract in the final 15 minutes of the boil.

BEER HALL HEFEWEIZEN
MUNICH-STYLE GERMAN HEFEWEIZEN

This is a recipe for a German Hefeweizen. Hefeweizens are pale, hazy, wheat beers known for their impressive foam and complex, yeast-derived aroma. Two prominent components of the aroma are banana and clove. These are the result of isoamyl acetate and 4-vinyl guaiacol, compounds produced by the special yeast strains used to ferment these types of beers. This recipe produces a Hefeweizen that is balanced, but slightly favors the clove aroma over the banana.

5.0 GALLONS (19 L) AT 5.1% ABV
OG =1.053, FG = 1.013
20 IBU, 5 SRM

+ Wyeast 3068 (Weihenstephan Wheat) or White Labs WLP300 (Hefeweizen) yeast
+ A 1.5-qt. (1.4-L) yeast starter is recommended
+ 7.0 lb. (3.2 kg) red wheat malt
+ 3.0 lb. (1.4 kg) Pilsner malt
+ 1.4 oz. (40 g) Hallertau hopsat 4% alpha acids, boiled for 60 minutes (20 IBU)
+ 11 oz. (300 g) corn sugar, to prime bottles for 3.5 volumes of CO_2

Make your yeast starter two to three days ahead of time. In your kettle (not your mash tun), heat 3.75 gallons (14 L) of water to 120°F (49°C). Stir in the crushed grains, yielding a mash thickness of 1.5 quarts/pound (3.1 L/kg). Your initial mash temperature should be 109°F (43°C), although it is okay if you don't hit this mark exactly. Heat the mash slowly—over about 10 minutes—to 113°F (45°C). Then, heat the mash to 122°F (50°C). Do this more quickly, increasing the temperature by about two degrees per minute. Rest at 122°F (50°C) for 20 minutes.

Begin the decoction mash by pulling a thick decoction from the main mash, roughly one-quarter of the total volume. Heat the decoction to 162°F (72°C) in a separate brew pot. Hold this for 5 minutes, and then boil the decoction until the 20-minute rest in the main mash is done. (Stir the decoction constantly.) Stir the decoction back into the main mash, which should yield a temperature of 153°F (67°C). Rest at 153°F (67°C) for 45 minutes. Then heat the full mash to 162°F (72°C) at a rate of about two degrees per minute. Hold at 162°F (72°C) for 5 minutes, then transfer the mash to your lauter tun, adding boiling water to raise temperature to 168°F (176°C). You will need about 1.0 gallon (3.84 L) of boiling water for this. Let mash settle for about 5 minutes, then recirculate the wort for 20 minutes.

(continued)

Run off wort, sparging with hot water to collect about 6.5 gallons (25 L) of wort. Boil the wort vigorously for 90 minutes. Add the hops with 60 minutes remaining in the boil. Chill wort, transfer to a bucket fermenter and aerate thoroughly. Pitch the yeast sediment from your yeast starter. Ferment at 68°F (20°C). Once fermentation starts, remove the bucket lid. (Take the fermentation lock off first so you don't suck airlock liquid into the beer.) Replace airlock and leave bucket lid on loosely for the next two to three days. Once the fermentation slows, and before the kräusen falls back into the beer, seal the bucket again and leave it sealed for the remainder of the fermentation.

Keg or add priming sugar and bottle. Bottle in heavy bottles, such as 500 ml Hefeweizen bottles. (You'll need about 40.) Siphon the beer into the dissolved sugar in your bottling bucket and stir well enough to even out the distribution of sugar. However, don't stir so hard as to splash or otherwise aerate the beer. Keep the bottles somewhere warm—optimally 70–75°F (21–24°C)—for a couple of weeks while carbonation develops. Move to cold storage when a test bottle indicates the beer is carbonated. As an option, you can add a teaspoon of dried lager yeast to your bottling bucket to help with bottle conditioning.

MALT EXTRACT OPTION

To produce your wort, replace the malts in the all-grain recipe with 1.40 pounds (0.63 kg) of red wheat malt, 0.60 pound (0.27 kg) of Pilsner malt and 5.75 pounds (2.6 kg) of liquid wheat malt extract. (Most wheat malt extracts are made from a 50:50 blend of wheat malt and barley malt and that is what you want.) In your brew pot, steep the malts in 2.8 quarts (2.6 L) of water at 113°F (45°C) for 10 minutes. Heat the steeping grains to 153°F (67°C) and hold for 45 minutes. Remove the grains and add water to your brew pot to make 3.0 gallons (11 L) and bring to a boil. Boil for 60 minutes, adding hops at the beginning of the boil. Stir in malt extract in the final 15 minutes of the boil. Chill wort, transfer to fermenter and top up with cool water to 5.0 gallons (19 L). Follow the instructions for fermentation in the all-grain recipe.

CLOVE AROMA AND THE FERULIC ACID REST

German wheat beers are brewed with special strains of yeast. The interesting aroma of a hefeweizen comes from the variety of yeast by-products these strains produce. The most important of these is 4-vinyl-guaiacol, or 4VG. This molecule imparts a clove-like aroma to the beer. In wheat beer yeast strains, the immediate precursor to 4VG is ferulic acid. If a mash contains a rest around 109–113°F (43–45°C), a comparatively large amount of ferulic acid is extracted from the grain.

Ferulic acid is present in both barley and wheat malt. It's normally bound to molecules called pentosans, and the ferulic acid rest favors a reaction that detaches the molecules. Free ferulic acid in the wort can later be converted to 4VG during fermentation. So, if you add a ferulic acid rest to your mash program, you've primed your wort to produce more of the clove-like aroma when fermented.

In any step or decoction mash, the ferulic acid rest—at 109–113°F (43–45°C)—is likely to be your first. You only need to hold the rest for about 10 minutes before proceeding with your mash program. Some hefeweizen recipes skip the ferulic acid rest altogether. It augments the levels of ferulic acid in your wort, but some ferulic acid would be present simply from taking a wheat beer grist and performing a single infusion mash.

It is interesting to note that the presence of 4VG is unwanted in most other beer styles. In fact, it has been bred out of "normal" brewer's yeast strains. In contrast, most wild yeast strains do produce 4VG.

BROTHERS GROSSBART ROGUE ROGGEN
ROGGENBIER

Roggenbier is similar to a dunkelweizen (dark German wheat beer, see page 214), but made with rye instead of wheat. They are brewed with the same specialized yeast strains as German wheat beers, so they share the same banana and clove aroma with those beers. Some crystal-type malt and a small amount of roasted malt gives them their dark amber color.

5.0 GALLONS (19 L) AT 5.1% ABV
OG = 1.053, FG = 1.013
17 IBU, 16 SRM

+ Wyeast 3068 (Weihenstephan Wheat) or White Labs WLP300 (Hefeweizen) yeast; A 1.4-qt. (1.3-L) yeast starter is recommended

+ 1 lb. 7 oz. (650 g) Vienna malt

+ 2 lb. 6 oz. (1.1 kg) Munich malt

+ 5 lb. 11 oz. (2.6 kg) rye malt

+ 8.0 oz. (230 g) CaraMunich malt (60°L)

+ 2.0 oz. (57 g) Carafa III Special malt (dehusked)

+ 1.0 oz. (28 g) Tettnanger hops at 4.5% alpha acids, boiled for 60 minutes (17 IBU)

+ 11 oz. (300 g) corn sugar, to prime bottles for 3.5 volumes of CO_2

Make your yeast starter two to three days ahead of time. In your kettle (not your mash tun), heat 3.75 gallons (14 L) of water to 120°F (49°C). Stir in the crushed grains, yielding a mash thickness of 1.5 quarts/pound (3.1 L/kg). Your initial mash temperature should be 109°F (43°C), although it is okay if you don't hit this mark exactly. Heat the mash slowly—over about 10 minutes—to 113°F (45°C). Then, heat the mash to 122°F (50°C). Do this more quickly, increasing the temperature by about two degrees per minute. Rest at 122°F (50°C) for 20 minutes.

Begin the decoction mash by pulling a thick decoction from the main mash, roughly one-quarter of the total volume. Heat the decoction to 162°F (72°C) in a separate brew pot. Hold this for 5 minutes, and then boil the decoction until the 20-minute rest in the main mash is done. (Stir the decoction constantly.) Stir the decoction back into the main mash, which should yield a temperature of 153°F (67°C). Rest at 153°F (67°C) for 45 minutes. Then heat the full mash to 162°F (72°C) at a rate of about two degrees per minute. Hold at 162°F (72°C) for 5 minutes, then transfer the mash to your lauter tun, adding boiling water to raise temperature to 168°F (176°C). You will need about 1.0 gallon (3.8 L) of boiling water for this. Let mash settle for about 5 minutes, then recirculate the wort for 20 minutes.

Run off wort, sparging with hot water to collect about 6.5 gallons (25 L) of wort. Boil the wort vigorously for 90 minutes. Add the hops with 60 minutes remaining in the boil. Chill wort, transfer to a bucket fermenter and aerate thoroughly. Pitch the yeast sediment from your yeast starter. Ferment at 68°F (20°C). Once fermentation starts, remove the bucket lid. (Take the fermentation lock off first so you don't suck airlock liquid into the beer.) Replace airlock and leave bucket lid on loosely for the next two to three days. Once the fermentation slows, and before the kräusen falls back into the beer, seal the bucket again and leave it sealed for the remainder of the fermentation.

Keg or add priming sugar and bottle. Bottle in heavy bottles, such as 500 ml hefeweizen bottles. (You'll need about 40.) Siphon the beer into the dissolved sugar in your bottling bucket and stir well enough to even out the distribution of sugar. However, don't stir so hard as to splash or otherwise aerate the beer. Keep the bottles somewhere warm—optimally 70–75°F (21–24°C)—for a couple of weeks while carbonation develops. Move to cold storage when a test bottle indicates the beer is fermented. As an option, you can add a teaspoon of dried lager yeast to your bottling bucket to help with bottle conditioning.

MALT EXTRACT OPTION

Add 5 pounds 4 ounces (2.4 kg) of liquid rye malt extract to the recipe. Omit the rye malt. Lower the amount of Munich malt to 1 pound 10 ounces (740 g). Lower the amount of Vienna malt to 13 ounces (370 g). In your brew pot, steep the 3.0 pounds (1.4 kg) total of crushed grains in 4.1 quarts (3.9 L) of water at 152°F (67°C) for 60 minutes. (This is really a mash, so follow the temperature and volume guidelines closely.) After steeping, place the grain bag in a large colander over your brew pot. Rinse the grains slowly with 2.0 quarts (1.9 L) of 170°F (77°C) water. Add roughly a third of the malt extract to the wort collected and adjust the wort volume with water to make 3.0 gallons (11 L) of wort. Boil for 60 minutes, adding hops at times indicated. Add remaining malt extract in the final 10 minutes of the boil.

LAUTERING WITH STICKY GRAINS

Rye has the reputation of being a "sticky" grain that is hard to lauter. It contains more beta glucans ("gums") than barley, and even more than wheat. When lautering a rye beer, several things can help you avoid a stuck mash. Most important, take it slow. If you are continuously sparging, collect the wort at a slow, steady rate. Aim to collect the entire wort over 60–90 minutes, and watch for the flow of wort suddenly slowing. When this happens, dial back even further on your collection speed and you should be able to recover.

Do not skip the mash out. The hotter the wort is, the less viscous it is, and the easier it is to lauter. Likewise, keep the sparge water hot enough to maintain the grain bed temperature at 168°F (76°C). Adding rice hulls to the mash can also make the grain bed more porous. Try adding 1.0–2.0 pounds (450–910 g) to the mash of a 5.0-gallon (19-L) batch.

There are enzymes that commercial brewers use to break down glucans, but these generally aren't available in a size that a homebrewer would use.

FLANDERS!
FLANDERS RED

Flanders red is a tart beer with a complex malt profile. This beer often has a wine-like astringency from being aged in wood. In this recipe, that is partly simulated by adding oak cubes. The hardest thing about making this beer is waiting for it to sour—this can take up to two years.

5.0 GALLONS (19 L) AT 5.3% ABV
OG = 1.053, FG = 1.012 (OR LOWER)
13 IBU, 10 SRM

+ Wyeast 3763 (Roeselare Ale Blend) or White Labs WLP655 (Belgian Sour Mix 1) yeast and bacteria blend
+ Do not make a yeast starter
+ 6 lb. 8 oz. (3.8 kg) Vienna malt
+ 2.0 lb. (910 g) Pilsner malt
+ 1.0 lb. (450 g) Munich malt (10°L)
+ 8.0 oz. (230 g) Munich malt (20°L)
+ 8.0 oz. (230 g) aromatic malt (23°L)
+ 3.0 oz. (85 g) crystal malt (120°L)
+ 0.75 oz. (21 g) Spalt Spalter hops at 4.5% alpha acids, boiled for 60 minutes (13 IBU)
+ 1.0 tsp. Irish moss, boiled for 15 minutes
+ 2.0 oz. (57 g) oak cubes (medium toast)
+ 7.0 oz. (200 g) corn sugar, to prime bottles for 3.0 volumes of CO_2

Heat 14 quarts (13 L) of brewing liquor to 163°F (73°C) and mash in grains. Mash at 152°F (67°C) for 60 minutes, stirring every 15 minutes if you can. Heat or add boiling water to mash out to 168°F (76°C). Recirculate wort until clear, and then run off. Sparge to collect about 7.0 gallons (26 L) of wort. If you'd like, you can sparge with water hot enough to raise the grain bed temperature to 176°F (80°C); this will extract more tannins than usual and give the beer a bit of a wine-like mouthfeel.

Boil wort for 90–120 minutes, to reduce volume to just over 5.0 gallons (19 L), adding hops and Irish moss at times indicated. Chill wort, then rack to bucket fermenter. Aerate wort thoroughly and pitch yeast starter and bacteria blend. Add oak cubes to fermenter. Ferment starting at 72°F (22°C), but let temperature drift up to 80°F (27°C) after the first week.

Let the beer sour for at least a year, or better yet a year and a half. You can choose to let the beer sit on the yeast for all or part of this time. I would recommend letting the beer sit on the yeast for six months, then decide whether to rack to a secondary fermenter. Check the airlock routinely and replace water, if needed. After fermentation stops, keg or add priming sugar and bottle and carbonate to 3.0 volumes of CO_2.

MALT EXTRACT OPTION

This option will produce a very similar beer. Add 5 pounds 2 ounces (2.3 kg) of liquid Munich malt extract to the recipe. Reduce the amount of Vienna malt to 1 pound 13 ounces (820 g). Omit Pilsner malt and Munich malt (10°L). "Steep" the crushed grains in 4.1 quarts (3.9 L) of water at 152°F (67°C) for 60 minutes. ("Steep" is in quotes because technically this is a partial mash.)

Place the grain bag in a colander over your brew pot and rinse the grains with 2.0 quarts (1.9 L) of 170°F (77°C) water. Add roughly one-third of the malt extract to this wort. Add water to bring brew pot volume to 3.0 gallons (11 L). Boil for 60 minutes, adding hops and Irish moss at times indicated. Add the remaining malt extract in the final 15 minutes of the boil.

SOUR FERMENTATIONS IN A BUCKET

Most Belgian sour beers are aged in barrels. The barrels "breathe" slightly, through the grain of the wood, letting in tiny amounts of air over the course of their souring. It is hard to replicate this at home, but you do not need to. Many homebrewers age their sour beers in buckets. The plastic in buckets actually "breathe" more than wooden barrels do. As such, some homebrewers will start the fermentation in a bucket and rack the beer to a glass carboy after several months. Others will simply leave the beer in the bucket. (I have successfully aged lambic three years in a bucket this way.) Still others will age the beer in the bucket until the pellicle falls into the beer, then rack to a glass carboy. There is no right or wrong way to age sour beers at home. Use the equipment you have and the method that appeals to you the most.

A Flanders red is sometimes sparged with hotter-than-usual sparge water.

DUNKLEOSTEUS DUNKELWEIZEN
DUNKELWEIZEN (DUNKLES WEISSBIER)

Dunkleweizen translates to dark wheat beer. Dunkelweizens are similar to hefeweizens, but with added color and malt character. The banana-clove character of a hefeweizen is present as they are fermented with the same types of yeast as hefeweizens are. The yeast strain, starter size and fermentation temperature recommended here are meant to produce a wheat beer with a slight balance towards the banana. For this reason, the ferulic acid rest (see page 208) is skipped.

5.0 GALLONS (19 L) AT 5.2% ABV
OG = 1.054, FG = 1.014
17 IBU, 14 SRM

+ Wyeast 3333 (German Wheat Yeast) White Labs WLP380 (Hefeweizen IV Ale) or Fermentis Safbrew WB-06 yeast
+ A 1.4-qt. (1.3-L) yeast starter is recommended
+ 6.0 lb. (2.7 kg) wheat malt
+ 2.0 lb. (910 g) Pilsner malt
+ 1 lb. 12 oz. (790 g) Munich malt (8°L)
+ 5.0 oz. (140 g) crystal malt (60°L)
+ 3.0 oz. (85 g) Carafa Special II malt (410°L)
+ 1.0 oz. (28 g) Tettnanger hops at 4.5% alpha acids, boiled for 60 minutes (17 IBU)
+ 11 oz. (300 g) corn sugar, to prime bottles for 3.5 volumes of CO_2

If you are using one of the liquid yeasts, make your yeast starter two to three days ahead of time. Heat 13 quarts (12 L) of brewing liquor to 163°F (73°C) and mash in grains. Mash at 152°F (67°C) for 60 minutes, stirring every 15 minutes if you can. Heat or add boiling water to mash out to 168°F (76°C). Recirculate wort until clear, and then run off. Sparge to collect about 6.7 gallons (25 L) of wort.

Boil wort for 60–90 minutes, to reduce the volume to just over 5.0 gallons (19 L), adding hops at times indicated. Chill wort, then rack to fermenter. Aerate wort thoroughly and pitch sediment from yeast starter. Ferment at 68°F (20°C). After fermentation stops, keg or bottle and carbonate to 3.5 volumes of CO_2. Bottle the beer in heavy bottles.

Wheat malt is huskless and can cause lautering problems at high percentages.

RECIPE OPTIONS AND NOTES

Some dunkelweizens are colored in whole or part by a malt color extract, such as Weyermann's SINAMAR. SINAMAR is an intensely colored (~3100°L) beer used for color adjustment. In this dunkelweizen, you could replace the 3.0 ounces (85 g) of Carafa Special II malt (410°L) with 0.025 fluid ounces (0.71 ml) of SINAMAR to reach the same color.

MALT EXTRACT OPTION

Add 4 pounds 4 ounces (1.9 kg) of dried wheat malt extract to the recipe. Reduce the amount of wheat malt to 1.5 pounds (680 g). Reduce the amount of Pilsner malt to 8.0 ounces (230 g). Reduce the amount of Munich malt to 8.0 ounces (230 g). "Steep" the crushed grains in 4.1 quarts (3.9 L) of water at 152°F (67°C) for 60 minutes. ("Steep" is in quotes because technically this is a partial mash.)

Place the grain bag in a colander over your brew pot and rinse the grains with 2.0 quarts (1.9 L) of 170°F (77°C) water. Add roughly one-third of the malt extract to this wort. Add water to bring brew pot volume to 3.0 gallons (11 L). Boil for 60 minutes, adding hops and Irish moss at times indicated. Add the remaining malt extract in the final 15 minutes of the boil.

GOLDSCHMIDT'S HOPEFUL MONSTER
BRETTANOMYCES BEER

This is an experimental beer fermented with *Brettanomyces* instead of *Saccharomyces* yeast. The wort composition is based on a farmhouse ale, but the *Brettanomyces* species chosen will produce a fruity ale, with pear-like notes. *Brettanomyces* is one of the organisms usually involved in a lambic fermentation. For this reason, many homebrewers assume a "Brett" beer will be sour. In reality, this yeast does not produce much acid and does not make a sour beer.

Fermentations using only *Brettanomyces* can be finicky, so monitor yours closely. If the fermentation seems to suddenly falter, let the temperature rise to (hopefully) get the yeast back in the game. Also, do not skip making the yeast starter—the higher your pitching rate, the greater the chance of an ordered fermentation.

5.0 GALLONS (19 L) AT 5.9% ABV
OG = 1.058, FG = 1.013 (OR LOWER)
21 IBU, 5.1 SRM

+ White Labs WLP648 (Brettanomyces Bruxellensis Troi Vrai)
+ A 4.0-qt. (3.8-L) yeast starter is recommended
+ 7 lb. 4 oz. (3.3 kg) Pilsner malt
+ 1 lb. 8 oz. (680 g) Munich malt (10°L)
+ 1.0 lb. (450 g) CaraPils malt (1.5°L)
+ 12 oz. (340 g) wheat malt
+ 12 oz. (340 g) flaked oats
+ 1.0 oz. (28 g) Cascade hops at 5.5% alpha acids, boiled for 60 minutes (21 IBU)
+ 0.33 oz. (9.4 g) Cascade hops at 5.5% alpha acids, boiled for 0 minutes (0 IBU)
+ 1.0 tsp. Irish moss, boiled for 15 minutes
+ 5.3 oz. (150 g) corn sugar, to prime bottles for 2.5 volumes of CO_2

Make your yeast starter two to three days ahead of time. Heat 13 quarts (12 L) of brewing liquor to 163°F (73°C) and mash in malts and oats. Mash at 152°F (67°C) for 60 minutes, stirring every 15 minutes if you can. Heat or add boiling water to mash out to 168°F (76°C). Recirculate wort until clear, and then run off. Sparge to collect about 6.6 gallons (25 L) of wort. Boil wort for 60–90 minutes, to reduce volume to just over 5.0 gallons (19 L), adding hops and Irish moss at times indicated.

Chill wort, then rack to fermenter. Aerate wort thoroughly and pitch sediment from yeast starter. Ferment initially at 72°F (22°C). If the fermentation seems to falter, let the temperature rise a bit—up to 80°F (27°C). After fermentation stops, let the beer sit at 68–72°F (20–22°C) from two weeks to two months. (This increases the odds that the yeast has finished working and gives the beer a little time to condition.) Then, keg or bottle and carbonate to 2.5 volumes of CO_2.

MALT EXTRACT OPTION

Add 4 pounds 4 ounces (1.9 kg) of light dried malt extract to the recipe. Omit the Pilsner malt. "Steep" the crushed grains and flaked oats in 4.1 quarts (3.9 L) of water at 152°F (67°C) for 60 minutes. ("Steep" is in quotes because technically this is a partial mash.) Place the grain bag in a colander over your brew pot and rinse the grains with 2.0 quarts (1.9 L) of 170°F (77°C) water. Add roughly one-third of the malt extract to this wort. Add water to bring brew pot volume to 3.0 gallons (11 L). Boil for 60 minutes, adding hops and Irish moss at times indicated. Add the remaining malt extract in the final 15 minutes of the boil.

BRETTANOMYCES

Brettanomyces is a genus of fungi with many species that contaminate brewery fermentations. It was first isolated from British beer aged in wooden barrels and the Latin genus name it was given means British brewing fungus. Today, brewers are starting to purposely inoculate beer with "Brett," either along with *Saccharomyces* (brewer's yeast) or by itself to make some experimental beers.

Brettanomyces is best known as one of the organisms usually present in a lambic fermentation. In lambics, in which only a small population of Brett cells is introduced to the beer, it can lend a number of characteristics—from fruity esters, to spicy phenolics, to "horse blanket." It is a big component of the "funk" of a lambic. When a large amount of Brett is pitched, however, the yeast produces a much cleaner fermentation profile, often with interesting fruity esters. Comparatively little is known about using *Brettanomyces* as a primary brewing strain, but many craft brewers and homebrewers are experimenting with this British brewing fungus.

80 ACRES SAISON

SAISON

Saisons are farmhouse ales, usually fermented with characterful ale strains that are sometimes difficult to work with. They are usually fairly strong beers that are meant to stay in good shape for a fair amount of time. This recipe blends Vienna malt with some wheat and unmalted oats for an orange-golden, lightly hazy beer. An addition of sugar in the kettle adds strength to the beer without raising the final gravity.

5.0 GALLONS (19 L) AT 7.1% ABV
OG = 1.065, FG = 1.010
34 IBU, 6.1 SRM

+ Wyeast 3724 (Belgian Saison), White Labs WLP565 (Belgian Saison I) or Fermentis Safbrew T-58 yeast
+ A 3.2-qt. (3.0-L) yeast starter is recommended
+ 8 lb. 4 oz. (3.7 kg) Vienna malt
+ 2.0 lb. (910 g) wheat malt
+ 8.0 oz. (230 g) flaked oats
+ 1 lb. 4 oz. (570 g) cane sugar
+ 1.25 oz. (35 g) Styrian Goldings hops at 6% alpha acids, boiled for 60 minutes (28 IBU)
+ 0.75 oz. (21 g) Styrian Goldings hops at 6% alpha acids, boiled for 5 minutes (3.4 IBU)
+ 0.75 oz. (21 g) East Kent Goldings hops at 5% alpha acids, boiled for 5 minutes (2.8 IBU)
+ 1.0 tsp. Irish moss, boiled for 15 minutes
+ 5.3 oz. (150 g) corn sugar, to prime bottles for 2.5 volumes of CO_2

If you are using one of the liquid yeasts, make your yeast starter two to three days ahead of time. Heat 14 quarts (13 L) of brewing liquor to 163°F (73°C) and mash in malts and oats. Mash at 152°F (66°C) for 60 minutes, stirring every 15 minutes if you can. Heat or add boiling water to mash out to 168°F (76°C). Recirculate wort until clear, and then run off. Sparge to collect about collect 7.0 gallons (26 L) of wort. Boil wort for 90–120 minutes, to reduce volume to just over 5.0 gallons (19 L), adding hops and Irish moss at times indicated.

Add sugar in final 10 minutes of the boil. Chill wort, then rack to fermenter. Aerate wort thoroughly and pitch sediment from yeast starter, and then ferment starting at 80°F (27°C). A couple of days after high kräusen, let the temperature start creeping up by roughly 2°F (1°C), if it can on its own. It can go as high as 95°F (35°C), but doesn't need to. If the fermentation sticks—and it's prone to with this yeast—swirl the fermenter to rouse the yeast and raise the temperature 2–4°F (1–2°C). You can also add a dried neutral ale yeast to finish the fermentation if it is progressing too slowly. After fermentation stops, let the beer condition—at around 70°F (21°C)—for about two weeks. Then, keg or add priming sugar and bottle and carbonate to 2.5 volumes of CO_2.

MALT EXTRACT OPTION

Unless you can find Vienna malt extract, there's no way to reproduce the all-grain wort. However, this adaptation will come close. Add 2 pounds 4 ounces (1.0 kg) of light dried malt extract to the recipe. Add 2 pounds 12 ounces (1.3 kg) of liquid Munich malt extract to the recipe. Omit the Vienna malt.

"Steep" the crushed grains in 4.1 quarts (3.9 L) of water at 152°F (67°C) for 60 minutes. ("Steep" is in quotes because technically this is a partial mash.) Place the grain bag in a colander over your brew pot and rinse the grains with 2.0 quarts (1.9 L) of 170°F (77°C) water. Add roughly one-third of the malt extract to this wort. Add water to bring brew pot volume to 3.0 gallons (11 L). Boil for 60 minutes, adding hops and Irish moss at times indicated. Add the remaining malt extract in the final 15 minutes of the boil. Add sugar in the final 10 minutes of the boil.

HIGH-TEMPERATURE YEAST STRAINS

Most ales are fermented in the 68–72°F (20–21°C) range, with some strains working well down to around 60°F (16°C). There are two primary reasons for this. When many strains are used over 72°F (21°C), they produce a level of esters that are unappealing in beer. In addition, over a certain temperature—that varies by strain—high-temperature fermentations lead to the production of higher alcohols. These higher alcohols, sometimes called fusel oils, lend a solvent-like flavor to beer and can cause headaches if too much are consumed.

However, there are a minority of yeast strains that can ferment well above 72°F (21°C), and it can be handy for brewers in warm climates to be familiar with them.

Most of the German wheat beer strains available to homebrewers can be fermented at up to 75°F (24°C). In these yeasts, warmer temperatures correspond to more banana esters in the beer, but the brewer can lower them by increasing the pitching rate. Many Belgian ale strains will work at elevated temperatures. Several will work up to 80°F (27°C) and one—the strain used in this beer—is listed for up to 95°F (35°C)!

Finally, although the yeast manufacturers do not mention it, Wyeast 1056 (American Ale), White Labs WLP001 (California Ale) and Fermentis Safale U.S.-05—all putatively isolates of the "Chico" strain—ferment well at up to 80°F (27°C), assuming an adequate amount is pitched.

If you live where it's warm, summertime does not need to include a vacation from brewing. Try making a saison or other Belgian-style beer.

8

BEERS MADE WITH SPECIAL INGREDIENTS: INTERESTING AND EXPERIMENTAL FLAVORED BREWS

The section gives the recipes for 21 beers brewed with ingredients other than malt, other grains, hops, yeast and water. These include spiced beers, fruit beers, vegetable beers and others—there's even a bacon beer! They range from an OG 1.038 (3.8 percent ABV) coffee stout to an OG 1.110 (12 percent ABV) imperial braggot—with chocolate beers, a honey wheat beer and others in between.

There is more than one way a special ingredient can be used. For starters, it can be mashed, boiled or added in the fermenter. How you handle the ingredient affects the intensity and character of its flavor and the aroma in your beer. In many cases, there are multiple ways the added ingredient could be used. For best results, follow the instructions to get the best presentation of the ingredient.

For most of these beers, the added flavor or aroma is meant to blend with the characteristics of the beer, not overshadow them. The spruce beer, for example, is meant to taste like beer with a hint of spruce. In a few cases, the unusual flavor is the dominant flavor. For most of these recipes, I explain how much of the special ingredient to add or subtract if you want to tone down the flavor or take it up a notch.

Remember that other ingredients will vary in how potent or flavorful they are. Use only fresh spices, ripe fruit, etc., when brewing these. A flavored beer is not the place to get rid of ingredients that are beyond their prime. (You can use fruit with bad spots if you take a knife and excise the bruised, rotting or otherwise questionable areas.) Conversely, attempting to save a failed beer by adding something in the fermenter is just throwing good ingredients after bad.

For beers in which the special ingredient is added in secondary, you can split the batch—less than 5.0 gallons (19 L) of flavored beer while retaining some of the base beer. Just scale the added ingredient proportionally. This gives you some diversity and, in the case of expensive ingredients, will save you a little money. In some cases, the base beer has been modified so it will blend with the special ingredient.

For example, the roast malt character in the coffee stout is dialed down a notch as it is expected to gain some roast character when blended with coffee. Also, in most cases, late hopping is minimal so the special ingredient is prominently featured in the aroma of the beer. If you intend to split the batch, review the recipe of the base beer and consider if you want to make some changes.

CUP OF JOE STOUT
COFFEE STOUT

This is a dry stout blended with coffee. It's a coffee stout for coffee lovers, not for people who think coffee is too bitter. Before brewing this beer, try blending a commercial stout (such as Guinness) with coffee to see if you like the 1:4 blend, or if there is another ratio you prefer.

5.0 GALLONS (19 L) AT 3.8% ABV
OG = 1.038, FG = 1.008
32 IBU, 30+ SRM

+ Wyeast 1056 (American Ale) or White Labs WLP001 (California Ale) yeast
+ A 1.1-qt. (1.0-L) yeast starter is recommended
+ 6.0 lb. (2.7 kg) U.S. 2-row pale malt
+ 1.0 lb. (450 g) flaked barley
+ 12 oz. (340 g) roasted barley (500°L)
+ 1.0 oz. (28 g) Northdown hops at 8.5% alpha acids, boiled for 60 minutes (32 IBU)
+ 0.75 tsp. Irish moss, boiled for 15 minutes
+ 8.0 oz. (230 g) coffee beans (roasted)
+ 5.0 oz. (140 g) corn sugar, to prime bottles for 2.5 volumes of CO_2

Make your yeast starter two to three days ahead of time. Heat 10 quarts (9.0 L) of brewing liquor to 161°F (72°C) and mash in grains. Mash at 150°F (66°C) for 60 minutes, stirring every 15 minutes if you can. Heat or add boiling water to mash out to 168°F (76°C). Recirculate wort until clear, and then run off. Sparge to collect about 5.0 gallons (19 L) of wort. Boil wort for 60 minutes to reduce volume to just over 4.0 gallons (15 L), adding hops and Irish moss at times indicated. Chill wort, which should be at about SG 1.047, then rack to fermenter.

Aerate wort thoroughly and pitch sediment from yeast starter. Ferment at 68°F (20°C). After fermentation stops, brew 1.0 gallon (3.8 L) of coffee from the coffee beans. (You can do this in increments, if needed.) Cool coffee and add to secondary fermenter. Rack stout into coffee, making 5.0 gallons (19 L). Let the beer condition for three days, then keg or add priming sugar and bottle and carbonate to 2.5 volumes of CO_2.

(continued)

A dark wort comes to a boil.

MALT EXTRACT OPTION

Add 2 pounds 11 ounces (1.2 kg) of light dried malt extract to the recipe. Reduce the amount of 2-row pale malt to 1 pound 6 ounces (620 g). "Steep" the crushed grains in 4.1 quarts (3.9 L) of water at 150°F (66°C) for 60 minutes. ("Steep" is in quotes because technically this is a partial mash.) Place the grain bag in a colander over your brew pot and rinse the grains with 2.0 quarts (1.9 L) of 170°F (77°C) water.

Add roughly one-half of the malt extract to this wort. Add water to bring brew pot volume to 3.0 gallons (11 L). Boil for 60 minutes, adding hops and Irish moss at times indicated. Add the remaining malt extract in the final 15 minutes of the boil. Chill wort and transfer to fermenter. Add water to make 4.0 gallons (15 L) and pitch yeast.

CLIFFORD'S BROWN
COCOA BROWN ALE

This is a lightly sweet brown ale with a touch of real chocolate. The real chocolate mingles with the caramel flavor from the crystal malts and roast flavor from the chocolate malt to make a flavorful, yet fairly low-gravity, brew. Lactose sweetens the brew, to enhance the chocolate flavor.

5.0 GALLONS (19 L) AT 3.9% ABV
OG = 1.043, FG = 1.013
21 IBU, 18 SRM

+ Wyeast 1968 (London ESB) or White Labs WLP002 (English Ale) yeast
+ A 1.1-qt. (1.0-L) yeast starter is recommended
+ 7.0 lb. (3.2 kg) U.K. 2-row pale ale malt
+ 12 oz. (340 g) crystal malt (30°L)
+ 6.0 oz. (170 g) crystal malt (40°L)
+ 6.0 oz. (170 g) UK chocolate malt (400°L)
+ 6.0 oz. (170 g) cocoa powder (unsweetened)
+ 5.0 oz. (140 g) lactose
+ 1.25 oz. (35 g) East Kent Goldings hops at 5% alpha acids, boiled for 60 minutes (21 IBU)
+ 1.0 tsp. Irish moss, boiled for 15 minutes
+ 5.0 oz. (140 g) corn sugar, to prime bottles for 2.5 volumes of CO_2

Make your yeast starter two to three days ahead of time. Heat 11 quarts (10 L) of brewing liquor to 163°F (73°C) and mash in grains. Mash at 152°F (67°C) for 60 minutes, stirring every 15 minutes if you can. Heat or add boiling water to mash out to 168°F (76°C). Recirculate wort until clear, and then run off. Sparge to collect about 5.5 gallons (21 L) of wort.

Add 0.50 gallons (1.9 L) of water to wort. Boil wort for 60 minutes, to reduce volume to just over 5.0 gallons (19 L), adding hops and Irish moss at times indicated. Add lactose with 10 minutes left in the boil. Add cocoa for the final 2 minutes of the boil. Chill wort, then rack to fermenter. Aerate wort thoroughly and pitch sediment from yeast starter. Ferment at 68°F (20°C). After fermentation stops, keg or add priming sugar and bottle and carbonate to 2.5 volumes of CO_2.

Baking soda can be used to raise the pH of a dark mash.

RECIPE OPTIONS AND NOTES

Add one or two vanilla beans, sliced down the center, to a secondary fermenter. Rack the brown ale onto beans. Let infuse for seven to 10 days, and then package the beer.

MALT EXTRACT OPTION

Add 3 pounds 4 ounces (1.5 kg) of light dried malt extract to the recipe. Reduce the amount of 2-row pale ale malt to 1 pound 8 ounces (680 g). "Steep" the crushed grains in 4.1 quarts (3.9 L) of water at 152°F (67°C) for 60 minutes. ("Steep" is in quotes because technically this is a partial mash.) Place the grain bag in a colander over your brew pot and rinse the grains with 2.0 quarts (1.9 L) of 170°F (77°C) water. Add roughly one-third of the malt extract to this wort. Add water to bring brew pot volume to 3.0 gallons (11 L). Boil for 60 minutes, adding hops and Irish moss at times indicated. Add the remaining malt extract in the final 15 minutes of the boil. Add lactose in the final 10 minutes of boil. Add cocoa for the final 2 minutes of the boil.

RECIPE OPTIONS AND NOTES

Mountain Dew looks green, but it's an orange-flavored soda. You can brew this beer with other orange sodas, or with any other soda you think would work.

BEELZEBOSS
SODA POP SAISON

This is loosely a saison, brewed using the soda pop Mountain Dew as part of the brewing liquor. It makes a dry, fizzy ale with an unusual color. Like most sodas, Mountain Dew has a specific gravity around 1.046, and the high-fructose corn syrup used to make it is 100 percent fermentable. Mountain Dew does contain preservatives, but not at levels that will disrupt an active beer fermentation.

5.0 GALLONS (19 L) AT 5.2% ABV
OG = 1.045, FG = 1.004
21 IBU, 2.2 SRM

+ Fermentis Safbrew T-58 dried yeast
+ Fermentis Safale U.S.-05 dried yeast
+ 1.0 lb. (450 g) 2-row pale malt
+ 1.0 lb. (450 g) Vienna malt
+ 10 oz. (280 g) wheat malt
+ 6.0 oz. (170 g) flaked wheat
+ 6.0 oz. (170 g) flaked oats
+ 3.0 gallons (11 L) Mountain Dew soda
+ 1.25 oz. (35 g) Tettnanger hops at 4.5% alpha acids, boiled for 60 minutes (21 IBU)
+ 0.50 tsp. Irish moss, boiled for 15 minutes
+ 5.50 oz. (155 g) corn sugar, to prime bottles for 2.7 volumes of CO_2

Heat 4.2 quarts (4.0 L) of brewing liquor to 163°F (73°C) and mash in grains. Mash at 152°F (67°C) for 60 minutes, stirring every 15 minutes if you can. Heat or add boiling water to mash out to 168°F (76°C). Recirculate wort until clear, and then run off. Sparge to collect about 2.1 gallons (8.3 L) of wort.

Add water to make 3.0 gallons (11 L) of wort. Boil wort for 60 minutes, to reduce volume to 2.0 gallons (7.5 L), adding hops and Irish moss at times indicated. Chill wort, then rack to fermenter. Aerate wort thoroughly and pitch dried yeast (both packets). Ferment at 68°F (20°C). When the fermentation starts winding down, pour soda into secondary fermenter. Pour roughly to release some of the carbonation. Rack beer into soda, to make 5.0 gallons (19 L). When secondary fermentation finishes, keg or add priming sugar and bottle and carbonate to 2.7 volumes of CO_2.

MALT EXTRACT OPTION

Make 2.0 gallons (7.5 L) of wheat beer wort with 2.0 pounds (910 g) of wheat dried malt extract and the Tettnanger hops from the recipe. Ferment, then rack into soda.

SWEETE POTATOE BITTERE
SWEET POTATO BITTER

This is an English bitter, brewed with sweet potatoes as an adjunct. The sweet potatoes are simply stirred into the mash and their starches are degraded by the enzymes from the malt. They add an interesting orange hue to the beer, but no appreciable flavor—unless you roast them (see recipe option on the opposite page).

5.0 GALLONS (19 L) AT 4.3% ABV
OG = 1.046, FG = 1.013
35 IBU, 7.6 SRM

+ Wyeast 1968 (London ESB) or White Labs WLP002 (English Ale) yeast
+ A 1.1-qt. (1.0-L) yeast starter is recommended
+ 5.0 lb. (2.3 kg) sweet potatoes (peeled and cubed)
+ 6.5 lb. (3.0 kg) U.K. 2-row pale ale malt (3°L)
+ 9.0 oz. (260 g) crystal malt (60°L)
+ 1.25 oz. (35 g) First Gold hops at 7.5% alpha acids, boiled for 60 minutes (35 IBU)
+ 0.75 oz. (21 g) East Kent Goldings hops at 5% alpha acids, boiled for 0 minutes (0 IBU)
+ 1.0 oz. (28 g) East Kent Goldings hops (dry hops)
+ 1.0 tsp. Irish moss, boiled for 15 minutes
+ 4.5 oz. (130 g) corn sugar, to prime bottles for 2.4 volumes of CO_2

Make your yeast starter two to three days ahead of time. Peel the sweet potatoes and cut into cubes. Boil for about 20 minutes to soften. Pour off water and mash with a potato masher. Heat 10 quarts (9.5 L) of brewing liquor to 163°F (73°C) and mash in grains. Stir sweet potatoes into the mash. Mash at 152°F (67°C) for 60 minutes, stirring every 15 minutes if you can. If the sweet potatoes are still hot when you stir them in, they may raise the mash temperature a bit. If so, add cool water to return mash temperature to 152°F (67°C). Heat or add boiling water to mash out to 168°F (76°C).

Recirculate wort until clear, and then run off. Sparge to collect about 5.0 gallons (20 L) of wort. Add water to make 6.0 gallons (23 L). Boil wort for 60 minutes, to reduce volume to just over 5.0 gallons (19 L), adding hops and Irish moss at times indicated. Chill wort, then rack to fermenter. Aerate wort thoroughly and pitch sediment from yeast starter. Ferment at 68°F (20°C). Dry hop for seven–10 days. Keg or add priming sugar and bottle and carbonate to 2.4 volumes of CO_2.

RECIPE OPTIONS AND NOTES

Prepared boiled and mashed, the sweet potatoes add starches to the wort and color to the beer, but no appreciable flavor. If you want a hint of sweet potato flavor, peel the sweet potatoes, cut into cubes and roast on a baking sheet in a 350°F (176°C) oven until they pick up a bit of color, about 30 minutes.

APIS MELLIFERA ALE
HONEY WHEAT

This is an American wheat beer brewed with the aroma of honey. This is a subtly flavored beer, so—at 20 percent of the fermentables—the delicate aroma of honey will be detectable. There's also an option to add hibiscus, ginger and orange peel to make this a spiced beer. If you're making the beer with just honey, look around and find a type of honey with a relatively strong aroma you enjoy. If you're making the hibiscus, ginger, orange honey wheat, you can use any decent supermarket honey.

5.0 GALLONS (19 L) AT 4.7% ABV
OG = 1.045, FG = 1.009
19 IBU, 3.1 SRM

+ Wyeast 1056 (American Ale), White Labs WLP001 (California Ale) or Fermentis U.S.-05 yeast
+ A 1.1-qt. (1.0-L) yeast starter is recommended with liquid yeast
+ 3 lb. 4 oz. (1.5 kg) U.S. 2-row pale malt
+ 3.0 lb. (1.4 kg) white wheat malt
+ 4.0 oz. (110 g) flaked wheat
+ 1.0 oz. (28 g) Willamette hops at 5% alpha acids, boiled for 60 minutes (19 IBU)
+ 0.25 oz. (7.1 g) Willamette hops at 5% alpha acids, boiled for 0 minutes (0 IBU)
+ 1.0 tsp. Irish moss, boiled for 15 minutes
+ 1 lb. 12 oz. (790 g) honey
+ 5.2 oz. (150 g) corn sugar, to prime bottles for 2.6 volumes of CO_2

If you are using one of the liquid yeasts, make your yeast starter two to three days ahead of time. Heat 8.1 quarts (7.7 L) of brewing liquor to 161°F (72°C) and mash in crushed malts and flaked wheat. Mash at 150°F (66°C) for 60 minutes, stirring every 15 minutes if you can do so without losing too much heat from your mash tun. Heat or add boiling water to mash out to 168°F (76°C). Recirculate wort until clear, and then run off.

Sparge steadily over 90 minutes to collect about 4.2 gallons (16 L) of wort. Add water to make sufficient volume to yield 5.0 gallons (19 L) of wort after a 60-minute boil. Boil wort for 60 minutes. Add hops and Irish moss at times indicated. Stir in honey at knockout. Chill wort, then rack to fermenter. Aerate wort thoroughly and pitch sediment from yeast starter. Ferment at 68°F (20°C). Carbonate to 2.6 volumes of CO_2.

(continued)

RECIPE OPTIONS AND NOTES

You can color and spice this wheat beer by adding 12–18 ounces (340–510 g) of hibiscus (the red calyces from the roselle plant), along with 1.0–1.5 ounces (28–35 g) of freshly grated ginger. You could also add the zest of one orange. Add the ginger and orange zest somewhere between the last 2 minutes of the boil and knockout. Add the hibiscus in secondary, as you would dry hops.

Use good quality honey when making the spiced version of this drink.

MALT EXTRACT OPTION

Add 2.0 pounds (910 g) of dried wheat malt extract to the recipe. Lower the amount of 2-row pale malt to 1 pound 6 ounces (620 g). Also lower the amount of wheat malt to 1 pound 6 ounces (620 g). In your brew pot, steep the 3.0 pounds (1.4 kg) total of crushed grains and flaked wheat in 4.1 quarts (3.9 L) of water at 150°F (66°C) for 60 minutes. (This is really a mash, so follow the temperature and volume guidelines closely.) After steeping, place the grain bag in a large colander over your brew pot. Rinse the grains with 2.0 quarts (1.9 L) of 170°F (77°C) water.

Add roughly half of the malt extract to the wort collected and adjust the wort volume with water to make 3.0 gallons (11 L) of wort. Boil for 60 minutes, adding hops and Irish moss at times indicated. Add the remaining malt extract in the final 10 minutes of the boil. Add honey at knockout.

NUTTY PORTER
PEANUT BUTTER PORTER

PB2 is a powdered form of peanut butter. It contains 85 percent less fat than regular peanut butter. Letting the beer contact this powder for a few days infuses the beer with the flavor of peanuts, without adding detrimental amounts of oils to the beer. In this porter, the peanut butter flavor complements the dark, roasted-grain character.

5.0 GALLONS (19 L) AT 4.3% ABV
OG = 1.047, FG = 1.014
25 IBU, 32 SRM

+ Wyeast 1968 (London ESB) or White Labs WLP002 (English Ale) yeast
+ A 1.1-qt. (1.0-L) yeast starter is recommended
+ 7.5 lb. (3.4 kg) 2-row pale ale malt (3°L)
+ 10 oz. (280 g) caramel malt (30°L)
+ 6.0 oz. (170 kg) chocolate malt (350°L)
+ 8.0 oz. (230 g) black malt (500°L)
+ 1.0 lb. (450 g) PB2 (powdered, reduced-fat peanut butter)
+ 1.25 oz. (35 g) Kent Goldings hops at 5% alpha acids, boiled for 60 minutes (23 IBU)
+ 0.25 oz. (7.1 g) Kent Goldings hops at 5% alpha acids, boiled for 5 minutes (1.9 IBU)
+ 0.75 tsp. Irish moss, boiled for 15 minutes
+ 5.0 oz. (140 g) corn sugar, to prime bottles for 2.5 volumes of CO_2.

Make your yeast starter two to three days ahead of time. Heat 12 quarts (11 L) of brewing liquor to 163°F (73°C) and mash in grains. Mash at 152°F (67°C) for 60 minutes, stirring every 15 minutes if you can. Heat or add boiling water to mash out to 168°F (76°C). Recirculate wort until clear, and then run off. Sparge to collect about 5.9 gallons (22 L) of wort. Boil wort for 60 minutes, to reduce volume to just over 5.0 gallons (19 L), adding hops and Irish moss at times indicated. Chill wort, then rack to fermenter.

Aerate wort thoroughly and pitch sediment from yeast starter. Ferment at 68°F (20°C). After fermentation stops, place powdered peanut butter in a secondary fermenter and rack beer into it. Let beer contact peanut butter powder for five days. Gently swirl the fermenter once a day to rouse sedimented peanut butter. Then, rack the beer off the peanut butter sediment into a keg—or bottle the beer. Avoid racking the "oil slick" into the keg or bottling bucket. Keg or add priming sugar and bottle. Carbonate to 2.5 volumes of CO_2.

(continued)

Add some real chocolate flavor by adding 5.0 ounces (140 g) of unsweetened cocoa powder in the final 2 minutes of the boil.

The best time to clean your equipment is immediately after use.

MALT EXTRACT OPTION

Add 3 pounds 10 ounces (1.6 kg) of light dried malt extract to the recipe. Reduce the amount of 2-row pale ale malt to 1 pound 8 ounces (680 g). "Steep" the crushed grains in 4.1 quarts (3.9 L) of water at 152°F (67°C) for 60 minutes. ("Steep" is in quotes because technically this is a partial mash.) Place the grain bag in a colander over your brew pot and rinse the grains with 2.0 quarts (1.9 L) of 170°F (77°C) water. Add roughly one-third of the malt extract to this wort. Add water to bring brew pot volume to 3.0 gallons (11 L). Boil for 60 minutes, adding hops and Irish moss at times indicated. Add the remaining malt extract in the final 15 minutes of the boil.

RECIPE OPTIONS
AND NOTES

You can use lemonade to make a
hard lemonade–like beverage.

ZOMBIMA
MALTERNATIVE BEVERAGE

This is a recipe for a homebrewed "malternative beverage," or "alcopop." This recipe makes a nearly clear, fizzy, citrus-flavored beverage. See the recipe options on the photo on page 238 for a way to make hard lemonade.

5.0 GALLONS (19 L) AT 5.3% ABV
OG = 1.047, FG = 1.006
7.5 IBU, 2.0 SRM

+ Wyeast 1056 (American Ale) or White Labs WLP001 (California Ale) yeast
+ A 1.5-qt. (1.4-L) yeast starter is recommended
+ 5.0 lb. (2.3 kg) Pilsner malt
+ 0.75 oz. (21 g) Saaz hops at 3.5% alpha acids, boiled for 30 minutes (7.5 IBU)
+ 0.50 tsp. yeast nutrients, boiled for 15 minutes
+ 0.50 tsp. Irish moss, boiled for 15 minutes
+ 1 lb. 8 oz. (680 g) cane sugar
+ One 2-L bottle of Squirt or other grapefruit-flavored soda
+ Two 2-L bottles of Sprite or 7UP or other lemon-lime–flavored soda
+ 5.6 oz. (160 g) corn sugar, to prime bottles for 2.8 volumes of CO_2

Make your yeast starter two to three days ahead of time. Heat 6.3 quarts (5.9 L) of brewing liquor to 161°F (72°C) and mash in grains. Mash at 150°F (66°C) for 60 minutes, stirring every 15 minutes, if you can do so without losing too much heat from your mash tun. Heat or add boiling water to mash out to 168°F (76°C). Recirculate wort until clear, and then run off.

Sparge to collect about 3.3 gallons (12 L) of wort. Add water to make 5.3 gallons (20 L). Boil wort for 60 minutes, to reduce volume to just over 4.3 gallons (16 L), adding hops, Irish moss and yeast nutrients at times indicated. Add cane sugar in the final 10 minutes of the boil. Chill wort, then rack to fermenter. Aerate wort thoroughly and pitch sediment from yeast starter. Ferment at 68°F (20°C). When fermentation slows, pour soda into a secondary fermenter and rack beer into it, making 5.0 gallons (19 L). Pour soda roughly to release as much carbonation as is reasonably possible. When renewed fermentation is complete, keg or bottle and carbonate to 2.8 volumes of CO_2.

MALT EXTRACT OPTION

Replace the Pilsner malt with 3.0 pounds (1.4 kg) of extra-light dried malt extract. Dissolve malt extract and add water to make at least 3.0 gallons (11 L) of wort. Boil for 30 minutes, adding hops at beginning of boil. Add yeast nutrients and Irish moss in the final 15 minutes of the boil. Stir in sugar in the final 10 minutes of the boil. Chill wort and add water to make 4.3 gallons (16 L) of wort. Aerate and pitch yeast.

CRANBERRY ZINGER
CRANBERRY WHEAT BEER

This is a light wheat beer, made with honey and flavored with cranberry relish—cranberries, apples and oranges. The cranberries lend the beer a strong fruit flavor, with a hint of astringency that is accentuated by a dry character and a high level of carbonation.

5.0 GALLONS (19 L) AT 5.3% ABV
OG = 1.049, FG = 1.008
14 IBU, 3.5 SRM

+ Wyeast 1056 (American Ale) or White Labs WLP001 (California Ale) yeast
+ A 1.1-qt. (1.0-L) yeast starter is recommended
+ 3 lb. 4 oz. (1.5 kg) 2-row pale malt
+ 3.0 lb. (1.4 kg) wheat malt
+ 12 oz. (340 g) flaked wheat
+ 2.0 lb. (910 g) honey
+ 4.0 lb. cranberries
+ 2 medium navel oranges
+ 2 medium Granny Smith apples
+ 1.0 oz. (28 g) Willamette hops at 5% alpha acids, boiled for 30 minutes (14 IBU)
+ 1 tsp. Irish moss, boiled for 15 minutes
+ 6.0 oz. (170 g) corn sugar, to prime bottles for 2.9 volumes of CO_2

Make your yeast starter two to three days ahead of time. Heat 8.8 quarts (8.3 L) of brewing liquor to 163°F (73°C) and mash in grains. Mash at 152°F (67°C) for 60 minutes, stirring every 15 minutes if you can. Heat or add boiling water to mash out to 168°F (76°C). Recirculate wort until clear, and then run off. Sparge to collect about 4.5 gallons (17 L) of wort.

Add water make 6.0 gallons (23 L) and boil wort for 60 minutes. Aim to reduce wort volume to just over 5.0 gallons (19 L). Add hops and Irish moss at times indicated. Stir in honey with 10 minutes left in boil. Chill wort, then rack to fermenter. Aerate wort thoroughly and pitch sediment from yeast starter. Ferment at 68°F (20°C).

Grind cranberries, cored apples and whole oranges coarsely into a cranberry relish. Place in nylon steeping bag, and then put the bag in a bucket fermenter and rack beer into it. Let beer contact cranberry relish for five to seven days. After renewed fermentation stops, keg or add priming sugar and bottle and carbonate to 2.9 volumes of CO_2.

MALT EXTRACT OPTION

Add 4.0 pounds (1.8 kg) of dried wheat malt extract to the recipe. Omit the pale malt, wheat malt and flaked wheat. Make 5.0 gallons (19 L) of base beer from malt extract and honey.

BRUSSELS TO BASTROP WHITE
WITBIER

This is a Belgian white ale, brewed with wheat and lightly spiced with coriander and orange peel. Witbiers are hazy from the wheat, and sometimes have a slightly acidic tang. With a fairly high level of carbonation, they are a refreshing beer.

5.0 GALLONS (19 L) AT 4.9% ABV
OG = 1.049, FG = 1.011
16 IBU, 3.4 SRM

+ Wyeast 3944 (Belgian Witbier) or White Labs WLP400 (Belgian Wit Ale) yeast
+ A 1.1-qt. (1.0-L) yeast starter is recommended
+ 6.0 lb. (2.7 kg) Pilsner malt
+ 2 lb. 8 oz. (1.1 kg) wheat malt
+ 12 oz. (340 g) flaked wheat
+ 0.25 oz. (7.1 g) coriander (freshly ground)
+ 0.25 oz. (7.1 g) orange peel (fresh)
+ 1.25 oz. (35 g) Saaz hops at 3.5% alpha acids, boiled for 60 minutes (16 IBU)
+ 5.2 oz. (150 g) corn sugar, to prime bottles for 2.6 volumes of CO_2

Make your yeast starter two to three days ahead of time. Heat 12 quarts (11 L) of brewing liquor to 163°F (73°C) and mash in grains. Mash at 152°F (67°C) for 60 minutes, stirring every 15 minutes if you can. Heat or add boiling water to mash out to 168°F (76°C). Recirculate wort until clear, and then run off. Sparge to collect about 6.0 gallons (23 L) of wort. Boil wort for 60 minutes, to reduce volume to just over 5.0 gallons (19 L). Add hops at times indicated. Add spices in the final 2 minutes of the boil.

Chill wort, then rack to fermenter. Aerate wort thoroughly and pitch sediment from yeast starter. Ferment, starting at 62°F (17°C). After high kräusen, let temperature rise to 66°F (19°C). After fermentation stops, let beer condition at 50–60°F (10–16°C) for two to three weeks, then keg or bottle and carbonate to 2.6 volumes of CO_2.

Spicing is always tricky. If your beer shows less spice character than you'd like, you can try making a strong tea with hot water and blending it into your beer. Keep in mind any liquid you add will dilute the beer, so make the tea as strong as possible.

(continued)

RECIPE OPTIONS AND NOTES

You can experiment with adding small amounts of other spices, such as chamomile or lavender. Start with small amounts, 0.25 ounce (7.1 g) or less, and increase if needed for future batches.

Add the spices near the end of the boil. Boiling them too long may extract excess tannins.

MALT EXTRACT OPTION

Add 3 pounds 11 ounces (1.7 kg) of light dried malt extract to the recipe. Omit Pilsner malt. Reduce the amount of flaked wheat to 8.0 ounces (230 g). "Steep" the crushed grains in 4.1 quarts (3.9 L) of water at 152°F (67°C) for 60 minutes. ("Steep" is in quotes because technically this is a partial mash.) Place the grain bag in a colander over your brew pot and rinse the grains with 2.0 quarts (1.9 L) of 170°F (77°C) water. Add roughly one-third of the malt extract to this wort.

Add water to bring brew pot volume to 3.0 gallons (11 L). Boil for 60 minutes, adding hops at times indicated. Add the remaining malt extract in the final 15 minutes of the boil. Add spices in the final 2 minutes of the boil.

ERIC THE RED WHEAT
RASPBERRY WHEAT

This a German-style wheat beer with raspberries added for flavoring. A beer like this would have been forbidden by the Reinheitsgebot, when it was in force. And even today, I doubt any German brewery would consider brewing one. For homebrewers, however, this is a classic fruit beer—with the tart flavor of raspberries mingling with the banana esters from the wheat beer yeast.

5.0 GALLONS (19 L) AT 5.1% ABV
OG = 1.050, FG = 1.011
13 IBU, 3.8 SRM

+ Wyeast 3068 (Weinstephan Weizen) or White Labs WLP300 (Hefeweizen Ale) yeast
+ A 1.6-qt. (1.5-L) yeast starter is recommended
+ 3 lb. 2 oz. (1.4 kg) U.S. 2-row pale malt
+ 5 lb. 12 oz. (2.6 kg) wheat malt
+ 6.0 lb. (2.7 kg) raspberries
+ 0.75 oz. (21 g) Hallertau hops at 4.5% alpha acids, boiled for 60 minutes (13 IBU)
+ 7.7 oz. (220 g) corn sugar, to prime bottles for 3.5 volumes of CO_2

Make your yeast starter two to three days ahead of time. Heat 12 quarts (11 L) of brewing liquor to 163°F (73°C) and mash in grains. Mash at 152°F (67°C) for 60 minutes. Stir the mash every 15 minutes, if you can do so without losing too much heat from your mash tun. Heat or add boiling water to mash out to 168°F (76°C). Recirculate wort until clear, and then run off. Sparge to collect about 5.8 gallons (22 L) of wort.

Add water to make 6.0 gallons (23 L). Boil wort for 60 minutes, to reduce volume to just over 5.0 gallons (19 L). Add hops at beginning of boil. Chill wort, then rack to fermenter. Aerate wort thoroughly and pitch sediment from yeast starter. Ferment at 66°F (19 °C). After fermentation stops, place raspberries in a nylon steeping bag and place bag in a sanitized bucket fermenter. Use a potato masher, or anything similar, to crush berries. Rack beer to bucket. After secondary fermentation subsides, keg or add priming sugar and bottle and carbonate to 3.5 volumes of CO_2. Bottle the beer in heavy bottles.

(continued)

The diversity of available dried yeast strains is increasing.

You can change the flavor slightly and darken the color by swapping blackberries for some of the raspberries. Swapping in a pound (450 g) of blackberries for a pound (450 g) of raspberries will shift the color to an almost blood-like red and give a hint of the characteristic "tang" of blackberries.

Pitching less yeast and raising the fermentation temperature will force the yeast to produce more banana esters. Making a 1.1-quart (1.0-L) yeast starter and fermenting at 68°F (20°C) will bump the banana up a notch, without being excessive.

MALT EXTRACT OPTION

Add 3 pounds 6 ounces (1.5 kg) of light dried malt extract to the recipe. Omit the barley malt. Reduce the amount of wheat malt to 3.0 pounds (1.4 kg). "Steep" the crushed malt in 4.1 quarts (3.9 L) of water at 152°F (67°C) for 60 minutes. ("Steep" is in quotes because technically this is a partial mash.) Place the grain bag in a colander over your brew pot and rinse the grains with 2.0 quarts (1.9 L) of 170°F (77°C) water. Add roughly one-third of the malt extract to this wort. Add water to bring brew pot volume to 3.0 gallons (11 L). Boil for 60 minutes, adding hops at times indicated. Add the remaining malt extract in the final 15 minutes of the boil.

LUMBERJAMBER AMBER
MAPLE SYRUP AMBER ALE

This is a full-bodied, slightly sweet American amber ale with touch of maple flavor.

5.0 GALLONS (19 L) AT 5.0% ABV
OG = 1.052, FG = 1.013
25 IBU, 13 SRM

+ Wyeast 1272 (American Ale II) or White Labs WLP051 (California V Ale) yeast
+ A 1.7-qt. (1.6-L) yeast starter is recommended
+ 9.0 lb. (4.1 kg) U.S. 2-row pale malt
+ 12 oz. (340 g) caramel malt (30°L)
+ 8.0 oz. (230 g) caramel malt (40°L)
+ 2.0 oz. (57 g) black malt (500°L)
+ 1.25 oz. (35 g) Willamette hops at 5% alpha acids, boiled for 60 minutes (21 IBU)
+ 0.50 oz. (14 g) Liberty hops at 4% alpha acids, boiled for 10 minutes (2.5 IBU)
+ 0.50 oz. (14 g) Willamette hops at 5% alpha acids, boiled for 5 minutes (1.7 IBU)
+ 1.0 tsp. Irish moss, boiled for 15 minutes
+ 10 oz. (280 g) maple syrup
+ 5.0 oz. (140 g) corn sugar, to prime bottles for 2.5 volumes of CO_2

Make your yeast starter two to three days ahead of time. Heat 13 quarts (12 L) of brewing liquor to 165°F (74°C) and mash in grains. Mash at 154°F (68°C) for 60 minutes, stirring every 15 minutes if you can. Heat or add boiling water to mash out to 168°F (76°C). Recirculate wort until clear, and then run off. Sparge to collect about 6.7 gallons (26 L) of wort.

Boil wort for 90 minutes, to reduce volume to just over 5.0 gallons (19 L), adding hops and Irish moss at times indicated. Stir in maple syrup in the final 5 minutes of boil. Chill wort, then rack to fermenter. Aerate wort thoroughly and pitch sediment from yeast starter. Ferment at 68°F (20°C). After fermentation stops, keg or add priming sugar and bottle and carbonate to 2.5 volumes of CO_2.

MALT EXTRACT OPTION

Add 4 pounds 4 ounces (1.9 kg) of light dried malt extract to the recipe. Reduce the amount of 2-row pale malt to 1 pound 10 ounces (740 g). "Steep" the crushed grains in 4.1 quarts (3.9 L) of water at 154°F (68°C) for 60 minutes. ("Steep" is in quotes because technically this is a partial mash.) Place the grain bag in a colander over your brew pot and rinse the grains with 2.0 quarts (1.9 L) of 170°F (77°C) water.

Add roughly one-third of the malt extract to this wort. Add water to bring brew pot volume to 3.0 gallons (11 L). Boil for 60 minutes, adding hops and Irish moss at times indicated. Add the remaining malt extract in the final 15 minutes of the boil. Add maple syrup in the last 5 minutes of the boil.

RECIPE OPTIONS AND NOTES

You can make this a smoked maple and pecan amber ale by swapping 2.0–4.0 pounds (0.91–1.8 kg) of rauchmalz for the same amount of pale malt in the recipe. "Dry nut" with 0.75–1.0 pound (340–450 g) of pecans in a secondary fermenter. You can roast the pecans on a baking sheet to develop their flavor. Roast at 350°F (180°C) until they begin to smell and darken a shade or two.

RECIPE OPTIONS AND NOTES

You can use Briess cherrywood smoked malt or Weyermann rauchmalz in place of the home-smoked malt.

You may also consider adding table salt (NaCl) to the dry-porked growler until you can just detect the salty flavor. (The intensity should be at or below the level of salt in a gose.) Once blended back into the porter, you won't overtly taste the salt but it will intensify the bacon flavor. Approach salt additions with caution. Overly salty beer is horrible (and probably unhealthy).

HAMHOCK PORTER
BACON-SMOKED PORTER

This is a smoked porter with the flavor of bacon. Hickory is the hardwood most often associated with smoked bacon, and homemade hickory-smoked malt is used in the recipe. (See page 164 for how to smoke malt at home.) A sample of the beer is later "dry-porked" with bacon, then blended back into the porter.

5.0 GALLONS (19 L) AT 5.3% ABV
OG = 1.056, FG = 1.015
31 IBU, 30 SRM

+ Wyeast 1968 (London ESB) and White Labs WLP002 (English Ale) yeast
+ A 1-qt. (1-L) yeast starter is recommended
+ 5.0 lb. (2.3 kg) English pale ale malt
+ 4 lb. 2 oz. (1.9 kg) home-smoked malt (hickory)
+ 1.0 lb. (450 g) crystal malt (40°L)
+ 8.0 oz. (230 g) U.K. chocolate malt (400°L)
+ 4.0 oz. (110 g) black malt
+ 1.0 oz. (28 g) First Gold hops at 8% alpha acids, boiled for 60 minutes (30 IBU)
+ 0.25 oz. (7.1 g) East Kent Goldings hops at 5% alpha acids, boiled for 5 minutes (0.94 IBU)
+ 0.25 oz. (7.1 g) East Kent Goldings hops at 5% alpha acids, boiled for 0 minutes (0 IBU)
+ 0.75 tsp. Irish moss, boiled 15 minutes
+ 8.0 oz. (230 g) bacon
+ 5.0 oz. (140 g) corn sugar, to prime bottles for 2.5 volumes of CO_2

Make your yeast starter two to three days ahead of time. Smoke 2-row pale ale malt with hickory at least a week before brew day. Heat 14 quarts (13 L) of brewing liquor to 163°F (73°C) and mash in grains. Mash at 152°F (67°C) for 60 minutes, stirring every 15 minutes if you can. Heat or add boiling water to mash out to 168°F (76°C). Recirculate wort until clear, and then run off. Sparge to collect about 7.1 gallons (27 L) of wort.

Boil wort for 60 minutes, adding hops and Irish moss at times indicated. Chill wort, then rack to fermenter. Aerate wort thoroughly and pitch sediment from yeast starter. Ferment at 68°F (20°C). After fermentation stops, fry the bacon and cut off as much fat as you can. Place bacon pieces in a sanitized growler (or other sealable 2–3-quart [2–3-L] vessel). Fill growler with porter. (Go slowly as it will foam a bit.)

"Dry-pork" the beer in the growler for five to seven days. Taste the "bacon tea" from the growler and decide how much to blend back into your porter. (Strain out the pieces of bacon. You can also use a paper towel to absorb any fat floating on top of the "bacon tea.") Keg or add priming sugar and bottle and carbonate to 2.5 volumes of CO_2.

FRANKEN BERRY WEISSE
BREAKFAST CEREAL WHEAT BEER (BY JAMES SPENCER)

This is a Belgian wheat beer flavored with the breakfast cereal Franken Berry. If I had no shame, I'd describe it as frighteningly good.

5.0 GALLONS (19 L) AT 6.2% ABV
OG = 1.056, FG = 1.008
23 IBU, 4.2 SRM

+ Wyeast 3787 (Trappist High Gravity) or White Labs WLP530 (Abbey Ale) yeast
+ A 1.5-qt. (1.4-L) yeast starter is recommended
+ 5 lb. 12 oz. (2.6 kg) 2-row pale malt
+ 4 lb. 13 oz. (2.2 kg) wheat malt
+ 1.0 lb. (450 g) Franken Berry cereal
+ 1.75 oz. (50 g) Saaz hops at 3.5% alpha acids, boiled for 60 minutes (23 IBU)
+ 1.0 tsp. Irish moss, boiled for 15 minutes
+ 5.0 oz. (140 g) corn sugar, to prime bottles for 2.5 volumes of CO_2

Make your yeast starter two to three days ahead of time. Heat 15 quarts (14 L) of brewing liquor to 165°F (74°C) and mash in grains. Then, stir in breakfast cereal. Mash at 154°F (68°C) for 60 minutes. You will need to stir at least once, after the cereal has dissolved, to break it up. Heat or add boiling water to mash out to 168°F (76°C). Recirculate wort until clear, and then run off. Sparge to collect up to 6.9 gallons (26 L) of wort.

Boil wort to reduce volume to just over 5.0 gallons (19 L), adding hops and Irish moss at times indicated. Chill wort, then rack to fermenter. Aerate wort thoroughly and pitch sediment from yeast starter. Ferment at 70°F (21°C). After fermentation stops, keg or bottle and carbonate to 2.5 volumes of CO_2.

James Spencer is the host of Basic Brewing Radio *and* Basic Brewing Video*, which can be found at basicbrewing.com. He also is the cofounder of* Beer and Wine Journal.

SEAFOOD STOUT
OYSTER STOUT

This is a stout with oysters added. You can't really taste the oysters in it, although there is a very slight "briny" character they add to the beer. There are commercial beers labeled oyster stouts, but not all contain actual oysters. For some, it indicates that it's a stout that pairs well with oysters. In this case, once you've gone to the trouble of brewing with oysters, you might as well enjoy the final product with oysters.

5.0 GALLONS (19 L) AT 5.7% ABV
OG = 1.057, FG = 1.012
37 IBU, 48 SRM

+ Wyeast 1098 (British Ale), White Labs WLP007 (Dry English Ale) or Fermentis Safale S-04 yeast
+ A 1.5-qt. (1.4-L) yeast starter is recommended
+ 8.0 lb. (3.6 kg) 2-row pale malt
+ 1.0 lb. (450 g) flaked oats
+ 12 oz. (340 g) flaked barley
+ 4.0 oz. (110 g) caramel malt (120°L)
+ 7.0 oz. (200 g) chocolate malt (350°L)
+ 1 lb. 2 oz. (510 g) roasted barley (500°L)
+ 1.25 oz. (35 g) First Gold hops at 8% alpha acids, boiled for 60 minutes (37 IBU)
+ 0.75 tsp. Irish moss, boiled for 15 minutes
+ 12 oz. (340 g) oysters (canned, plus brine)
+ 5.0 oz. (140 g) corn sugar, to prime bottles for 2.5 volumes of CO_2

Make your yeast starter two to three days ahead of time. Heat 15 quarts (14 L) of brewing liquor to 163°F (73°C) and mash in grains. Mash at 152°F (67°C) for 60 minutes, stirring every 15 minutes if you can do so without losing too much heat from your mash tun. Heat or add boiling water to mash out to 168°F (76°C). Recirculate wort until clear, and then run off. Sparge to collect about 7.5 gallons (28 L) of wort.

Boil wort to reduce to just over 5.0 gallons (19 L), adding hops and Irish moss at times indicated. Add oysters, and brine from the can, with 15 minutes left in the boil. Chill wort, then rack to fermenter. (Do not let the oysters carry over into the fermenter.) Aerate wort thoroughly and pitch sediment from yeast starter. Ferment at 68°F (20°C). After fermentation stops, keg or add priming sugar and bottle and carbonate to 2.5 volumes of CO_2.

Smoked oysters in a stout made with some smoked malt add an interesting character to the beer.

RECIPE OPTIONS AND NOTES

As an option, you could use smoked oysters and some smoked malt—say, about 2.0–3.0 pounds (0.91–1.4 kg), swapped for an equal amount of pale malt—for a lightly smoked oyster stout.

MALT EXTRACT OPTION

Add 4 pounds 6 ounces (2.0 kg) of light dried malt extract to the recipe. Reduce the amount of 2-row pale malt to 7.0 ounces (200 g). Follow the general procedures for a countertop partial mash, as described on page 36, with these specifics: Mash at 152°F (67°C) for 60 minutes. Recirculate, run off, and sparge to collect 2.6 gallons (9.8 L).

Add roughly one-third of the malt extract to this wort. Add water to bring brew pot volume to at least 3.0 gallons (11 L). Boil for 60 minutes, adding hops and Irish moss at times indicated. Add the remaining malt extract in the final 15 minutes of the boil. Add oysters immediately after adding the remaining malt extract.

Three pounds (1.4 kg) of candy is a lot. You may want to consider keeping 2.0 gallons (7.6 L) as a light (OG 1.046, 4.4 percent ABV) American wheat beer and dissolving 1.5 pounds (680 g) of candies in 2.0 quarts (1.9 L) of water to make 2.5 gallons (9.5 L) of watermelon wheat beer.

You can use other flavors of Jolly Ranchers or other hard candies to flavor this beer. You can also consider souring the wheat beer and making a more tart watermelon wheat. And finally, you can blend the beer with fruit juices that have an SG around 1.037–1.046 instead of the candy for a flavored American wheat beer. You can always make a test blend using a commercial beer first to figure out a blending ratio that pleases you.

POOLSIDE WATERMELON WHEAT
JOLLY RANCHER WATERMELON WHEAT

This is an American wheat beer flavored with the (powerfully artificial) flavor of Jolly Rancher Watermelon hard candies. The (powerfully artificial) aroma of watermelon essence dominates the flavor and disguises the fact that the beer is actually fairly dry and 6.6 percent ABV.

5.0 GALLONS (19 L) AT 6.6% ABV
OG = 1.059, FG = 1.008
22 IBU, 3.2 SRM

+ Wyeast 1056 (American Ale) or White Labs WLP001 (California Ale) yeast; A 1.1-qt. (1.0-L) yeast starter is recommended
+ 3 lb. 8 oz. (1.6 kg) U.S. 2-row pale malt
+ 3.0 lb. (1.4 kg) wheat malt
+ 8.0 oz. (230 g) flaked wheat
+ 1.0 oz. (28 g) Mt. Hood hops at 6% alpha acids, boiled for 60 minutes (22 IBU)
+ 0.75 tsp. Irish moss, boiled for 15 minutes
+ 3.0 lb. (1.4 kg) Jolly Rancher Watermelon hard candy
+ 5.0 oz. (140 g) corn sugar, to prime bottles for 2.5 volumes of CO_2

Make your yeast starter two to three days ahead of time. Heat 8.8 quarts (8.3 L) of brewing liquor to 161°F (72°C) and mash in grains. Mash at 150°F (66°C) for 60 minutes, stirring every 15 minutes if you can. Heat or add boiling water to mash out to 168°F (76°C). Recirculate wort until clear, and then run off. Sparge to collect about 4.6 gallons (17 L) of wort.

Add roughly 2.0 quarts (1.9 L) of water and boil wort for 60 minutes to reduce volume to 4.0 gallons (15 L) at around SG 1.046. Add hops and Irish moss at times indicated. Chill wort, then rack to fermenter. Aerate wort thoroughly and pitch sediment from yeast starter. Ferment at 68°F (20°C). After fermentation stops, dissolve hard candy in 1.0 gallon (3.8 L) of water in secondary fermenter. This can take up to 30 minutes. You can use hot water, but then you'll need to cool it down. Rack beer into candy water. After secondary fermentation ceases, keg or add priming sugar and bottle and carbonate to 2.5 volumes of CO_2.

MALT EXTRACT OPTION

Keep it simple. Add 4.0 pounds (1.8 kg) of dried wheat malt extract to the recipe. Omit all the other grains and make 4.0 gallons (15 L) of wort with the wheat dried malt extract and Mt. Hood hops.

DARK AND DECADENT STOUT
CHERRY STOUT

This is a sweet stout, brewed with a mix of black malt and chocolate malt. It is flavored with cherries. The sweet background accentuates the cherry flavor, which blends well with the roasted, dark-grain character. This is a flavorful, full-bodied beer.

5.0 GALLONS (19 L) AT 5.4% ABV
OG = 1.062, FG = 1.020
28 IBU, 35 SRM

+ Wyeast 1084 (Irish Ale) or White Labs WLP004 (Irish Ale) yeast
+ A 1.3-qt. (1.2-L) yeast starter is recommended
+ 7.0 lb. (3.2 kg) U.S. 2-row pale malt
+ 10 oz. (280 g) caramel malt (40°L)
+ 6.0 oz. (170 g) chocolate malt (350°L)
+ 10 oz. (280 g) black malt (500°L)
+ 1.0 lb. (450 g) lactose
+ 1.25 oz. (35 g) Santiam hops at 6% alpha acids, boiled for 60 minutes (28 IBU)
+ 0.50 tsp. Irish moss, boiled for 15 minutes
+ 9.0 lb. (4.1 kg) cherry purée
+ 5.0 oz. (140 g) corn sugar, to prime bottles for 2.5 volumes of CO_2

Make your yeast starter two to three days ahead of time. Heat 11 quarts (10 L) of brewing liquor to 163°F (73°C) and mash in grains. Mash at 152°F (67°C) for 60 minutes, stirring every 15 minutes if you can. Heat or add boiling water to mash out to 168°F (76°C). Recirculate wort until clear, and then run off. Sparge to collect about 5.6 gallons (21 L) of wort. Add water to make 6.0 gallons (23 L).

Boil wort for 60 minutes, to reduce volume to just over 5.0 gallons (19 L). Add hops and Irish moss at times indicated. Add lactose in the final 10 minutes of boil. Chill wort, then rack to fermenter. Aerate wort thoroughly and pitch sediment from yeast starter. Ferment at 68°F (20°C). After fermentation stops, place cherry purée in a sanitized bucket fermenter. Rack stout into cherries and stir gently—enough to mix the beer and purée, but not so much as to aerate the mix. When secondary fermentation is complete, keg or add priming sugar and bottle and carbonate to 2.5 volumes of CO_2.

(continued)

RECIPE OPTIONS AND NOTES

You can add some real chocolate flavor to complement the cherries by adding 5.0 ounces (140 g) of unsweetened cocoa in the final 5 minutes of the boil.

Fruit purée is a great way to add fruit to beer.

MALT EXTRACT OPTION

Add 3 pounds 4 ounces (1.5 kg) of light dried malt extract to the recipe. Reduce the amount of 2-row pale malt to 1 pound 6 ounces (620 g). "Steep" the crushed grains in 4.1 quarts (3.9 L) of water at 152°F (67°C) for 60 minutes. ("Steep" is in quotes because technically this is a partial mash.) Place the grain bag in a colander over your brew pot and rinse the grains with 2.0 quarts (1.9 L) of 170°F (77°C) water. Add roughly one-third of the malt extract to this wort. Add water to bring brew pot volume to 3.0 gallons (11 L). Boil for 60 minutes, adding hops and Irish moss at times indicated. Add the remaining malt extract in the final 15 minutes of the boil. Add the lactose in the final 10 minutes of the boil.

REVENANT VIKING ALE
GOTLANDSDRICKA

Gotlandsdricka is a fairly strong rustic farmhouse ale from the Swedish island of Gotland. The wort for Gotlandsdricka is made with malt, smoked malt, some unmalted grains and honey. It is strained through juniper boughs, which gives it a faintly gin-like taste.

5.0 GALLONS (19 L) AT 6.8% ABV
OG = 1.064, FG = 1.012
23 IBU, 5.1 SRM

+ Wyeast 3787 (Trappist High Gravity) or White Labs WLP520 (Abbey Ale) yeast
+ A 1.5-qt. (1.4-L) yeast starter is recommended
+ 4 lb. 8 oz. (2.0 kg) U.K. 2-row pale ale malt (3°L)
+ 4.0 lb. (1.8 kg) Weyermann rauchmalz (beechwood-smoked malt)
+ 1.0 lb. (450 g) flaked wheat
+ 12 oz. (340 g) flaked oats
+ 1.25 oz. (35 g) East Kent Goldings hops at 5% alpha acids, boiled for 60 minutes (23 IBU)
+ 1.0 tsp. Irish moss, boiled for 15 minutes
+ 1 lb. 12 oz. (790 g) honey
+ 1.0 lb. (450 g) juniper boughs (the ends, with berries) or 0.50 oz. (14 g) juniper berries
+ 5.2 oz. (150 g) corn sugar, to prime bottles for 2.5 volumes of CO_2

Make your yeast starter two to three days ahead of time. Heat 13 quarts (12 L) of brewing liquor to 163°F (73°C). If you are brewing with juniper boughs, place them in the bottom of your mash tun, so the wort must pass though them when lautering. Mash at 152°F (67°C) for 60 minutes, stirring only the top layer every 15 minutes if you can do so. Add boiling water to mash out to 168°F (76°C). Stir in, but don't disturb the juniper. Recirculate the wort until clear, then run off.

Sparge to collect about 6.7 gallons (25 L) of wort. Boil wort for 60 minutes, adding hops and Irish moss at times indicated. Add honey in the final 5 minutes of the boil. If you are brewing with just the juniper berries, add to the boil for the final 5 minutes. Chill wort, then rack to fermenter. Aerate wort thoroughly and pitch sediment from yeast starter. Ferment at 70°F (21°C). After fermentation stops, keg or add priming sugar and bottle and carbonate to 2.5 volumes of CO_2.

RECIPE OPTIONS AND NOTES

In brewing Gotlandsdricka, farmers would use whatever grains they had available to make the malt and for the unmalted grains. They would not stick to a set recipe year after year. So, feel free to adjust the ratio of pale malt to rauchmalz (smoked malt). You can use other unmalted grains instead of or in addition to the wheat and oats. Keep the percentage of unmalted grains under 25 percent and aim for an ABV of 6.0–8.0 percent.

If you add rye to the recipe, and ferment with a German wheat beer yeast, your beer will be similar to Sahti, a Finnish beer brewed with juniper.

A HYMN TO NINKASI
NINKASI ALE

This beer is made from an ancient Sumerian beer recipe that appears within a poem dedicated to Ninkasi, the Sumerian goddess of beer. The mix of grains, bappir (beer bread), fruit and honey was fermented, then drunk young through straws (to filter out the solids).

5.0 GALLONS (19 L) AT 7.3% ABV
OG = 1.064, FG = 1.008 (OR LOWER)
00 IBU, 3.8 SRM

+ 1.0 gallon (3.8 L) date wine (see instructions below); You will need 3 lb. 8 oz. (1.6 kg) of dates for this

+ Wyeast 1056 (American Ale) or White Labs WLP001 (California Ale) yeast; No yeast starter

+ 1 lb. 8 oz. (680 g) honey

+ 4.0 lb. (1.8 kg) rauchmalz (smoked malt)

+ 3.0 lb. (1.4 kg) bappir ("beer bread," see instructions below); You will need 3.0 lb. (1.4 kg) pale malt, 1.0 lb. (450 g) unbleached wheat flour and 1 lb. 4 oz. (570 g) honey for this

+ 1 lb. 8 oz. (680 g) rice hulls

Make the wine by placing 3.5 pounds (1.6 kg) of dates in a nylon grain bag. In a pot or crock with a lid, mash the fruit and then add enough water to just cover it. Place the lid on the crock and set it somewhere warmer than room temperature. The next day, pitch the ale yeast to the wine. The fruit may already show signs of spontaneous fermentation.

Make the beer bread by grinding the malt into flour and combining it with the wheat flour. Fold the honey into this mix, then slowly add water and knead until the dough is roughly the consistency of cookie dough. On nonstick baking sheets, flatten the dough into roughly half-inch (1.3-cm) thick layers of dough. Bake at 350°F (180°C) until the outside starts to brown. Let the bread cool, then cut into small "fingers" (like biscotti) about 2.0 inches (5.1 cm) long by 0.50 inches (1.3-cm) wide. Bake the "fingers" at 350°F (180°C) until they almost harden.

When the date wine is strongly fermenting, or a day or two later, make the wort by mixing the crushed rauchmalz and crumbled bread "fingers" with 11 quarts (10 L) of water.

Mash this mixture at 152°F (67°F) for 60 minutes, then stir in the rice hulls and 2.3 quarts (2.1 L) of boiling water. Collect 4.6 gallons (17 L) of wort and boil for 30 minutes. Add honey in the final 10 minutes of the boil. Cool wort and transfer to fermenter. Aerate wort and pitch with fermenting date wine. Squeeze the bag of fruit pulp to yield all the liquid you reasonably can. Add water to make 5.0 gallons (19 L), if needed, and ferment at 68°F (20°C). When fermentation stops, bottle the beer without priming sugar. Enjoy young, but be aware that continued fermentation might yield highly carbonated bottles over time.

EVERGREEN AMBER ALE
OLD ALE (WITH SPRUCE TIPS)

This is an amber ale with a hint of spruce flavor. The flavor of spruce is hard to describe, with fruity, sometimes citrus-like notes, but generally not piney (as many would expect). Spruce has been a part of the brewing tradition in Scandinavian countries for centuries.

5.0 GALLONS (19 L) AT 6.4% ABV
OG = 1.064, FG = 1.014
34 IBU, 14 SRM

+ Wyeast 1275 (Thames Valley Ale) or White Labs WLP023 (Burton Ale) yeast; A 1.9-qt. (1.8-L) yeast starter is recommended
+ 11 lb. 8 oz. (5.2 kg) UK pale ale malt (3°L)
+ 12 oz. (340 g) crystal malt (40°L)
+ 3.0 oz. (85 g) chocolate malt (350°L)
+ 4.0 oz. (110 g) spruce tips (fresh)
+ 8.0 oz. (230 g) cane sugar
+ 1.0 oz. (28 g) Challenger hops at 8% alpha acids, boiled for 60 minutes (34 IBU)
+ 1.0 oz. (28 g) Fuggles hops at 5% alpha acids, boiled for 0 minutes (0 IBU)
+ 1.0 tsp. Irish moss, boiled for 15 minutes
+ 5.0 oz. (140 g) corn sugar, to prime bottles for 2.5 volumes of CO_2

Make your yeast starter two to three days ahead of time. Heat 16 quarts (15 L) of brewing liquor to 163°F (73°C) and mash in grains. Mash at 152°F (67°C) for 60 minutes, stirring every 15 minutes if you can do so without losing too much heat from your mash tun. Heat or add boiling water to mash out to 168°F (76°C). Recirculate wort until clear, and then run off. Sparge to collect up to 8.1 gallons (30 L) of wort.

Boil wort for 60 minutes, adding hops and Irish moss at times indicated. Add sugar for final 10 minutes of the boil. Add spruce tips throughout the final 5 minutes of the boil. Chill wort, then rack to fermenter. Aerate wort thoroughly and pitch sediment from yeast starter. Ferment at 70°F (21°C). After fermentation stops, keg or add priming sugar and bottle and carbonate to 2.5 volumes of CO_2.

MALT EXTRACT OPTION

Add 5 pounds 10 ounces (2.6 kg) of light dried malt extract to the recipe. Reduce the amount of 2-row pale ale malt to 2 pounds 1 ounce (930 g). "Steep" the crushed grains in 4.1 quarts (3.9 L) of water at 152°F (67°C) for 60 minutes. ("Steep" is in quotes because technically this is a partial mash.) Place the grain bag in a colander over your brew pot and rinse the grains with 2.0 quarts (1.9 L) of 170°F (77°C) water. Add roughly one-third of the malt extract to this wort. Add water to bring brew pot volume to 3.0 gallons (11 L). Boil for 60 minutes, adding hops and Irish moss at times indicated. Add the remaining sugar and malt extract in the final 15 minutes of the boil. Add spruce tips throughout the final 5 minutes of the boil.

FROST GIANT JULE ØL
SPIKED WINTER WARMER

This is a strong, dark winter beer. An ale—øl, in Norwegian—made stronger by the addition of aquavit, a Scandinavian liquor spiced with caraway. Perfect for sitting by the fireplace on a snowy night and snacking on some cheese.

5.0 GALLONS (19 L) AT 8.0% ABV
(5.2 GALLONS [20 L] AT 9.0% ABV, AFTER SPIKING)
OG = 1.081, FG = 1.019
42 IBU, 31 SRM

+ Wyeast 1056 (American Ale) or White Labs WLP001 (California Ale) yeast

+ A 3.2-qt. (3.0-L) yeast starter is recommended

+ 4 lb. 4 oz. (1.9 kg) U.K. pale ale malt

+ 10 lb. 8 oz. (4.8 kg) German Munich malt (8°L)

+ 1.0 lb. (450 g) melanoidin malt (27°L)

+ 11 oz. (310 g) chocolate malt (400°L)

+ 20 fl. oz. (590 ml) aquavit (Scandinavian caraway-flavored liquor)

+ 1.25 oz. (35 g) Northern Brewer hops at 9% alpha acids, boiled for 60 minutes (42 IBU)

+ 0.33 oz. (9.4 g) Perle hops at 8% alpha acids, boiled for 0 minutes (0 IBU)

+ 1.0 tsp. Irish moss, boiled for 15 minutes

+ 5.2 oz. (150 g) corn sugar, to prime bottles for 2.5 volumes of CO_2

Make your yeast starter two to three days ahead of time. Heat 21 quarts (20 L) of brewing liquor to 165°F (74°C) and mash in grains. Mash at 154°F (68°C) for 60 minutes, stirring every 15 minutes if you can. Heat or add boiling water to mash out to 168°F (76°C). Recirculate wort until clear, and then run off. Sparge to collect up to 11 gallons (50 L) of wort.

Boil wort to reduce to just over 5.0 gallons (19 L), adding hops and Irish moss at times indicated. Chill wort, then rack to fermenter. Aerate wort thoroughly and pitch sediment from yeast starter. Ferment at 68°F (20°C). After fermentation stops, add aquavit. Let sit for a day to blend, then keg or add priming sugar and bottle and carbonate to 2.5 volumes of CO_2.

A three-tiered brewing system.

MALT EXTRACT OPTION

Add 9.0 pounds (4.1 kg) of liquid Munich malt extract to the recipe. Omit the pale ale malt. Reduce the amount of Munich malt to 1 pound 5 ounces (590 g). "Steep" the crushed grains in 4.1 quarts (3.9 L) of water at 152°F (67°C) for 60 minutes. ("Steep" is in quotes because technically this is a partial mash.) Place the grain bag in a colander over your brew pot and rinse the grains with 2.0 quarts (1.9 L) of 170°F (77°C) water. Add roughly one-third of the malt extract to this wort. Add water to bring brew pot volume to 3.0 gallons (11 L). Boil for 60 minutes, adding hops and Irish moss at times indicated. Add the remaining malt extract in the final 15 minutes of the boil.

RECIPE OPTIONS AND NOTES

There are other flavors of booze to consider—mint, cinnamon, citrus, etc.—If you think another flavor would work well in a dark ale base, then try it. If the liquor is 80 proof (40 percent alcohol) and you use the same amount as in this recipe, you will raise the beer's ABV from 8.0 to 9.0 percent.

If you want to get the spice level just right for your taste buds, you can make small test blends with any dark ale and adjust the blending ratio. As it is, the beer will have a moderately strong—although not overpowering—caraway flavor.

SCHOPPE'S TRIPEL BRAGGOT
(BY MARK SCHOPPE)

Mark Schoppe says, "This is a fairly simple all-grain Belgian tripel recipe that is turned into a braggot by the addition of a large amount of honey at the end of the boil. The recipe calls for orange blossom honey, but just about any characterful honey can be used. Some other good choices are mesquite, huajillo, yaupon holly, blackberry blossom and cotton blossom. You can also add spices to make a spiced tripel braggot (e.g., coriander, grains of paradise, black/red/green/white peppercorns, allspice)."

5.0 GALLONS (19 L) AT 12% ABV
OG = 1.110, FG = 1.020
45 IBU, 4.7 SRM

+ Wyeast 3787 (Trappist High Gravity) yeast or White Labs WLP530 (Abbey Ale) yeast
+ A 2.1-qt. (2.0-L) yeast starter is recommended
+ 14 lb. 3 oz. (6.4 kg) Pilsner malt
+ 5 lb. 5 oz. (2.4 kg) orange blossom honey
+ 0.75 oz. (21 g) Magnum hops at 14% alpha acids, boiled for 60 minutes (39 IBU)
+ 0.50 oz. (14 g) Saaz hops at 3.0% alpha acids, boiled for 30 minutes (4.3 IBU)
+ 0.50 oz. Saaz hops at 3.0% alpha acids, boiled for 10 minutes (2.0 IBU)
+ 1.0 tsp. Irish moss, boiled for 15 minutes
+ 0.50 tsp. yeast nutrients, boiled for 15 minutes
+ 5.75 oz. (160 g) corn sugar, to prime bottles for 2.7 volumes of CO_2

Make your yeast starter two to three days ahead of time. On brew day, heat 19 quarts (18 L) of brewing liquor to 161°F (72°C) and mash grains, at 150°F (66°C), for 60–75 minutes. Stir the mash a couple times, if you can do so and maintain temperature (via heating mash tun or adding hot water). Add boiling water to mash out to 168°F (76°C). Recirculate wort until clear, and then run off. Sparge to collect about 7.0 gallons (27 L) of wort. Vigorously boil wort for 90 minutes, to yield post-boil volume around 5.25 gallons (20 L).

Add hops, Irish moss and yeast nutrients at times indicated. Add the honey at flame out. Chill wort, then rack to fermenter. Aerate wort thoroughly and pitch sediment from yeast starter. Ferment at 72°F (22°C). After fermentation stops, let beer settle for two to three days, then rack to keg or bottling bucket. Carbonate to 2.7 volumes of CO_2.

MALT EXTRACT OPTION

Add 6 pounds 10 ounces (3.0 kg) of dried Pilsner malt extract to the recipe. Reduce the amount of Pilsner malt to 3.0 pounds (1.4 kg). "Steep" the crushed grains in 4.1 quarts (3.9 L) of water at 150°F (66°C) for 60 minutes. ("Steep" is in quotes because technically this is a partial mash.) Place the grain bag in a colander over your brew pot and rinse the grains with 2.0 quarts (1.9 L) of 170°F (77°C) water. Add roughly one-quarter of the malt extract to this wort. Add water to bring brew pot volume to 3.5 gallons (13 L). Boil for 60 minutes, adding hops and Irish moss at times indicated. Add the remaining malt extract in increments over the final 30 minutes of the boil.

Mark Schoppe is a member of the Austin ZEALOTS. He won the Ninkasi award—the top individual award at the National Homebrew Contest in 2012 and 2015. He also won the individual award for the Lone Star Circuit (the circuit of Texas homebrew competitions) in 2011, 2012 and 2014.

Choose a good-quality, aromatic honey for this braggot.

ACKNOWLEDGMENTS

I'd like to start by thanking every brewer who has inspired me over the years. I'd definitely like to single out my homebrew club, the Austin ZEALOTS, whose enthusiastic brewers are a constant inspiration.

Four homebrewers—James Spencer, Denny Conn, Dan Ironside and Mark Schoppe—contributed recipes to this book, and I thank them. Additional thanks go to James Spencer for our collaboration on *Beer and Wine Journal* (beerandwinejournal.com) and for cutting out the bits where I'm yelling at my cats when he interviews me for his podcast, *Basic Brewing Radio* (basicbrewing.com). Other recipes in this book are heavily influenced by the homebrews of Dan and Joelle Dewberry (Belgian IPA), Joe Walton and Jim Michalk (Oyster Stout), and Corey Martin (Munich Dunkel) and I thank them.

The rest of the recipes are inspired by a long line of brewers, maltsters, hop breeders, brewing scientists, brewing authors etc., spanning the whole of brewing history, who have advanced the science and art of brewing. To paraphrase Sir Isaac Newton, "If I have brewed a tasty fermented grain beverage, it is because someone has held my beer while I climbed onto the shoulders of a giant." I hope other brewers, in turn, will take these recipes and brew, tweak, twist, mutate and re-envision them to continue to expand our brewing horizons.

Thanks to Ted Axelrod for the beautiful photos in the book. Thanks to Matthew Chrispen for letting us take pictures of his amazing homebrew setup. (He has a cool blog, incidentally. It's called *Accidentalis Brewing*, and can be found at accidentalis.com.) Thanks to my in-laws, Ray and Diane Long, for letting us take pictures of beer glasses in and around their beautiful home.

Writing a book can be a solitary pursuit, but getting a book published involves the work of numerous people. I'd like to thank everyone at Page Street for this opportunity and for the work they've put into the book. I briefly worked for an educational book publisher, so I know all the hard work that must occur after a manuscript arrives. Special thanks to my editor Elizabeth Seise for putting up with a first-time book author's incessant questions.

Finally, I'd like to thank my parents, Joseph and Mary Colby. As a kid, they made sure I had access to books. If they hadn't, this book wouldn't exist.

ABOUT THE AUTHOR

Chris Colby has been a homebrewer since 1991, ever since a fellow graduate student at Boston University introduced him to homebrew. He began by brewing malt extract–based beers by himself in his apartment in Boston. Early on in his pursuit of the hobby, he visited a friend —John Weerts—in Kansas City and taught him how to brew. Years later, "Weertsie" was an accomplished all-grain brewer and a visit to Boston—with a keg of rye beer in tow—inspired Colby to jump into all-grain brewing. A few years after that—after moving to Bastrop, Texas—he joined the Austin ZEALOTS (the homebrew club) and began enjoying the social aspect to being a homebrewer.

Over the years, Colby has brewed numerous types of beers ranging from English and American-style ales, to German-style lagers, to Belgian-inspired sour beers. His gueuze won Best of Show at the Austin ZEALOTS Homebrew Inquisition (their annual contest) in 2004, and that's the brewing award he is most proud of. This beer was blended from 3-year-old, 2-year-old and 1-year-old batches of lambic and was thus 4 years in the making (See the recipe on page 203.)

Although his favorite beers are "just plain beers"—moderate-strength beers brewed from just malt, hops, yeast and water—Colby does like to experiment with special ingredients. He also likes brewing beers using interesting procedures. He refined the idea of using wort as brewing liquor into an idea he calls reiterated mashing, a method for brewing very strong, very pale beers entirely from malted grains. (See the recipe on page 149.) He has also experimented with brewing very strong ales and lagers, using special techniques to coax the yeast to new heights.

Colby has written more than 200 magazine articles about homebrewing and was the editor of *Brew Your Own* magazine for 15 years. He currently produces *Beer and Wine Journal* (beerandwinejournal.com), an online publication dealing with homebrewing, in collaboration with James Spencer. (He also writes frequently about gardening in *GRIT* magazine, if you're into that sort of thing.)

Colby's formal education includes BAs in biology and chemistry from Augustana College, Sioux Falls, South Dakota, and a PhD in biology from Boston University. He and his wife live in Bastrop, Texas, with an undisclosed number of cats.

INDEX